W9-DFX-278

"From the first page, the reader of *How to Read a Poem* realises that this, at last, is a book which begins to answer Adrian Mitchell's charge: 'Most people ignore most poetry because most poetry ignores most people'. Eagleton introduces himself as 'a politically minded literary theorist'. The remarkable achievement of this book is to prove that such a theorist is the only person who can really show what poetry is for. By a brilliant and scrupulous series of readings – of Yeats and Frost and Auden and Dickinson – framed in a lively account of the function of criticism as perhaps only he could expound it, Eagleton shows how literary theory, seriously understood, is the ground of poetic understanding. This will be the indispensable apology for poetry in our time."

Bernard O'Donoghue, Wadham College, University of Oxford

Terry Eagleton

The author is John Edward Taylor Professor of English Literature at the University of Manchester. His recent publications include *The English Novel* (2004), *Sweet Violence: The Idea of the Tragic* (2003), *The Idea of Culture* (2000), *Scholars and Rebels in Nineteenth-Century Ireland* (1999), *Literary Theory: An Introduction* (second edition, 1996) and *The Illusions of Postmodernism* (1996), all published by Blackwell Publishing.

To Peter Grant,
who taught me poetry and a good deal more

How to Read a Poem

Terry Eagleton

Blackwell
Publishing

BLACKWELL PUBLISHING
350 Main Street, Malden, MA 02148-5020, USA
9600 Garsington Road, Oxford OX4 2DQ, UK
550 Swanston Street, Carlton, Victoria 3053, Australia

First published 2007 by Blackwell Publishing Ltd

5   2008

Library of Congress Cataloging-in-Publication Data

Eagleton, Terry, 1943–
    How to read a poem / by Terry Eagleton.
        p. cm.
    Includes bibliographical references and index.
    ISBN-13: 978-1-4051-5140-5 (hbk. : alk. paper)
    ISBN-13: 978-1-4051-5141-2 (pbk. : alk. paper)
1. English poetry—History and criticism.
2. American poetry—History and criticism. 3. Poetry—Explication.
4. Poetics. I. Title.

    PR502.E23 2007
    808.1—dc22

                                                        2006008194

A catalogue record for this title is available from the British Library.

Set in 10.5/13pt Dante
by Graphicraft Ltd, Hong Kong
Printed and bound in the United Kingdom
by TJ International Ltd, Padstow, Cornwall

The publisher's policy is to use permanent paper from mills that operate a sustainable forestry policy, and which has been manufactured from pulp processed using acid-free and elementary chlorine-free practices. Furthermore, the publisher ensures that the text paper and cover board used have met acceptable environmental accreditation standards.

For further information on
Blackwell Publishing, visit our website:
www.blackwellpublishing.com

Contents

Preface		vii
Acknowledgements		viii
1	**The Functions of Criticism**	**1**
	1 The End of Criticism?	1
	2 Politics and Rhetoric	8
	3 The Death of Experience	17
	4 Imagination	22
2	**What is Poetry?**	**25**
	1 Poetry and Prose	25
	2 Poetry and Morality	28
	3 Poetry and Fiction	31
	4 Poetry and Pragmatism	38
	5 Poetic Language	41
3	**Formalists**	**48**
	1 Literariness	48
	2 Estrangement	49
	3 The Semiotics of Yury Lotman	52
	4 The Incarnational Fallacy	59
4	**In Pursuit of Form**	**65**
	1 The Meaning of Form	65
	2 Form versus Content	70
	3 Form as Transcending Content	79

	4	Poetry and Performance	88
	5	Two American Examples	96
5	**How to Read a Poem**		**102**
	1	Is Criticism Just Subjective?	102
	2	Meaning and Subjectivity	108
	3	Tone, Mood and Pitch	114
	4	Intensity and Pace	118
	5	Texture	120
	6	Syntax, Grammar and Punctuation	121
	7	Ambiguity	124
	8	Punctuation	130
	9	Rhyme	131
	10	Rhythm and Metre	135
	11	Imagery	138
6	**Four Nature Poems**		**143**
	1	William Collins, 'Ode to Evening'	143
	2	William Wordsworth, 'The Solitary Reaper'	149
	3	Gerard Manley Hopkins, 'God's Grandeur'	153
	4	Edward Thomas, 'Fifty Faggots'	157
	5	Form and History	161
		Glossary	165
		Index	169

Preface

This book is designed as an introduction to poetry for students and general readers. I have tried to make what some find an intimidating subject as lucid and accessible as possible; but some bits of the book are inevitably harder going than others. Less experienced readers might therefore prefer to start with Chapter 4 ('In Pursuit of Form'), Chapter 5 ('How To Read A Poem') and Chapter 6 ('Four Nature Poems'), before moving on to the more theoretical chapters. Even so, I think the book makes more sense if it is read from start to finish.

I am deeply grateful to John Barrell at York University, Stan Smith at Nottingham Trent University, Emma Bennett, Philip Carpenter and Astrid Wind at Blackwell, and William Flesch at Brandeis University for their helpful suggestions.

TE
Dublin, 2005

Acknowledgements

The editor and publisher gratefully acknowledge the permission granted to reproduce the copyright material in this book:

W. H. Auden, 'Musée des Beaux Arts,' from Edward Mendelson (ed.), *Collected Poems*. New York: Random House, 1976. Copyright 1940 and renewed 1968 by W. H. Auden. Used by permission of Random House, Inc.

Alan Brownjohn, 'Common Sense,' from *Collected Poems*. London: Enitharmon Press, 2005. Reprinted by permission of Enitharmon Press.

H. D. (Hilda Doolittle), 'Sea Violet,' from Louis L. Martz, *Collected Poems 1912–1944*. New York: New Directions, 1983. Copyright © 1982 by The Estate of Hilda Doolittle. Reprinted by permission of New Directions Publishing Corp. and Carcanet Press Ltd.

Philip Larkin, 'Days,' from *The Whitsun Weddings*. London: Faber & Faber, 1964. Copyright © 1988, 2003 by The Estate of Philip Larkin. Reprinted by permission of Farrar, Straus and Giroux LLC.

Bernard O'Donoghue, 'Pencil it in,' from *Here nor There*. London: Chatto & Windus, 1999. Reprinted by permission of The Random House Group Ltd.

John Pudney, 'For Johnny' from *For Johnny: Poems of World War II*. London: Shepheard-Walwyn, 1976. Reprinted by permission of David Higham Associates Limited.

Stevie Smith, 'Not Waving but Drowning,' from *Collected Poems of Stevie Smith*. New York: Shepheard-Walwyn, 1975. Copyright © 1972 by Stevie Smith; copyright the Estate of James MacGibbon. Reprinted by permission of James & James (Publishers) Ltd and New Directions Publishing Corp.

Dylan Thomas, 'A Refusal to Mourn the Death, by Fire, of a Child in London,' from *The Poems of Dylan Thomas*. New York: New Directions, 1971. Copyright © 1945 by The Trustees for the Copyrights of Dylan Thomas. Reprinted by permission of New Directions Publishing Corp. and David Higham Associates.

William Carlos Williams, 'This is Just to Say,' from Christopher MacGowan (ed.), *The Collected Poems of William Carlos Williams, Volume I, 1909–1939*. New York: Carcanet, 2000. Copyright © 1938, by New Directions Publishing Corp. Reprinted by permission of New Directions Publishing Corp. and Carcanet Press Limited.

Every effort has been made to trace copyright holders and to obtain their permission for the use of copyright material. The publisher apologizes for any errors or omissions in the above list and would be grateful if notified of any corrections that should be incorporated in future reprints or editions of this book.

Chapter 1

The Functions of Criticism

1.1   The End of Criticism?

I first thought of writing this book when I realised that hardly any of the students of literature I encountered these days practised what I myself had been trained to regard as literary criticism. Like thatching or clog dancing, literary criticism seems to be something of a dying art. Since many of these students are bright and capable enough, the fault would seem to lie largely with their teachers. The truth is that quite a few teachers of literature now-adays do not practise literary criticism either, since they, in turn, were never taught to do so.

This charge may seem pretty rich, coming as it does from a literary theorist. Wasn't it literary theory, with its soulless abstractions and vacuous gener-alities, which destroyed the habit of close reading in the first place? I have pointed out elsewhere that this is one of the great myths or unexamined clichés of contemporary critical debate.[1] It is one of those 'everybody knows' pieties, like the assumption that serial killers look just like you and me, keep themselves to themselves, but always have a polite word for their neighbours. It is as much a shop-soiled banality as the claim that Christmas has become dreadfully commercialised. Like all tenacious myths which refuse to vanish whatever the evidence, it is there to serve specific interests. The idea that literary theorists killed poetry dead because with their shrivelled hearts and swollen brains they are incapable of spotting a metaphor, let alone a

---

[1]   See, among other places, Terry Eagleton, *After Theory* (London, 2003), p. 93.

tender feeling, is one of the more obtuse critical platitudes of our time. The truth is that almost all major literary theorists engage in scrupulously close reading. The Russian Formalists on Gogol or Pushkin, Bakhtin on Rabelais, Adorno on Brecht, Benjamin on Baudelaire, Derrida on Rousseau, Genette or de Man on Proust, Hartman on Wordsworth, Kristeva on Mallarmé, Jameson on Conrad, Barthes on Balzac, Iser on Henry Fielding, Cixous on Joyce, Hillis Miller on Henry James, are just a handful of examples.

Some of these figures are not only eminent critics, but literary artists in their own right. They produce literature in the act of commenting on it. Michel Foucault is another such outstanding stylist. It is true that thinkers like these have sometimes been ill served by their disciples, but the same goes for some non-theoretical critics. But the point, in any case, is irrelevant. For it is not as though many students of literature today do not read poems and novels fairly closely. Close reading is not the issue. The question is not how tenaciously you cling to the text, but what you are in search of when you do so. The theorists I have mentioned are not only close readers, but are sensitive to questions of literary form. And this is where they differ from most students today.

It is significant, in fact, that if you broach the question of form with students of literature, some of them think that you are talking simply about metre. 'Paying attention to form', in their eyes, means saying whether the poem is written in iambic pentameters, or whether it rhymes. Literary form obviously includes such things; but saying what the poem means, and then tagging on a couple of sentences about its metre or rhyme scheme, is not exactly engaging with questions of form. Most students, faced with a novel or poem, spontaneously come up with what is commonly known as 'content analysis'. They give accounts of works of literature which describe what is going on in them, perhaps with a few evaluative comments thrown in. To adopt a technical distinction from linguistics, they treat the poem as *language* but not as *discourse*.

'Discourse', as we shall see, means attending to language in all of its material density, whereas most approaches to poetic language tend to disembody it. Nobody has ever heard language pure and simple. Instead, we hear utterances that are shrill or sardonic, mournful or nonchalant, mawkish or truculent, irascible or histrionic. And this, as we shall see, is part of what we mean by form. People sometimes talk about digging out the ideas 'behind' the poem's language, but this spatial metaphor is misleading. For it is not as though the language is a kind of disposable cellophane in which the ideas come ready-wrapped. On the contrary, the language of a poem is *constitutive* of its ideas.

It would be hard to figure out, just by reading most of these content analyses, that they were supposed to be about poems or novels, rather than about some real-life happening. What gets left out is the *literariness* of the work. Most students can say things like 'the moon imagery recurs in the third verse, adding to the sense of solitude', but not many of them can say things like 'the poem's strident tone is at odds with its shambling syntax'. A lot of them would just think that this was funny. They do not speak the same language as the critic who said of some lines of T. S. Eliot: 'There is something very sad about the punctuation.' Instead, they treat the poem as though its author chose for some eccentric reason to write out his or her views on warfare or sexuality in lines which do not reach to the end of the page. Maybe the computer got stuck.

Let us take the first stanza of W. H. Auden's 'Musée des Beaux Arts':

> About suffering they were never wrong,
> The Old Masters: how well they understood
> Its human position; how it takes place
> While someone else is eating or opening a window or just walking dully
> along;
> How, when the aged are reverently, passionately waiting
> For the miraculous birth, there always must be
> Children who did not specially want it to happen, skating
> On a pond at the edge of the wood:
> They never forgot
> That even the dreadful martyrdom must run its course
> Anyhow in a corner, some untidy spot
> Where the dogs go on with their doggy life and the torturer's horse
> Scratches its innocent behind on a tree.

A summary of this would be fairly straightforward. The Old Masters or great painters, so the poem claims, understood the incongruous nature of human suffering – the contrast between the sheer intensity of it, which seems to point to some momentous meaning, and the way its everyday surroundings appear so casually indifferent to it. All this, we might suspect, is an allegory of the contingent nature of modern existence. Things no longer form a pattern which converges on the hero or martyr at its centre, but collide quite randomly, with the trivial and the momentous, the guilty and the innocent, lying casually side by side.

What matters, however, is how all this shapes up verbally. The poem begins in casual style, as though we have just dropped in on someone's after-dinner conversation; yet there is a certain understated drama about this opening as well. It sidles obliquely into its theme rather than starting off with a fanfare: the first line and a half reverse the noun, verb and predicate, so that 'The Old Masters were never wrong about suffering', which would be far too bald a proposition, becomes the more angled, syntactically interesting 'About suffering they were never wrong, / The Old Masters'.

A more elaborate version of this syntactical sidling, in which the regular order of grammar is inverted, can be found in the loftily throwaway opening sentence of E. M. Forster's novel *A Passage to India*: 'Except for the Marabar Caves – and they are twenty miles off – the city of Chandrapore presents nothing extraordinary.' These first words are actually a choice piece of irony, since the caves will prove to be central to the entire action. The novel opens with what sounds like a parody of a rather snooty guidebook. A mild air of patrician languor broods over the entire, exquisitely balanced sentence.

Auden's poem is not in the least snooty or kid-gloved; but it has an air of well-bred worldliness about it. A faint sense of dramatic expectancy is created by the opening lines, as we have to step across the line-ending to find out who exactly was never wrong about suffering. 'The Old Masters' is in apposition to 'they', which lends the lines a relaxedly conversational air – as in a sentence like 'They're noisy, those freight trains.' The same colloquial idiom is obvious a little later in words like 'doggy' and 'behind', though this kind of speech is more the raciness of the gentleman than the vulgarity of the plebeian.

The weighty trisyllabic word 'suffering' sounds out resonantly at the very start, rather than being tucked away at the end of the clause as the sense might seem to dictate. The tone of the piece is urbane but not hard-boiled. It is civilised, but not camp or overbred, as some of Auden's later poetry can be. 'Dreadful' is a typical English upper-class adjective, as in 'Darling, he was perfectly dreadful!', but we do not feel it to be an affectation, however ineffectual a description of martyrdom it may be. The poem has an authority about it which seems to spring from mature experience, and to which we are therefore inclined to listen. If the poet can see how well the Old Masters understood the truth of human affliction, then he must surely be on equal terms with them, at least in this respect. The poem seems to speak on behalf of a very English common sense and normality; yet it also asks implicitly how certain extreme situations can be fitted into this familiar frame of reference. Is that normality therefore to be questioned as too narrow, or is it just in the nature of things that the ordinary and the exotic lie side by side, with no particular connection between them?

The stanza stretches literally from human agony to a horse's backside, and so involves a sort of bathos. We are cranked down a tone or two from the solemn 'How, when the aged are reverently, passionately waiting / For the miraculous birth', to the deliberately flat 'there always must be / Children who did not specially want it to happen', a line which has too many words of different shapes and sizes to flow smoothly. The syntax conspires with this deflationary effect: the comma after 'How' holds the sentence in suspense, allowing us an uplifting moment ('when the aged are reverently, passionately waiting . . .') only to bump us prosaically down again.

Yet even here the verse maintains its civility: 'did not specially want it to happen' may mean just what it says: the children are not opposed to the birth, but not enthused by the prospect either. But it could also be a polite way of saying that they couldn't give a damn about the miraculous birth, rather as 'not a little boring' is polite English understatement for 'unbelievably boring'. The poem preserves its good manners by a kind of verbal indirection. It isn't clear, though, quite how it moves from the idea of suffering to the idea of the aged reverently waiting for the miraculous birth. How exactly is reverent expectancy a matter of suffering? Because suspense is painful? Or is the suffering in question the birth itself?

One problem the piece faces is how to be suitably wry about suffering without being cynical about it. It has to tread a fine line between a lightly ironic wisdom and sounding merely jaded. It needs to demythologise human pain, but without seeming to devalue it. So the tone – mannered, but not callous or cavalier – has to be carefully managed. This is not the kind of voice whose possessor is likely himself to believe in miraculous births, indulge in excessive reverence, or get himself martyred. It is too secular and commonsensical for that, as well as too sceptical of grand designs. It wants to take the false heroics out of suffering by 'decentring' it, insisting on how marginal and haphazard it generally is. Yet there is also a humaneness about the speaking voice which suggests an understated sympathy.

So the stanza is disenchanted but not debunking. It is as though the poem wants to honour human torment by being coolly realistic about it, rather than subscribing to some sentimental myth for which such torment brings the whole world to a dramatic halt. It may feel like this to the sufferer herself, but the poem's hard-headed realism refuses to identify with the unimaginable anguish of another. (Another of Auden's poems, one about wounded soldiers, enquires: 'For who when healthy can become a foot?', meaning no doubt that the healthy are those who are able to take their bodies for granted.) When it comes to suffering, neither the perspective of the patient nor that of the observer is wholly reliable. The deepest respect we can pay to the afflicted, Auden seems to suggest, is to acknowledge the unbridgeable gap between their distress and our normality. There is what one might call an absolute epistemological break between sickness and health. Like many a literary work of the 1930s, 'Musée des Beaux Arts' would rather be thought heartless than sentimental. Its anti-heroism is also a typical 1930s stance. It is just that this toughness of mind, pressed to an extreme, can be a devious form of the very sentimentalism it repudiates.

There is another bit of dramatic suspense in the phrase 'its human position', whose meaning is not really clear until we step past the semicolon and find out. We then get a rather plodding, straggling sort of line – 'While someone else is eating or opening a window or just walking dully along' – which in its inelegant slinging together of clauses seems just to jog dully along. 'Where the dogs go on with their doggy life and the torturer's horse . . .' is another such stumbling, overpopulated line, its untidiness suggestive of the clutter of human experience itself. Children, dogs and horses go on doing their child-like, doggy or horsey things in the midst of massacre and martyrdom, and this, so the poetic voice seems to intimate, is just the way things are. They could no more be different than dogs could behave like children. Human existence is an unavoidable matter of irony, as the trifling and the terrible exist cheek by jowl. How something looks from the outside is not how it feels on the inside, and what is central to you is peripheral to me. Irony here is not just a tone but a clash of perspectives. It is as though it is built into the world, rather than simply an attitude towards it. And this adds to the sense of inevitability. You could no more change this condition than you could grow an extra limb overnight.

We might, however, take leave to question this outlook. It may well be true of some sorts of suffering, but isn't the poet rather dubiously universalising his claims? Is this really the 'human position', pure and simple? In the poem's second stanza, Auden implicitly compares an indifference to human disaster to the sun shining, as though the former were as natural as the latter. Yet the poem appeared in 1940, at a time when Europe had lived through the Spanish Civil War (in which Auden was briefly involved) and was now in the throes of a global war against fascism. This kind of suffering was surely not always a private, hole-in-the-corner affair. On the contrary, it could be a collective experience. If death and grief showed up the unbridgeable gaps between people, they were also realities that could be publicly shared. Catastrophe and the common life came together in the bombing of British cities. Suffering was not just something people got on with privately, like a hobby; there was to some extent a common language between sufferer and spectator, soldier and civilian.

So the poem's technical brilliance and worldly-wise tone may persuade us into accepting too readily a highly contentious proposition: that the private life is one thing, while the public world is quite another. Suffering is a private event, to which no public language could be adequate. Behind the work lurks the view that each of us is the private possessor of our own experience, eternally walled off from the sensations of others. A good deal of modern philosophy has been devoted to exposing the fallacy of this apparently commonsensical view; and there is no reason why criticism should not appeal to such arguments. We do not have to take the beliefs of a poet on trust.

If this is a 'modern' poem, it is partly because of its scepticism of grand narratives. Suffering is not part of any overall design, even if its intensity makes us suspect that it ought to be. It is arbitrary and contingent, and it is the contrast between this objective status and its subjective dreadfulness which is so shocking. The poem itself, by contrast, is intricately designed, but in a way which makes us feel that it isn't. Its conversational tone belies its subtle artistry. It is possible to read it, for example, without realising that it rhymes. The rhyme scheme, however, is pretty irregular, rather like the rhythm, which is one reason why we may not notice it. It provides the merest skeleton of form across which the poet can drape his apparently free-flowing thoughts. The rhymes are discreet and diplomatic to the point of semi-invisibility; and part of what makes them so unobtrusive is the constant enjambement, as the flow of thought overrides the line-endings.

The same goes for the syntax. This first stanza is actually a single, impressively sustained sentence, full of sub-clauses and grammatically complex constructions, but we hardly notice this as we read it. (Auden cheats a little here, however: there are a number of colons and semicolons which could in fact function as full stops.) The poem is highly shaped, but surreptitiously so, so as to foster an impression of colloquial spontaneity. It is artfully artless. And this sense of listening in on a well-tempered voice conversationally unfolding its reflections on life somehow confirms us in our scepticism of grand designs. The anti-heroism of the poem's argument finds an echo in the low-key anti-rhetoric of its style.

Auden wrote a poem in the same year as 'Musée des Beaux Arts' entitled 'In Memory of W. B. Yeats', the first stanza of which casts an interesting light on the former poem:

> He disappeared in the dead of winter:
> The brooks were frozen, the airports almost deserted,
> And snow disfigured the public statues;
> The mercury sank in the mouth of the dying day.
> What instruments we have agree
> The day of his death was a dark cold day.

Rather than turning casually away from the disaster of Yeats's death, the world seems to conspire in its sorrowfulness. But this, of course, is gravely tongue-in-cheek. It is as though the poet makes a courteous pretence that the brooks were frozen, the statues disfigured and the airports almost deserted *because* of his fellow poet's death, while knowing perfectly well that the connection between suffering and its surroundings is just as arbitrary here as it is in 'Musée des Beaux Arts'. There is a kind of poetic licence at work here, as the so-called pathetic fallacy – the belief that Nature shares our own moods and feelings – is invoked ironically, as a kind of solemn wit. The verse carefully does not claim that the day was a bleak one on account of Yeats's death; it simply allows us to infer the possibility. The very next stanza of the poem undercuts this apparent solidarity between humanity and the world in general: 'Far from his illness / The wolves ran on through the evergreen forests . . .' Reality is what turns its back upon us, resisting our infantile demand that the world should serve as our looking glass.

1.2   Politics and Rhetoric

I have argued that literary theorists may safely plead not guilty to the charge of having sabotaged literary criticism. Even so, there may seem something strange about a politically minded literary theorist like myself recalling us to the words on the page. Surely punctuation is one thing and politics is another? It is doubtful, in fact, that this distinction holds water. It would not be hard, for example, to show how the punctuation of D. H. Lawrence's writing, creating as it does an effect of flow and spontaneity, is related to his 'organic' vision of the world, and that in turn to his critique of industrial capitalism. There is a politics of form as well as a politics of content. Form is not a distraction from history but a mode of access to it. A major crisis of artistic form – let's say, the shift from realism to modernism in the late nineteenth and early twentieth centuries – is almost always bound up with an historical upheaval. In this case, the upheaval in question was the period of political and economic turmoil which culminated in the First World War. This is not to claim that modernism was no more than a symptom of something else. But a deep enough crisis of cultural form is usually an historical crisis as well.

To look at the historical high points of literary criticism is to witness a kind of dual attentiveness: to the grain and texture of literary works, and to those works' cultural contexts. This is as true of Romantic criticism as it is of the so-called Cambridge school of F. R. Leavis, I. A. Richards and William Empson. It is the hallmark of some of the twentieth century's towering literary scholars: Mikhail Bakhtin, Eric Auerbach, Walter Benjamin, Ernst Robert Curtius, Kenneth Burke, Edmund Wilson, Lionel Trilling, Edward Said. For almost all of these critics, there is a politics implicit in the painstaking investigation of the literary text. It is no accident that William Empson, who analysed poems more scrupulously than any critic had ever done before, was also a political liberal with socialist leanings, who was expelled from the University of Cambridge for supposed sexual misconduct and subsequently taught in conditions of considerable hardship in China and Japan. Empson's alertness to poetic ambiguities was also an openness to conflicting kinds of cultural meaning, including those which might well seem alien to most English gentlemen of his kind. A son of the Yorkshire landed squirearchy, Empson rebelled against his hunting-and-shooting background to become an oddball, a dissident and an outsider; and his fascination with textual dissonances and multiple meanings was closely bound up with this spiritual nonconformism.

In a similar way, F. R. Leavis's focus on the sensuous detail of a poem reflected among other things his opposition to an industrial order which was governed, so he felt, by abstraction and utility. Poetry, however indirectly, was thus a form of political critique. For I. A. Richards, the delicate equipoise of a poem offered a corrective to an urban society in which human impulses were no longer harmoniously integrated. All of these critics, along with the others I have mentioned, were deeply responsive to social history, in how-ever nostalgic or idealist a fashion. Yet all of them, to adopt a phrase of Fredric Jameson's, felt at the same time an 'obligation to come to terms with the shape of the individual sentences themselves'.[2] It is just that in their view, this obligation also involved coming to terms with the forces which helped shape the sentences, forces which include a good deal more than the author. For these critics, there was no simple-minded option between 'history' and 'the words on the page'. As philologists or 'lovers of language', their passion for literature was bound up with an engagement with entire civilisations. What else is language but the bridge which links the two? Language is the medium in which both Culture and culture – literary art and human society – come to consciousness; and literary criticism is thus a sensitivity to the thickness and intricacy of the medium which makes us what we are. Simply by attend-ing to its own distinctive object, it can have fundamental implications for the destiny of culture as a whole.

---

[2] Fredric Jameson, *Marxism and Form* (Princeton, NJ, 1971), p. xii.

Another great philologist, Friedrich Nietzsche, constantly preached the value of knowing how to read well. He presents himself as a teacher of 'slow' reading, and regards this as cutting against the grain of an age obsessed with speed.[3] Close reading for Nietzsche is a critique of modernity. To attend to the feel and form of words is to refuse to treat them in a purely instrumental way, and thus to refuse a world in which language is worn to a paperlike thinness by commerce and bureaucracy. The Nietzschean Superman is not an e-mail user. Yet this relation between politics and textuality goes a good deal further back – all the way, in fact, to the oldest form of literary criticism we know, the rhetoric of the ancient world.

Throughout late antiquity and the Middle Ages, what we know today as criticism was in effect known as rhetoric; and the word in the ancient world had both a textual and a political sense.[4] It meant both the study of verbal tropes and figures, and the art of persuasive public speech. The two were closely interrelated: professional rhetoricians were on hand to instruct you in what verbal devices could best achieve the political effects you were seeking. In ancient Roman schools, this was at times practically equivalent to education as such. The ancients recognised a special variety of discourse known as poetry; but there was no hard-and-fast distinction between this and other species of language. Rhetoric was the science of them all, and poetry, like history, was just a sub-branch of it. It was a kind of meta-discourse, defining the procedures of successful communication for any mode of language whatsoever. The point of studying stylistic strategies was a political one: it was to know how to put them to use most effectively in your own rhetorical practice. Speaking gracefully and thinking wisely were thought to be closely allied. An aesthetic error could lead to a political miscalculation.

Rhetoric, then, was a kind of discourse theory, one inseparable from the political, legal and religious institutions of the ancient state. It was born at the intersection of discourse and power. The Roman historian Tacitus tells us that Julius Caesar, along with the emperors Augustus, Tiberius, Caligula and Claudius, were all accomplished orators.[5] But the art of rhetoric was not simply a weapon of emperors. In its belief that all citizens must be taught to speak well, it was closely bound up with ancient Greek democracy. For

---

[3] See Keith Ansell Pearson, *Nietzsche* (London, 2005), p. 2.

[4] For studies of rhetoric, see George Kennedy, *The Art of Persuasion in Ancient Greece* (Princeton, NJ, 1963); Brian Vickers, *In Defence of Rhetoric* (Oxford, 1988); Terry Eagleton, 'A Small History of Rhetoric', in *Walter Benjamin, Or Towards a Revolutionary Criticism* (London, 1981).

[5] Tacitus, *The Annals of Imperial Rome* (London, 1996), p. 285.

the Greeks, a free man was one who was to be persuaded by speech rather than, like slaves or foreigners, to be coerced by violence. Language was thus the supreme capacity which differentiated free, equal citizens from their human or non-human subordinates.

Once these political conditions had passed away, a decline that can already be observed in the late Roman Empire, rhetoric was cut off from practical social life, to dwindle in the Middle Ages to a sterile inventory of literary devices. It was now a scholastic rather than a civic pursuit, one which belonged to the study rather than to the public sphere. Generally speaking, rhetoric was now subordinate to logic. The art enjoyed a triumphant revival with Renaissance humanism, which brandished rhetoric as its chief weapon against the medieval scholastics. Once again, in an epoch of wars, imperial expansion and deep-seated social change, the question of persuasive political speech shifted to centre-stage. Gradually, however, rhetoric became reduced to the question of style or subsumed into poetics, thus shedding its public, political functions. Later still, as eloquence and metaphor came under suspicion in an age of scientific rationalism, the word 'rhetoric' began to gather some of the negative connotations it has for us today: bombast, hot air, specious manipulation. The wheel, in fact, had come full circle, since this was pretty much what rhetoric had meant to Plato in his wranglings with the Sophists.

Rhetoric for the ancient world was language as public event and social relationship. If it was performative, it was also dialogical, as a form of speech which constantly overheard itself in the ears of others. It was not a way of seeing which would long survive either the invention of printing or the growth of rationalism. By the seventeenth century, rhetoric's figurative flourishes and passionate eloquence were seen by some as an obstacle to truth, not as a means of access to it. Both passions and metaphors clouded an objective vision of the world, and rhetoric involved both. John Locke, the father of modern philosophy, condemns rhetoric in his *Essay Concerning Human Understanding* as a 'powerful instrument of error and deceit'. There was still a scholarly fascination with rhetoric in the eighteenth century, not least among Scottish Enlightenment writers. In general, however, truth in the age of Enlightenment had become non-oral, non-dialogical, non-poetic, non-contextual and non-affective. Ideally, it was independent of language altogether, since language – the very medium of truth – was also a potential obstacle to it. The fuzziness of words got in the way of the lucidity of meanings. Truth was also growing a good deal more specialised and compartmentalised; and since rhetoric claimed to be a universal discourse, it was increasingly thrust out of business.

For the rationalists and empiricists, verbal embellishment distracted you from the facts of the matter. Formal flourishes were giving way to concrete investigations. If, for example, you were keen to tackle social injustices, you needed to know in soberly prosaic spirit how things stood with men and women; and flights of rhetoric or fantasy were unlikely to help. They were the privilege of those who could indulge their fancies while others lacked food. Wordplay was the enemy of welfare. Feelings were not a mode of access to the world, but a sentimental or demagogic distraction from it. An emergent democracy was nervous of rhetoric's authoritarian overtones – ironically, given rhetoric's political origins; but it was also wary of the kind of populist rhetoric which might stir the anarchic passions of the mob.

Romanticism, among other things, was the revenge of the poetic on this rather bloodless brand of Enlightenment reason. Now, however, poetry was pitted *against* rhetoric, as it is in the programmatic preface to Wordsworth and Coleridge's *Lyrical Ballads*. Rhetoric still meant deceitful, manipulative public discourse; it was just that what would resist it now was not rational inquiry or disinterested scholarship, but the truths of the human heart. Poetry was at war with the kind of discourse which has palpable designs on us. Unlike classical rhetoric, which meant nothing without a public to respond to it, it was in grave doubt about whether it actually had an audience at all. Perhaps the poet, in Shelley's fine phrase, was simply a nightingale singing in the dark. In the absence of an assured audience, there was a new cult of the inspired author. With English Romantics like Wordsworth, Coleridge, Blake, Shelley, Keats and Byron, poetry was still strenuously engaged with the public sphere; but the word 'public' was now beginning to assume pejorative overtones, and poetry was coming to speak a language altogether different from commerce, science and politics. It was part of what one might call a counter-public sphere; but it had not yet been privatised, as it would be, in effect, by some later Romantic artists.

It was about this point that a phenomenon called Literature was brought to birth. The word 'Literature' had previously covered various forms of writing, both factual and fictional; but now it was a signal that the virtues of all writing were epitomised in one, peculiarly privileged species of it: poetry. Poetry was the condition to which all the most authentic kinds of writing aspired. 'Literature' was a matter of feeling rather than fact, of the transcendent rather than the mundane, of the unique and original rather than the socially conventional. Poetry abhorred abstractions, and dealt only in the specific and the individual. It was concerned with what you could feel on the pulses, not with general notions. From this viewpoint, a *theory* of poetry is really a contradiction in terms. You cannot have a science of the concrete. There can be no systematic knowledge of the individual. You can have a science of several million individuals, known as demography or sociology or anthropology, but you cannot make a scientific study of the retired admiral in the cottage down the road.

So the prejudice that poetry deals above all in concrete particulars is actually fairly recent. In one sense, to be sure, it runs back all the way to Plato, who saw poetry as an ungovernable mob of unruly particulars, and banished it from his ideal state for much the same reasons that he expelled democracy. Aristotle, by contrast, saw poetry as dealing in universals; while for some early Christian thinkers like St Augustine, to attend to the particular as an end in itself, rather than to read it 'semiotically' as a sign of God's presence in the world, was an act of impiety. It is really with the growth of modern aesthetics in the mid-eighteenth century, and then with the flourishing of Romanticism, that the idea of concrete particularity as precious in itself burst upon the literary scene in a big way. The assumption that poetry busies itself with the sensuously specific, and is sceptical of general ideas, would no doubt have come as a mighty surprise to Aristotle, Dante, Shakespeare, Milton, Pope and Johnson. It would even have been news to a good many Romantics. There is hardly much sensuous specificity in Wordsworth. Not all poets have subscribed to the dangerous doctrine that only what we feel on the pulses is true. It is a belief at least as typical of neo-fascists as it is of creative artists. A nervousness of general ideas is as much a mark of the philistine as the poet.

In any case, if some Romantics insisted on the sensuous particularity of the poem, they were also inclined to speak of its universal nature. And the two would seem hard to reconcile. Even so, a resolution lay conveniently to hand, known as the symbol. The Romantic symbol is supposed to flesh out a universal truth in a uniquely specific form. In some mysterious fashion it combines the individual and the universal, setting up a direct circuit between the two which bypasses language, history, culture and rationality. To penetrate to the essence of what makes a thing uniquely itself is to discover the part it plays in the cosmic whole. This idea runs steadily through Western civilisation, all the way from Plato's Forms and Leibniz's monads to Hegel's World Spirit, Coleridge's symbols and Hopkins's 'inscapes'. What it meant in the case of poetry, translated into rather less exalted terms, was that poets now had two ways at their disposal of avoiding actual history. They could look 'below' it, to the ineffably particular; or they could rise above it to universal truths. With the aid of the symbol, they could even do both at the same time.

In going transcendent, poetry in the Romantic period cut increasingly adrift from the public world, moving both upward and inward. Yet it was also its very distance from that public sphere which allowed it to act as a critique of it, and so to engage with it after a fashion. The imagination soared higher than prosaic reality, but in poets like Blake and Shelley it still figured as a transformative political force. It could conjure up enthralling new possibilities of social existence; or it could insist upon the contrast between its own sublime energies and a drably mechanistic social order. Poetry could model a type of human creativity, along with 'organic' rather than instrumental relationships, which were less and less to be found in industrial society as a whole.

In Victorian England, this sense of the imagination as a political force gradually faded. It was still eloquently at work in the writings of John Ruskin and William Morris; but poetry, according to John Stuart Mill, was now to be overheard rather than heard. It had retreated from the public forum to the parlour. Having begun life as a sub-branch of rhetoric, it was now the precise opposite of it. Despite the enormous public esteem bestowed on the most eminent poets of the age, poetry itself had essentially been privatised. Tennyson might hold the public post of Poet Laureate, but his finest writing was more lyrical than epic, more tremulously introspective than robustly *engagé*. Challenged by the most powerful public genre of the age (the novel), and spurned by the dominant philosophy of Utilitarianism, poetry was in danger of being overlooked rather than overheard. In a new division of literary labour, the novel was now seen as a social form, dealing in ideas and institutions, while poetry had become the preserve of personal feeling. It was as though the lyric poem defined the entire genre. So it would remain, until modernists like Eliot, Yeats, Pound and Stevens sought to revive it as a major genre. Perhaps poetry might become a central art form once again in a modern age whose sense of solitude and spiritual anxiety matched its own. Perhaps it was in articulating this intensely private experience that it could, ironically, become most publicly representative.

The story of rhetoric, then, is not an encouraging one. After a promising start in the ancient city-states, it was fossilised by the medieval scholars, suppressed by scientific rationalism, and finally routed by a privatised poetics. A sophisticated ancient art ended up as synonymous with tub-thumping, brazen cajolery and the cynical inciting of mass emotion. In the United States today, it means teaching freshmen where to insert semicolons. The art of rhetoric did, however, exact a belated sort of revenge. In his notes on the subject, Friedrich Nietzsche argues that the study of rhetoric as the art of public persuasion should play second fiddle to the study of it as a set of tropes and figures – figures, he comments, which are the 'truest nature' of language as such. What Nietzsche did was to generalise rhetoric (in the sense of figurative or non-literal discourse) to the whole of our speech. All language worked by metaphor, metonymy, synecdoche, chiasmus and the like; and this meant that from the viewpoint of truth and communication, all language was thoroughly unreliable.

Post-structuralist thinkers like Jacques Derrida and Paul de Man then took up this case to demonstrate that communication could never quite take place, meaning never quite hit the mark.[6] Rationalism had denounced rhetoric as a purely ornamental affair; but rhetoric now returned the compliment by claiming that reason itself was infiltrated by figurative devices from end to end. Rhetoric was a fifth columnist in the enemy camp. It was the hidden truth of all language. Now, however, it worked to undermine truth, meaning, communication and political action, which was hardly the case for Cicero or Demosthenes. We have seen that the ancient art of rhetoric brought together the study of figurative language with the art of communication; but the former meaning of rhetoric was now turned against the latter. You could have metaphors or you could have stable meanings, but you could not have both together.

Since poetry was the home of figurative language, it was now once again seen as rhetoric – but rhetoric in the Nietzschean sense of slippery speech, not in the ancient sense of public utterance. In poetry, so the theory went, truth and meaning are fatally undermined by the metaphorical nature of the medium in which they are expressed. As de Man comments: 'poetry gains a maximum of convincing power at the very moment that it abdicates any claim to truth'.[7] We will see a little later how poetry can be regarded as the truth of language in general, in that it reveals how verbal form shapes meaning. Now, however, it was as though poetry revealed the truth of the untruth of language in general.

Yet this was only one theoretical current to emerge in the 1970s and 1980s. From feminist criticism to cultural materialism, the devotees of Mikhail Bakhtin to the New Historicism, there were other lines of inquiry which sought to keep faith with the project of classical rhetoric. Ironically, it was these supposedly newfangled theorists who were most in line with tradition. They, too, set out to investigate literary works as both patterns of meaning and historical events, places where power and signification converged. Yet as the new millennium approached, and the prevailing political system grew arrogantly convinced that it had seen off all challengers, this enterprise became harder to sustain. The very idea of a political criticism was coming under fire. A few decades ago, for example, it was acceptable to speak of literature

---

[6] For a useful introduction to post-structuralist thought, see Christopher Norris, *Deconstruction: Theory and Practice* (London, 1982); Catherine Belsey, *Critical Practice* (London, 1980) and Terry Eagleton, *Literary Theory: An Introduction* (Oxford, 1983), Ch. 4.

[7] Paul de Man, *Allegories of Reading* (New Haven, CT and London, 1979), p. 50.

in terms of social class. In fact, it was hard to see how one could not. The English novel, for example, is preoccupied with class, status, property, finance, marriage, reproduction and inheritance from one end to another.

Nowadays, however, to speak of the English novel in these terms provokes the charge of being 'sectarian', to quote one particular literary hack. The Victorians were quite prepared to hold forth on such subjects, whereas it seems that we moderns are rather more coy. In a world of burgeoning violence and dispossession, critics and reviewers have become for the most part 'post-political'. From the Russian Formalists to the American New Critics, Northrop Frye to Roland Barthes, the great formalist critics who contested historicist views of literature did so in provocative, theoretically sophisticated ways. Political criticism today, however, is not privileged to be up against such bracing antagonists. With some honourable exceptions, it is up against prejudice and ignorance.

We face, then, an alarming situation. Literary criticism is at risk of reneging on both of its traditional functions. If most of its practitioners have become less sensitive to literary form, some of them also look with scepticism on the critic's social and political responsibilities. In our own time, much of this political inquiry has been offloaded on to cultural studies; but cultural studies, conversely, has too often ditched the traditional project of close formal analysis. Each branch of study has learned too little from the other.

In both ways, then, literary criticism is in danger of breaking faith with its origins in classical rhetoric. It is equally in danger of breaking faith with the heritage of Renaissance humanism, whose exponents, as Joseph Schumpeter points out, 'were primarily philologists but . . . they quickly expanded into the fields of manners, politics, religion and philosophy'.[8] Something similar is true of modern criticism's august beginnings in England, in the form of what has been called the eighteenth-century public sphere.[9] Writers like Joseph Addison, Richard Steele and Samuel Johnson conceived of criticism as among other things a form of social and moral critique. So did the so-called men of letters of the nineteenth century, from Samuel Taylor Coleridge to Matthew Arnold. And so, too, did the twentieth-century lineage which stretches from Leavis, Richards and Empson to George Orwell, E. P. Thompson and Raymond Williams. What is known today as cultural theory is a modern version of traditional criticism. It is the 'traditionalist' opponents of such theory who are the blow-ins and interlopers. The slogan of a radical literary criticism, then, is clear: Forward to antiquity!

---

[8] Joseph A. Schumpeter, *Capitalism, Socialism, and Democracy* (New York, 1942), p. 148.
[9] See Terry Eagleton, *The Function of Criticism* (London, 1984).

1.3   The Death of Experience

It is ironic, in this light of his philological passion, that Nietzsche should figure in so many ways as the grandfather of postmodernist culture, since there is a plausible case to be made that it is this, not cultural theory, which has helped to sabotage the sensitive readings of texts. As one might expect, it is a specific way of life, not a set of abstract ideas, which is the culprit here. What threatens to scupper verbal sensitivity is the depthless, commodified, instantly legible world of advanced capitalism, with its unscrupulous way with signs, computerised communication and glossy packaging of 'experience'. There is, to be a sure, a theory that computers are actually a cunning way of trying to slow modern life down, as anyone who has tried to buy an air ticket or check into a hotel might testify. There are even those who are nostalgic for good, old-fashioned speed and bustle – for the whirlwind days when the hotel clerk simply took five seconds to slap your name down in a book, before modern technology put the brakes on such reckless rapidity. Writing your name in a book was also a process unlikely to crash.

The warning that experience itself is fading from the world has been issued all the way from Heidegger to Benjamin and beyond. Astonishingly, what is in peril on our planet is not only the environment, the victims of disease and political oppression, and those rash enough to resist corporate power, but *experience itself*. And this is a relatively new threat of extinction, one which would scarcely have been familiar to Chaucer or Samuel Johnson. On this theory (which as we shall see in a moment is strictly one side of the story), modernity has stripped us of many things – myth, magic, kinship, tradition, solidarity; but now it has finally succeeded in denuding us of ourselves. It has delved into the recesses of our very subjectivity, and emptied us out like so many rich plums ripe for scooping. The Eternal Now of modern urban existence, for which everything that happened up to ten minutes ago is ancient history, has eroded what for Walter Benjamin was the most precious medium of experience: tradition.[10] Experience for Benjamin meant the stories which the old recount to the young; and its disintegration in modern times was in his eyes one of the most grievous forms of human poverty. In a world of fleeting perceptions and instantly consumable events, nothing stays still long enough to lay down those deep memory traces on which genuine experience depends.

[10]   See, for example, his essay 'The Storyteller', in Hannah Arendt (ed.), *Illuminations* (London, 1973).

Benjamin, for whom even nostalgia could serve as a revolutionary weapon, did not live long enough to witness such cultural phenomena as the Grand Canyon Experience, or the Thomas Hardy's Double-Bed Experience. It is sobering to reflect how many deprived souls in the past visited the Grand Canyon without knowing that they were having the Grand Canyon Experience. What we consume now is not objects or events, but our experience of them. Just as we never need to leave our cars, so we never need to leave our own skulls. The experience is already out there, as ready-made as a pizza, as bluntly objective as a boulder, and all we need to do is receive it. It is as though there is an experience hanging in the air, waiting for a human subject to come along and have it. Niagara Falls, Dublin Castle and the Great Wall of China do our experiencing for us. They come ready-interpreted, thus saving us a lot of inconvenient labour. What matters is not the place itself but the act of consuming it. We buy an experience like we pick up a T-shirt.

A large part of what we are purchasing is not the immediate experience of the place, but (like a T-shirt) the fact that we will have had it. We experience the present in the future perfect tense. It is the act of having had the experience which matters, which removes us from the reality twice over. What is important about the event is its aftermath. And since what all these packaged spots have in common is the fact that they are experienced, they become, like commodities, indifferently interchangeable. Experience, which was once a way of resisting the commodity form in all of its rich specificity, is now just another species of it. A word which can mean an event of exceptional value ends up as a dead leveller. If the commodity form has impoverished our experience, postmodernism seeks to repair this destitution with a commodified experience. So the word 'experience' dwindles to an empty signifier, as in the sentence 'I am having the experience of boiling an egg', where the words 'having the experience of' could drop out with no detriment to the meaning. Experience gives way to information, which can be screwed up and tossed aside like a soiled tissue.

For post-structuralist thinkers like Foucault, Derrida and Lyotard, the death of experience is more commonly known as the death of Man. And this, for them, is a demise to be celebrated rather than mourned. For tradition and experience are not just repositories of value; they are also vehicles of violence and oppression. The whole idea of the 'full' human subject, replete in his stored sensations, cultivating his fine feelings like a bed of exotic plants and collecting his experiences like so many lovingly fondled art-objects, belongs to an earlier form of middle-class society – one which consumerist capitalism is now in the process of superseding. On this view, the passing of 'experience' is also the passing of the classical bourgeoisie – of the kind of men and women who figure in the novels of Proust and Thomas Mann, and who have now been replaced by an army of soulless stock-exchange traders and real-estate agents.

The Death of Man, then, is really the death of Bourgeois Man, who was a kind of private entrepreneur of his own experience. On this more traditional view, the self was to be regarded as an enormous whisky vat, in which experiences fermented quietly until they were mellow and mature. And this, in its own way, was as much a form of fetishism as the Ernest Hemingway's Gun-Room Experience. In its privileged way, it saw the self as a proprietor of its own perceptions. What mattered was a kind of rich, contemplative inwardness, to which practical action was strictly secondary.

The name of this inwardness was Culture. As an idea, it depended on a sense of unity, equipoise, self-assurance, unbroken continuity and harmonious self-development, as well as on a belief in the human subject as the controlling centre of reality. Since this model of Man assumed that everything in one's experience fundamentally hangs together, and that one's life is a smoothly unruptured narrative, it could make little room for dissonance and contradiction. Those who saw life in this way were inclined to the view that all experience was valuable, an article of faith not generally shared by the inhabitants of death row.

It is also the model of experience which underlies a good deal of modern talk about poetry. For what, so the critics inquire, is more unified and harmonious than a poem? Isn't it part of the very definition of poetry that absolutely nothing is out of place, that no word is idle or superfluous, that every element conspires with every other to form an integrated whole? This, by and large, is the view of poetry common to a great many commentators, from Coleridge to I. A. Richards, Goethe to the American New Critics. The poem is secretly a version of the well-ordered state. Like a hierarchical society, it has both dominant and subordinate levels. It is an organic society all of its own, a paradigm of unity and coherence. And therefore – at least for such iconoclastic thinkers as Freud – it is also the very image of a fetish. It is a reified response to a reified reality.

Poetry is supposed to be the place where words could only conceivably occur in the order in which we find them. As T. S. Eliot puts it in *Four Quartets*:

> . . . And every phrase
> And sentence that is right (where every word is at home,
> Taking its place to support the others,
> The word neither diffident nor ostentatious,
> An easy commerce of the old and the new,

The common word exact without vulgarity,
The formal word precise but not pedantic,
The complete consort dancing together)
Every phrase and every sentence is an end and a beginning,
Every poem an epitaph. . . .

If its words are locked so unchangeably into place, it is not surprising that the poem has an epitaph-like air of deathliness about it. Language, and the meanings it bears with it, are lent a disconcerting air of finality, almost of fateful necessity. Whereas the truth is that one of the most striking aspects of language is not only its slipping and sliding, as Eliot recognises elsewhere in the *Quartets*, but its unpredictability. No one bit of it can be rigorously deduced from any other bit. Even if I rise from the dinner table, tap a glass with my spoon and announce 'Ladies and . . .', it does not inexorably follow that my next word will be 'gentlemen'. It might always be 'headbangers'. Is poetry, then, a way of suppressing such linguistic possibilities? Does it encourage us to feel that a certain way of looking at the world is unalterable? And if this is so, is it a form of ideology rather than a critique of it?

It is significant that political radicals like Walter Benjamin did not *only* mourn the decay of experience in the age of mechanical reproduction. Had that been the case, Benjamin would be indistinguishable from a long lineage of cultural conservatives from Martin Heidegger and T. S. Eliot to Leo Strauss and George Steiner, for whom modernity is little more than a degenerate narrative of alienated science, vulgar democracy and mindless mass culture. It is not easy to imagine Heidegger sporting an i-pod, or Steiner browsing in the video store. On the contrary, radicals like Benjamin were aware that the death of certain forms of experience meant the possibility of bringing others to birth.[11] If modern technology can be oppressive, it can also be emancipatory. If it can dilute experiences, it can also increase their accessibility. Even the Giant's Causeway Experience can help to educate us, in however formulaic a fashion. History-as-heritage is arguably preferable to no history at all. Such cultural technology opens up a world of possibility unimaginable to our ancestors. Only a dialectical viewpoint, one which weighs the gains of modernity along with its losses, can do justice to it. And this is inimical alike to the cultural Jeremiahs, for whom civilisation has been going downhill ever since the invention of the wheel, and the wide-eyed cultural progressivists, for whom REM has thankfully put paid to Rembrandt.

[11]   See his essay 'The Work of Art in the Age of Mechanical Reproduction', in Arendt 1973.

Avant-garde artists like the Futurists and Surrealists plucked new kinds of art from the very speed, flatness, flux, randomness, irregularity, fragmentation and multiplicity of modern experience. A whole new poetics seemed possible. The most celebrated poem of the twentieth century, T. S. Eliot's *The Waste Land*, registers this haemorrhaging of experience from modern urban life, but views it as a spiritual catastrophe. Poets like Mayakovsky, Brecht and Breton, by contrast, did not look upon the emptying of the human subject with horror. Maybe being scooped out and dismantled might prove a prelude to being put together again, this time more productively. To learn something, as George Bernard Shaw remarked, always feels at first like losing something.

Yet that something had also been lost is surely beyond question; and part of the point of poetry was to seek to restore it. In a world of instant legibility, we had lost the experience of language itself. And to lose our sense of language is to lose touch with a great deal more than language. The largely pragmatic uses to which we put our speech had staled its freshness and blunted its force; and poetry, among other things, could allow us to relish and savour it anew. Rather than simply allow us to consume the stuff, it forced us to wrestle with it; and this was especially true of modern poetry. The notorious difficulty of such writing had much to do with the poem's objection to slipping down too easily. Instead, it thrust us into what T. S. Eliot called 'the intolerable wrestle with words and meanings'.

Poetry is a kind of phenomenology of language – one in which the relation between word and meaning (or signifier and signified) is tighter than it is in everyday speech. There are several different ways of saying 'Take a seat', but only one way of saying 'The hare limped trembling through the frozen grass.' Poetry is language in which the signified or meaning is *the whole process of signification itself.* It is thus always at some level language which is about itself. There is something circular or self-referential about even the most publicly engaged of poems. The meaning of a poem is far less abstractable from its total process of signification than is the meaning of a road sign. This is not to say that you cannot give a summary of a poem's content, just as you can of a police cadet's manual. But the former résumé is always likely to be less informational than the latter. Poetry is something which is done to us, not just said to us. The meaning of its words is closely bound up with the experience of them.

There is another distinctive feature of the poetic. The modern age has been continually divided between a sober but rather bloodless rationalism on the one hand, and a number of enticing but dangerous forms of irrationalism on the other. Poetry, however, offers to bridge this gap. More than almost any other discourse, it deals in the finer nuances of meaning, and thus pays its dues to the value of reasoning and vigilant awareness. At its best, it is a supremely refined product of human consciousness. But it pursues this devotion to meaning in the context of the less rational or articulable dimensions of our existence, allowing the rhythms, images and impulses of our subterranean life to speak through its crisp exactitudes. This is why it is the most complete sort of human language that one could imagine – though what constitutes language, ironically, is exactly its incompleteness. Language is what there is always more of.

1.4 Imagination

We may return, finally, to the question of the imagination. The imagination is one of those terms, like 'community' or 'Nelson Mandela', which it would seem almost impious to subject to criticism. It is as much a universally approved truth as the idea that young people who have been murdered were invariably bubbly and fun-loving with hordes of friends and a passionate zest for life. Everybody is for the imagination, just as everybody is for peace and an end to poverty. That studying literature is supposed to make the imagination more supple and dynamic is often advanced as a vital reason for doing it. And we are certainly in need of such rationales. For the problem with literary studies from an academic viewpoint is that they are simply not unpleasant enough to qualify as a *bona fide* academic discipline. Literary critics live in a permanent state of dread – a fear that one day some minor clerk in a government office, idly turning over a document, will stumble upon the embarrassing truth that we are actually paid for reading poems and novels. This would seem as scandalous as being paid for sunbathing or having sex.

But it is not only that we are paid for reading books. Even more outrageously, we are paid for reading books about people who never existed and events that never took place. In everyday life, talking about imaginary people as though they were real is known as psychosis; in universities, it is known as literary criticism. Quantum physicists work on entities which may not exist, and so do theologians. There are debates among sociologists about whether the Bank of England exists in the same sense that banknotes do, or whether it is just a fictional name for an assemblage of people, desks, practices, filing cabinets and so on. Mathematicians of a Platonic turn of mind hold that numbers are somehow actually out there, while for other mathematicians they are no more actually out there than the concept of crimson is. Even maverick archaeologists in search of the lost island of Atlantis, or astrophysicists who surmise that there may be an infinity of universes, may just be on to something real.

Literary critics, however, cannot reap the advantages of such doubts and ambiguities. For it is undeniable that there never was anyone called Emma Woodhouse or Emma Bovary – and that even if there were, for reasons too complex to examine here, it would make no difference to the kind of things that critics say about them. Critics do not have the satisfaction of working on things that actually exist, like sick dogs or dental cavities. So they are tempted to pluck a virtue out of necessity and claim that they toil in an altogether superior realm, that of the imagination. This implies, rather oddly, that things which do not exist are inevitably more precious than those that do, which is a fairly devastating comment on the latter. What kind of a world is it in which possibility is unquestionably preferable to actuality?

In making such claims, however, critics tend to assume, like almost everyone else on the planet, that the imagination is an unequivocally positive faculty, which is far from the case. For one thing, possibility clearly isn't always undoubtedly preferable to actuality. The imagination is able to project all sorts of dark, diseased scenarios, along with a number of utopian ones. It is revered as one of the 'highest' of human capacities; yet it is also embarrassingly close to fantasy, which is one of the most infantile and regressive. As Jonathan Swift was aware, sublimity and monstrosity border closely upon each other in human affairs.

The imagination is also sometimes commended for offering us in vicarious form experiences which we are unable to enjoy at first hand. If you can't afford an air ticket to Kuala Lumpur, you can always read Conrad and imagine yourself in South-East Asia. If you have been monotonously married for forty years, you can always lay furtive hands on a copy of James Joyce's letters. Literature on this view is a kind of supplement to our unavoidably impoverished lives – a sort of spiritual prosthesis which extends our capabilities beyond their normal restricted range. It is true that everyone's experience is bound to be limited, and that art can valuably augment it. But why the lives of so many people should be imaginatively impoverished is then a question that can easily be passed over. It is surely no accident that this theory of the imagination was gaining ground in the years of early industrial society, when the experience of a great many men and women was being warped and narrowed by inhuman conditions.

The modern idea of the imagination first emerged in English society when it became clear that everyday life was increasingly governed by an ethic of selfish individualism. If all I can really know is my sense-impressions, then how can I ever know you? Are we not forever cut off from each other by the walls of our bodies? If this is so, then there would seem a need for some special, intuitive faculty which would allow me to soar beyond my senses, plant myself within you and empathise with your feelings; and this remarkable capability was known to some eighteenth-century thinkers as the imagination. Human compassion was possible only by virtue of this quirky, enigmatic, somewhat fragile power. The imagination was a form of compensation for our natural insensibility to one another. We could not change that common-or-garden callousness, but we could always supplement it. If only I could know what it was like to be you, I would cease to be so brutal to you, or come to your aid when others were treating you badly.

So brutality, on this view, is just a breakdown of imagination. The only drawback with this doctrine is that it is obviously false. Sadists know exactly how their victims are feeling, which is what spurs them on to more richly imaginative bouts of torture. Even if I am not a sadist, knowing how wretched you feel does not necessarily mean that I will feel moved to do something about it. Conversely, people who come to the aid of others may be, so to speak, imaginatively tone-deaf, unable to re-create in themselves in any very vivid way the feelings of those they help out. The fact that they are unable to do so is morally speaking neither here nor there.

Acts of imagination are by no means always benign. Organising genocide takes a fair bit of imagination. Bank robbers need to be reasonably imaginative about making good their escape. Serial killers may indulge in unspeakable flights of fancy. Every lethal invention on record came about through the envisaging of unrealised possibilities. If William Blake ranks among the visionaries, so does Pol Pot. There is nothing creative in itself about the imagination, which launches wars as well as volumes of poetry. The imagination, like memory, is indispensable in an everyday sort of way: we would not tread warily on a slippery path without having a dim picture in our heads of how we might come to grief on it.[12] Nothing is more commonplace than this noble faculty. It is essential to our survival. But some exercises of it are no more positive than some acts of memory. Studying literature, then, may require a rather stronger rationale than this appeal to fantasy. Before we ask ourselves what this might be, however, we may pause to wonder why it should need a rationale at all, any more than sex or sunbathing.

So far, we have been speaking of poems and poetry without pausing to define our terms. Before we go any further, then, we need to see if we can arrive at some workable definition of what we are dealing with.

---

[12] For further critical comments about the imagination, see Terry Eagleton, *The Idea of Culture* (Oxford, 1983, pp. 45–6).

Chapter 2

What is Poetry?

2.1 Poetry and Prose

A poem is a fictional, verbally inventive moral statement in which it is the author, rather than the printer or word processor, who decides where the lines should end. This dreary-sounding definition, unpoetic to a fault, may well turn out to be the best we can do. Before we dissect it piece by piece, however, let us note what it doesn't say, rather than what it does.

To begin with, it makes no reference to rhyme, metre, rhythm, imagery, diction, or symbolism and so on. This is because there are plenty of poems which do not use these things, and quite a lot of prose that does. Prose may use internal rhymes, and quite commonly raids the resources of rhythm, imagery, symbolism, word-music, figures of speech, heightened language and the like. Wallace Stevens is rhythmical, but so is Marcel Proust. Virginia Woolf's prose is much more metaphorically charged than John Dryden's poetry, not to mention Gregory Corso's. There is more rhetorically heightened language in Joseph Conrad than there is in Philip Larkin.

It is true that prose does not generally use metre. On the whole, metre, like end-rhymes, is peculiar to poetry; but it can hardly be of its essence, since so many poems survive quite well without it. We are left, then, with line-endings, which the poet herself gets to decide on. Even this is only true up to a point: a particular kind of metre may itself determine where the lines have to end. But the poet gets to choose the metre, at least within certain constraints. A dramatist writing around 1600 was normally expected to use blank verse, while a satirist writing around 1750 would probably find heroic couplets the most appropriate form.

Line-endings in poetry may not always signify, but they can always be made to. They can even act as a kind of image, of the kind F. R. Leavis discerns in these lines from John Keats's ode 'To Autumn':

> And sometimes like a gleaner thou dost keep
> Steady thy laden head across a brook . . .

'As we pass across the line-division from "keep" to "steady"', Leavis observes, 'we are made to enact, analogically, the upright steadying carriage of the gleaner as she steps from one stone to another.'[1] The reader may find the comment genuinely perceptive, or just a more subtle version of the kind of criticism that claims to hear the cut and thrust of the rapiers in the swishing sibilants of some poetic description of a duel.

Prose, by contrast, is the kind of writing in which where the lines end is a matter of indifference. It is a purely technical affair. All the same, there is hardly a device thought of as 'poetic' which some piece of prose somewhere does not exploit. Prose may be lyrical, introspective and brimming with delicate feeling, while poetry may recount narratives about the land wars in nineteenth-century Ireland. The distinction between the two is ripe for dismantling.

Take, for example, this sourly misogynistic piece by D. H. Lawrence:

> The feelings I don't have, I don't have.
> The feelings I don't have, I won't say I have.
> The feelings you say you have, you don't have.
> The feelings you would like us both to have, we neither of us have.
>
> The feelings people ought to have, they never have.
> If people say they've got feelings, you may be pretty sure they haven't
>   got them.
>
> So if you want either of us to feel anything at all,
> You'd better abandon all idea of feelings altogether.
>   ('To Women, As Far As I'm Concerned')

What makes this a poem? Surely not the quality of the language, which is aggressively prosaic. The piece is as rough-and-ready in its language as it is in its attitudes. The poem doesn't rhyme (unless repeating 'have' counts as a rhyme), or employ metre (it is in so-called free verse). It also avoids

---

[1] F. R. Leavis, *The Common Pursuit* (Harmondsworth, 1962), p. 17.

symbolism, allegory, figurative speech, ambiguity, metaphor, suggestive connotation and the rest. Rather than exploring intricate states of feeling, it wrathfully rejects that whole enterprise. It does, however, manipulate rhythm and repetition to make its point. And setting up this rhythmical pattern involves an attention to line-endings. If the lines were strung out together like prose, this vital rhythmic pounding, like someone banging his fist on a table, might well be lost. So composing the piece as a poem has a point. By breaking it up like this on the page, the abrasive, staccato impact of the lines, each of which seems to end with a series of irascible thumps, is thrown into high relief. So is the parallelism between them, as each line weaves a variation on the last. And this sense of mechanical repetition captures something of the speaker's emotionally depleted state, as well as his sexual irritability.

The repetition also plays a major part in another of the poem's effects, which is that despite its dyspeptic quality, it is mildly funny. Its cut-the-crap bluntness, its bull-headed refusal to qualify or elaborate, make us smile, as we might at someone carelessly paring his corns on a Queen Anne chair. There is something wryly amusing about the poem's downrightness, which allows us to enjoy a momentary relief from the exacting complexities of feeling. It is the kind of brutal candour we might be tempted to go in for ourselves, if only we weren't so cravenly civil. The lines are wonderfully unsubtle. Indeed, the fact that the piece is comic and disgusted at the same time is part of its peculiar emotional impact. If it is deadly serious in its savage dismissal of fine feelings, there is a sense in which it is also sending itself up, or at least is ironically aware of its own exasperation. The emphatic refrain 'I don't have', 'you don't have', 'we don't have', 'neither of us have' is a kind of heavy-handed wit. It has the air of a comic riddle about it. The wordplay shows the poet as slightly detached from his own exasperation.

No doubt there should be a brief, suspenseful pause in the middle of each line after the first 'have', as with a stand-up comic about to deliver a punch line. (In English poetry, as opposed to some other kinds, a pause can come anywhere in the line.) Each line is in this sense a minor drama, cruelly pulling the carpet out from under whomever the speaker is addressing. One can imagine the speaking voice rising suggestively with 'The feelings you say you have', only to crash bathetically down with the matter-of-fact flatness of 'you don't have'. It is not the kind of piece you could vocalise very successfully in standard English. There is a lot about the language which suggests Lawrence's own provincial speech.

So one can see why it suits the poem to be in the form of verse. It is also poetry because it is a 'moral' statement, an idea we shall be examining in a moment. And calling it a poem, a title which the author acquires for it simply by organising his words on the page in this way, also suggests that it has a bearing beyond himself and his partner, or whoever the addressee may be. We shall be examining this idea in a moment as well. Even so, the lines have as little in common with the usual stereotype of the poetic as they can get away with. And to this extent, their form reflects their content. Their brusque way with self-conscious cults of feeling comes through in their calculatedly artless language, with its sense of rasping immediacy.

2.2   Poetry and Morality

The word 'moral' usually poses a problem, not least in Anglo-Saxon cultures. It suggests codes and prohibitions, grim strictures and civilised behaviour, rigorous distinctions between right and wrong. This forbidding notion of morality was what inspired the philosopher Bertrand Russell to remark that the Ten Commandments ought to come with the sort of rubric which is sometimes to be found on examination papers of ten questions: 'Only six need be attempted'. If poetry is about pleasure, morality would seem to be its opposite. In fact, morality in its traditional sense, before the advocates of duty and obligation got their hands on it, is the study of how to live most fully and enjoyably; and the word 'moral' in the present context refers to a qualitative or evaluative view of human conduct and experience. Moral language does not only include terms like good and bad, or right and wrong: its lexicon extends to such epithets as 'rash', 'exquisite', 'placid', 'sardonic', 'vivacious', 'resilient', 'tender', 'blasé' and 'curmudgeonly'. All these are as much moral terms as 'saintly' or 'genocidal'. Morality has to do with behaviour, not just with good behaviour. Moral judgements include such statements as 'Her protestations were more disquieting than reassuring', as well as statements like 'this evildoer ought to have his eyes gouged out'. The vocabulary of criticism is for the most part a moral one, with an admixture of technical or aesthetic terms.

'Moral', in this traditional usage, contrasts not with 'immoral', but with terms like 'historical', 'scientific', 'aesthetic', 'philosophical' and so on. It refers not to a distinct domain of human experience, but to the whole of that experience as considered from a particular angle. Physiologists, for example, may be interested in the muscular contractions which caused my arm to rise in the air; political scientists in how many other people were voting on my side; aestheticians in the way this sudden motion set the light on my jacket sleeve dappling and shimmering; and philosophers in how free this arm movement could be said to be. But the moralist is interested in the values which informed my decision, the human ends it was intended to serve, the extent to which it might promote human welfare and the like. To this extent, we are all moralists; and artists, who necessarily deal in values and qualities, are no doubt more so than most.

Poems are moral statements, then, not because they launch stringent judgements according to some code, but because they deal in human values, meanings and purposes. So another opposite of the word 'moral' here might be 'empirical'. A statement like 'She stood before the great carved door of the cathedral, her head bowed', is factual or empirical, whereas a statement like 'She stood before the great carved door of the cathedral, her head bowed in grief' is a moral one. A line like 'I rode my cycle into town' is not yet quite a poem, even though technically speaking it is an iambic tetrameter. So I could add a second line: 'And ran a short-legged sailor down'. This is more promising, since we now have another iambic tetrameter, along with a rhyme and an alliteration. But what we have so far is purely descriptive: it doesn't make any moral point. So I might add:

> Death falls like lightning from the sky;
> Nothing too small to 'scape its eye.

So now we have a poem, albeit a pretty wretched one.

Almost all works of literature include factual propositions, but part of what makes them works of literature is that these propositions are not present for their own sake, in the manner of statements like 'Keep Left' on English roads. Factual statements like this can always be used for non-factual effects, as happens in symbol and metaphor. 'Keep Left' can have political as well as empirical connotations. There is now a fat archive of poems which exploit the London Underground sign 'Mind the Gap' to symbolic effect. In these cases, two meanings – an empirical and a 'moral' one – are folded into unity. But factual or empirical statements might crop up in literary works because they play a part in their overall moral design. Balzac might need to give us a certain amount of information about the Parisian sewers, for example, simply to further his plot. These facts are not there simply for information, any more than 'You're an ugly-looking bastard' is there simply for information. This is why it isn't so important if poets, as opposed to brain surgeons or aeronautical engineers, get their facts wrong.

Even so, to get one's facts *wildly* wrong can make a 'moral' difference. Samuel Johnson, for example, could not enjoy a piece of literature which he thought immoral; but neither could he enjoy one which seemed to him in some obvious sense untrue. This is why he complains when Milton, in his poem *Lycidas*, speaks of Lycidas (the poet Edward King) and himself as having 'drove afield, and both together heard / What time the grayfly winds her sultry horn, / Battening our flocks with the fresh dews of night . . .' Johnson observes irritably in his *Lives of the Poets* that we know perfectly well that the two men did nothing of the kind. In fact, they hardly knew one another. Readers today are more ready to grant Milton a spot of poetic licence; but this is not to say that we will genially tolerate any old factual blunders in our poetry. Our enjoyment of literary works can be impaired if they commit serious empirical errors. If the poet really does appear to believe that Abraham Lincoln was a Tuareg tribeswoman, or that Stockholm sank without trace in the fifth century BC, we would probably be less enthralled by whatever rhetorical ends these facts were being mobilised to serve.

A convenient example is Dylan Thomas's line about a dead woman: 'Her fist of a face died clenched on a round pain.' For all its metaphorical audacity and panache, this comes unstuck because pains are plainly not round. The image only works if we subscribe to a version of the way the world is which we know to be false. As a consequence, the line is more grotesque than illuminating. Though it is meant to be abrasively physical, it is conceived in the head rather than in the guts. It is the kind of conceit that might occur to you after a hard night on the town, one you might even scribble down excitedly at two o'clock in the morning; but to commit it to paper in the sober light of day and release it to the general public betrays an alarming lack of judgement. This is not to say that while reading literary works we do not sometimes provisionally accept assumptions or hypotheses which we would not readily sign up to in real life. This is known as the suspension of disbelief. But there are limits to our disbelief, just as there are to our faith.

It is not always easy to draw a line between moral and empirical statements. Some moral philosophers, known as realists, insist that moral statements describe what is the case just as much as empirical or scientific ones do. On this theory, to say 'You are a loathsome sycophant' is to give just as factually accurate an account as to say 'you are five foot seven'. It is not just a way of describing my feelings about you, or recommending a way of behaving towards you, as some other moral theories hold. A similar blurring of the moral and empirical can be found in literature. There are pieces of writing like Lucretius's six-volume *De Rerum Natura*, which is an early scientific treatise, or Virgil's *Georgics*, which is a kind of agricultural manual. It is true that the *Georgics* is also a 'moral' work, a panegyric to a politically unified Italy which is intent on fostering certain conservative Roman values. But great stretches of it are devoted to such apparently unpoetic matters as beekeeping and cattle breeding. In fact, from antiquity to the Enlightenment, the distinction between the moral and the empirical is less of a hard-and-fast one than it generally is for us. Literature in the eighteenth century could include works of science, history and philosophy.

2.3   Poetry and Fiction

The distinction between the empirical and the moral is not the same as the difference between fact and fiction. There are plenty of moral statements, such as 'certain members of the Royal Family are oafish individuals of philistine tastes and remarkably low intelligence', which are not fictional – not only because they are true, but because they belong to the real world rather than to poems and novels. A poem does not only deal in moral truths; it deals with them in a fictional kind of way. What do we mean by this?

Let us look back at the Lawrence poem. One thing we mean by calling this a poem is that we are not to take it simply as about a real-life situation – one, say, between Lawrence and his partner. Lawrence might not have had a partner at all, and it would make no difference to the piece. The poem does not have the same status as an extract from a letter by Lawrence to his wife, even though it might actually be such an extract. It could be that Lawrence lifted a passage from a letter he wrote to his wife and reorganised it on the page in this way; but in doing so he altered its status by inviting a different kind of 'uptake' from the reader. By breaking the lines up on the page, as well as by using rhythm and repetition as obtrusively as he does, he is expecting the reader to relate to his words in a different way from how we might address ourselves to a letter. The carved-up shape of the lines on the page signals what would count as an appropriate interpretation of them. It proclaims, for example, that this is the kind of genre where what is primarily at stake is moral rather than factual truth. And in this sense it differs from a weather report, or the instructions on a can of soup. We are meant to take the verse not primarily as shedding light on the author's marriage, a relationship which may interest us as little as it appears to interest him, but on human feelings and relationships in general. This is one illustration of the fact that what an utterance means depends quite a bit on what sort of reading it anticipates.

To 'fictionalise', then, is to detach a piece of writing from its immediate, empirical context and put it to wider uses. To call something a poem is to put it into general circulation, as one wouldn't with one's laundry list. The very act of writing a poem, however desperately private its materials may be, is a 'moral' one, since it implies a certain communality of response. Which is not to say a certain uniformity of one. Simply by being arranged on the page as it is, it offers a meaning which is potentially sharable. Because it has come loose from its original context, or because that situation was an imaginary one, a poem's meaning cannot be rigorously determined by it. I can be fairly sure of what 'Keep Clear of the Crater's Edge' signifies when I am standing on the summit of Mount Etna; but a poem does not come complete with a ready-made context for making sense of its words. Instead, we have to bring such a context to it, and there is always a repertoire of different possibilities here. This is not to say that poems can mean just anything you like. 'And justify the ways of God to men' cannot mean 'And fix my puncture with some chewing gum', at least not as the English language is at present constituted. (Though there is absolutely no reason in principle why the word 'gum' could not mean 'men'. Maybe it does in some African language; or maybe it is slang for 'men' in some little known English idiom. In Northern English dialect, 'gum' is a euphemism for 'God', as in 'By gum'.)

So we are not speaking of a verbal free-for-all. But to say that poems have come loose from their original contexts is to say that ambiguity is somehow built into them, since they are more free-floating than, say, applications for planning permission. A poem is a statement released into the public world for us to make of it what we may. It is a piece of writing which could by definition never have just one meaning. Instead, it can mean anything we can plausibly interpret it to mean – though a great deal hangs on that 'plausibly'. To some extent, this is true of all writing, 'imaginative' or not. Writing just is language which can function perfectly well in the physical absence of its author, as pillow talk cannot. It is transportable from one context to another. But this is more obvious in the case of fictional writing, where there is no actual material context for us to check it against. Even if a poem does concern an actual event like the Boston Tea Party, the fact that it has such an oblique relation to empirical truth means that it still cannot simply be checked off against it. Poetry is language trying to signify in the absence of material cues and constraints.

So a poem is the kind of writing which can work perfectly well in the absence of a reader or addressee. Not in the absence of *any* addressee (there are no unread poems), but in the absence of a specific one, like one's plumber or sexual partner. A poet may write verses especially for a specific reader, such as Catherine the Great or Ringo Starr, but to call them a poem implies that they must in principle be intelligible to someone else as well. Unless a poem was potentially intelligible to someone else, it would not be meaningful to the poet either. You could write in a private language known only to yourself; but to code and decode your experience in this way, indeed to have the concepts of 'code' and 'decode' in the first place, you would already need a language learned from and shared with others, who could therefore in principle come to decipher what you had written.

Many poems do not actually have an original context, since the experiences they portray are purely imaginary. There was no real situation in the first place. We have no idea whether Shakespeare ever called down frightful curses upon his treacherous daughters while crazed and naked on a heath, and from a critical viewpoint it does not matter whether he did or not. It is not the experience 'behind' *Lear* which concerns us, but the experience which *is* the play. T. S. Eliot once remarked that a genuine poet was one who wrote about experiences before they had happened to him.[2] In any case, not all poems register 'experiences'; what 'experience' does Homer's *Iliad* or Alexander Pope's *Essay on Criticism* reflect?

Even so, this is not quite what we mean by calling these works fictional. 'Fictional' does not primarily mean 'imaginary'. As far as fictionalising goes, it does not really matter whether the experience in question actually happened or not. Even if we discovered that there was a real-life Victorian orphan called Oliver Twist, it would make no difference to our 'uptake' of the work in which he appears. Some of the experiences recorded in Charlotte Brontë's novels actually happened to her, and some did not; but we do not need to know which is which in order to respond to her writing. An historically challenged reader could enjoy *War and Peace* without knowing that Napoleon actually existed.

If 'fiction' and 'imaginary' are not the same thing, it is partly because not all imaginary experiences are fiction (hallucinations, for example), but also because you can 'fictionalise' a piece of writing which was originally intended as factual. Notes to the milkman are usually terse, to the point, and written in plain, economical style; but this would not prevent a poetically inclined milkman from noting that 'Two skimmed, two semi-skimmed and one full cream' is an iambic pentameter. The meaning of a statement is partly determined by what sort of reception it anticipates; but this does not guarantee that it will get that sort of reception. We can read fictions non-fictionally, as when I am convinced that *Crime and Punishment* is a secret message about the unhealthy state of my feet addressed to me alone. Or we can read factual discourse fictionally, as when we read a meteorological report so as to

---

[2] Quoted in John Haffenden, *William Empson: Vol. 1: Among the Mandarins* (Oxford, 2005), p. 112.

stimulate in ourselves a sublime sense of the vastness of the skies and the mighty powers of Nature.

A different kind of example can be found in Alan Brownjohn's poem 'Common Sense':

> An agricultural labourer, who has
> A wife and four children, receives 20s a week.
> $^3/_4$ buys food, and the members of the family
> Have three meals a day.
> How much is that per person per meal?
> *—From Pitman's Common Sense Arithmetic, 1917*

> A gardener, paid 24s a week, is
> Fined $^1/_3$ if he comes to work late.
> At the end of 26 weeks, he receives
> £30.5.3. How
> Often was he late?
> *—From Pitman's Common Sense Arithmetic, 1917*

> . . . The table printed below gives the number
> Of paupers in the United Kingdom, and
> The total cost of poor relief.
> Find the average number
> Of paupers per ten thousand people.
> *—From Pitman's Common Sense Arithmetic, 1917*

> . . . Out of an army of 28,000 men,
> 15% were
> Killed, 25% were
> Wounded. Calculate
> How many men were there left to fight?
> *—From Pitman's Common Sense Arithmetic, 1917*

The poem is presumably not primarily aimed at those with an interest in the history of arithmetical textbooks. Instead, it sheds some light on what counts at various times as common sense, which is a moral rather than empirical matter, and thus the kind of stuff in which poems trade. The supposedly most dispassionate of human languages – mathematics – is revealed to be interwoven with ideological assumptions. Why should one take it for granted, for example, that those left alive should carry on fighting? Why not surrender? By breaking lines from the textbook up on the page, Brownjohn can turn them into a moral statement without altering a word. Pitman's phrases have now been reoriented. They have accrued a different sort of meaning from the one they would have for a school pupil in the First World War trying to solve these sums.

Fiction, then, does not mean in the first place 'factually false'. There are lots of falsehoods which are not fictional, and, as we have seen, there are also lots of factually true statements in literary works. The word 'fiction' is a set of rules for how we are to *apply* certain pieces of writing – rather as the rules of chess tell us not whether the chess pieces are solid or hollow, but how we are to move them around. Fiction instructs us in what we are to do with texts, not in how true or false they are. It suggests, for example, that we should not take them primarily as factual propositions, or worry overmuch about whether what factual claims they do contain are true or false. These claims, fiction informs us, are there mostly in the service of moral truth; they are not present for their own sake.

Fiction, then, is the kind of place in which the moral holds sway over the empirical – in which what holds our attention is, say, the significance of Fagin's matted red hair, not how many red-haired Jewish child-corrupters there actually were in Victorian London. This is not to dismiss such questions as pointless: it says quite a bit about Dickens that he should make one of the only two Jewish characters in his novels a villain. (The other was portrayed favourably in a feeble attempt to compensate for the first.) The way literary works rig the empirical evidence may be part of their moral meaning. And you cannot identify this rigging without empirical research.

Even so, if we read *Oliver Twist* for historical information about Victorian workhouses, we are not reading the novel as fiction – even though everything in it, including the information it provides about Victorian workhouses, *is* fiction. This information is fictional, as we have seen already, because it is there not for its own sake but as part of an overall rhetorical design. It is there to help construct what we might call a moral vision or way of seeing; and it is certainly possible for us to say whether we think *this* is true or false, feeble or powerful, frivolous or illuminating. But moral visions are not true or false in the same way that statements of fact are.

The fact that what is mainly at stake in literature are moral rather than empirical claims means that writers can bend the latter to fit the former. Aristotle remarks that the poet, unlike the historian, does not have to stick to the way things are. Because literary works, including historical novels, are not obliged to conform closely to the historical facts, they can reorganise those facts so as to highlight their moral significance. Narratives usually reconfigure the world in order to make a point about it. If you are writing a novel about Byron, you might feel it more appropriate to have him die fighting in the struggle for Greek national independence rather than unheroically succumbing to a fever in the midst of it, which was how he actually met his end. It might even seem more 'true'. History does not always get the facts in the most satisfactory order, or stage its events in the most convincing way. It was an absurd oversight on history's part to make Napoleon so stunted, or to cram so many wars into the twentieth century rather than spacing them out a bit more.

If we do not treat *Oliver Twist* 'fictionally', there is a danger that we will read it as just another real-life biography, and so fail to grasp its deeper implications. Its moral impact might be muffled if we take it too literally. Yet for the work to make such an impact, it needs to have an air of reality about it. The more realist it is, the more its moral significance is intensified; but for just the same reason, the more it is endangered. The ambiguous message of a work of literature, then, is 'Take me as real, but don't take me as real.' In one sense, poems, particularly post-Romantic ones, can seem *more* real, in the sense of more vitally present, more sensuously specific and emotionally intense, than the tarnished, abstraction-ridden everyday world. In another sense, as we have seen, they are less real, in the sense of less empirical, than most other forms of writing.

Just as there are risks in reading poems too literally, so there are dangers in generalising their meaning too far. We might come to believe, disastrously, that all the moral truths we encounter in literature are universally valid ones. We might read *Oliver Twist* not as portraying a situation which is in some sense remediable, but as an unalterable part of the human condition. We would thus find ourselves taking the view of the Victorian Poor Law Commissioners, who held for the most part that poverty was divinely ordained. This would be particularly ironic, since some of the social abuses which Dickens's novel depicts had in fact disappeared by the time it was published.

To generalise the meaning of a poem does not mean to treat the poem as an allegory of universal truth. On the contrary, part of the point of Romantic and post-Romantic poetry, as we have seen already, is to restore a sense of specificity in an increasingly abstract society. It is something like this, perhaps, which the delicate poem 'Sea Violet' by H. D. (Hilda Doolittle) intends to do:

> The white violet
> is scented on its stalk,
> the sea-violet
> fragile as agate,
> lies fronting all the wind
> among the torn shells
> on the sand-bank.

The greater blue violets
flutter on the hill,
but who would change for these
who would change for these
one root of the white sort?

Violet
your grasp is frail
on the edge of the sand-hill,
but you catch the light –
frost, a star edges with its fire.

The violet is not particularly meant to be 'symbolic'. But this does not mean that the poem is simply a description of an individual flower, without deeper, more complex resonances. Indeed, one of those resonances lies in the very sensuous detail of the piece – in the unwaveringly focused attention it trains upon this fragile, vulnerable form of life. It is this tender sensitivity to the particular, if you like, which is part of its more general significance.

One might say the same of some of John Clare's Nature poetry:

When midnight comes a host of dogs and men
Go out and track the badger to his den,
And put a sack within the hole, and lie
Till the old grunting badger passes by.
He comes and hears – they let the strongest loose.
The old fox hears the noise and drops the goose.
The poacher shoots and hurries from the cry,
And the old hare half wounded buzzes by.
They get a forked stick to bear him down
And clap the dogs and take him to the town,
And bait him all the day with many dogs,
And laugh and shout and fright the scampering hogs.
He runs along and bites at all he meets:
They shout and hollo down the noisy streets.
                    ('Badger')

The strength of these jagged, busily energetic lines lies not just in the way they casually turn their back on verbal adornment, but also in the way they resist any attempt to 'symbolise' the experience in question, making it speak portentously of more than itself. Clare's language is sinewy rather than suggestive. Both aspects of the piece are all the more effective for being quite unselfconscious. There is no programmatic, *Lyrical Ballads*-like attempt at 'plain language' here, simply a taken-for-granted trust in the robustness and resilience of common speech. 'Buzzes' is an especially fine stroke, one which (like 'old' fox and 'old' hare) captures less a quality of the animal itself than the poet's sense of affectionate familiarity with it.

Here as elsewhere, Clare stitches some of his lines together with a simple, repetitive copula ('And') – a device you can also find, though much more cultically and self-consciously, in a good deal of post-Hemingway American prose. He avoids stately or convoluted syntax for a sense of headlong narrative excitement. Unlike more 'polite' eighteenth-century poets, for example, he tends to steer well clear of sub-clauses. There is very little grammatical subordination of one thing to another, or sense of foreground and background. Instead, everything seems to exist on the same level, without proportion or perspective. The verse is written in a rapid, tumbling sort of iambic pentameter: we take in a line, but as we do so look expectantly to what's round the next line-ending.

The structure of the poem is metonymic (a matter of linking items together) rather than metaphorical (grasping affinities between them). There is no apparent concern for overall structure. Things sit haphazardly side by side simply because that is the way they occur in real life. Apart from a general air of fun and riot, one perhaps a little offensive to our more ecologically sensitive ears, the verse seems to feel no need to imply any complex attitude to what it records. Instead, its language effaces itself before what it registers. Its present tense catches the turmoil of the hunt as it happens, but it is also a timeless present which suggests that the badger-baiting has a venerable tradition behind it. So our sense of dramatic high jinks is blended with a bolstering sense of custom and stability.

2.4   Poetry and Pragmatism

Another way of putting the point about fiction is to claim that poems invite us to treat what they say 'non-pragmatically'. They are not about getting something done in a practical, immediate sense, even if they may get things done in some more indirect sense. The British national anthem 'God Save The Queen' is a kind of prayer – one which, like any petitionary prayer, expresses a hope that God will be gracious enough to do what we ask (namely, save the monarch) as a direct result of our mouthing the words. But the speech act is really non-pragmatic: it gives voice to this hope in order to express one's reverence for the head of state. Most British people who sing the national anthem are not cast into suicidal disillusion when, having lustily bellowed out these lines, they discover that the Queen remains as stubbornly unsaved as ever, every bit as stingy to her servants as she was when they started.

We could imagine the legendary anthropologist from Alpha Centauri listening to our speech and not realising that it was meant, among other things, to get things done – not grasping the connections between what we said and what we did, or even that such connections existed. In a sense, he would be hearing our language as poetry – as a verbal ceremony which existed for its own sake. Yet this ceremony itself is part of what we do, and has practical consequences for the rest of our way of life. Poetry is a social institution. It has complex affinities with other parts of our cultural existence. Treating language as not directly related to a material situation, for example, demands a great deal of material stage-setting.

The idea of poetry as a non-pragmatic discourse might be illuminated by this William Carlos Williams poem, which reads like a message to his wife:

> This is Just to Say
>
> I have eaten
> the plums
> that were in
> the icebox
>
> and which
> you were probably
> saving
> for breakfast
>
> Forgive me
> they were delicious
> so sweet
> and so cold

The poem might even have *been* a message to his wife. There is a parody of the piece by Kenneth Koch:

> I chopped down the house that you had been saving to live in next summer.
> I am sorry, but it was morning, and I had nothing to do
> and its wooden beams were so inviting.
>
> We laughed at the hollyhocks together
> and then I sprayed them with lye.
> Forgive me, I simply do not know what I am doing.

I gave away the money that you had been saving to live on for the next
  ten years.
The man who asked for it was shabby
and the firm March wind on the porch was so juicy and cold.

Last evening we were dancing and I broke your leg.
Forgive me. I was clumsy, and
I wanted you here in the wards, where I am a doctor!

(Williams was a physician as well as a poet.) That final exclamation mark is
superfluous, but Koch's parody, as well as being mildly funny, makes an interesting implicit comment on the Williams original. It seems (or pretends) to
see Williams's poem as seeking to excuse selfish and irresponsible behaviour
by appealing to the privileges bestowed on him by the status of poet. Poets,
so the implication runs, believe themselves absolved from common moral
strictures. Their self-centred cult of feeling elevates their own needs over
the claims of others, and the naivety with which they acknowledge this is
simply part of their moral immaturity. Their much-vaunted sensitivity is thus
a kind of callousness.

Perhaps poets can acknowledge their faults as readily as they do because they
know that, like overindulged children, they will be forgiven. The exquisite
sensibility they pride themselves on is really just a form of moral regressive-
ness. In any case, Williams's apology for eating the plums is oddly incoher-
ent: he asks to be forgiven for the act of raiding the plums, appealing to the
fact that they turned out to be delicious. But he could not have known
this when he decided to eat them. What if they had not turned out to be
delicious? It is rather like saying: 'Forgive me for shooting your dog; I got such
a kick out of it.'

There is, however, another way of looking at the piece. This is to see it
less as a poem about the infantile egoism of poets than one about the nature
of poetry itself. The poem is cast in the form of a message, which is a pragmatic piece of language; and it concerns the equally pragmatic or instrumental
action of storing some fruit away in the fridge to eat for breakfast. Putting
the message in this chopped-up form, however, overrides its pragmatic function, rather as the speaker has overridden the pragmatic function of keeping
the fruit for later. What attracted him was the sensuous reality of the plums
themselves, their delectable coldness and sweetness. And this means that
his relation to the plums is more 'poetic' than instrumental. It might be objected
that eating something is quite as pragmatic an activity as putting it in the
icebox; but the point is that the poet 'uses' the plums with full attention to

their specific properties, rather than simply grabbing them as if any old food will do. It is this which forms the basis of his apology, not the more predictable excuse that he was hungry. In fact, he may well not have been; the poem does not propose this at all as a way of exonerating his behaviour.

One thing the poem does, then, apart from fostering in us scriptural reflections about the guilt of eating forbidden fruit, is to show us that the pragmatic and the poetic are not always mutually exclusive. This is also true, as it happens, of Karl Marx's concept of use-value, which involves using things in ways appropriate to their inherent properties. For Marx, the opposite of 'exchange-value', which means a purely instrumental use of objects without regard to their particular features, is not refraining from using things at all, but using them with an eye to their sensuous qualities. So the idea of use-value is an alternative to the aesthete on the one hand, for whom all use is a desecration, and the philistine on the other, who has no feeling for the inner life of things.

In so far as poems, like plums, yield us pleasure, they have a kind of pragmatic function. It is just that this function is closely bound up with their sensuous existence. We do not just use poems instrumentally, any more than the speaker is interested in the plums simply because he is hungry. And just as his relation to the plums is both poetic and pragmatic, so is the text itself, which has the form of a scribbled communication yet which in its last four lines touches on a deeper sort of intensity. 'Forgive me', for example, seems a little histrionic, when 'Sorry' might have done just as well. There is indeed guilt as well as gratification involved in being a poet: it means not relating to the world quite as others do, though this (contrary to popular mythology) springs from being more thoroughly attuned to it, not less. Koch, then, is perhaps not entirely mistaken: a poet can give us a sense of the coldness and sweetness of things, where we might simply see tomorrow morning's breakfast; but to do so involves a 'de-pragmatising' of the world which has its perils as well as its value. One would not usually assign the chair of the famine relief committee to a poet.

2.5   Poetic Language

The final part of our definition to consider is 'verbally inventive'. The phrase is a lame one, but it is probably more accurate than less feeble formulations such as 'verbally self-conscious'. Poetry is often characterised as language which draws attention to itself, or which is focused upon itself, or (as the semiotic jargon has it) language in which the signifier predominates over the signified.

On this theory, poetry is writing which flaunts its material being, rather than modestly effacing it before the Holy-of-Holies of meaning. It is heightened, enriched, intensified speech.

The only problem with this theory is that quite a lot of what we call poetry seems not to behave this way. Take, for example, this passage from Robert Lowell's 'My Last Afternoon with Uncle Devereux Winslow':

> My Uncle was dying at twenty-nine.
> 'You are behaving like children',
> said my Grandfather,
> when my Uncle and Aunt left their three baby daughters,
> and sailed for Europe on a last honeymoon . . .
> I cowered in terror.
> I wasn't a child at all –
> unseen and unseeing. I was Agrippina
> In the Golden House of Nero . . .
> Near me was the white measuring-door
> my Grandfather had pencilled with my Uncle's heights.
> In 1911, he had stopped growing at just six feet . . .

One could imagine this passage written out as prose without it sounding particularly odd, were it not for the suggestive elliptical leaps of lines like 'I cowered in terror. / I wasn't a child at all – unseen and unseeing. / I was Agrippina / In the Golden House of Nero . . .'. Poetry allows for these quick shifts of imaginative logic, in which language works more by compression and association than by fully spelt-out connections. But the first five and last three lines could well appear in the form of prose.

Or take these lines from Ezra Pound's *Cantos*:

> And he came in and said: 'Can't do it,
> Not at that price, we can't do it'.
> That was in the last war, here in England,
> And he was making chunks for a turbine
> In some sort of an army plane;
> An' the inspector says: 'How many rejects?'
> And Joe said: 'We don't get *any* rejects, our . . .'
> And the inspector says: 'Well then of course
>   you can't do it'.

It seems stretching a point to see this kind of thing as involving a peculiar verbal self-consciousness, of the kind that one could find, for example, almost anywhere in Gerard Manley Hopkins:

I caught this morning morning's minion, king-
dom of daylight's dauphin, dapple-dawn-drawn Falcon, in his riding
Of the rolling level underneath him steady air, and striding
High there, how he rung upon the rein of a wimpling wind
In his ecstasy! . . .
                                                    ('The Windhover')

This, admittedly, is a pretty exotic example of the play of the signifier – of language focused flamboyantly upon itself. It is the kind of thing one also finds in certain uses of metre:

Mine eyes have seen the glory of the coming of the Lord:
He is trampling out the vintage where the grapes of wrath are stored . . .
                    (Julia Ward Howe, 'Battle-Hymn of the Republic')

. . . While I nodded, nearly napping, suddenly there came a tapping,
As of someone gently rapping, rapping at my chamber door.
''Tis some visitor', I murmured, 'tapping at my chamber door –
                                Only this and nothing more'.
                                (Edgar Allan Poe, 'The Raven')

I went into a public-'ouse to get a pint o'beer,
The publican 'e up an' sez, 'We serve no red-coats here'.
The girls be'ind the bar they laughed and giggled fit to die,
I outs into the street again an' to myself sez I:
    O it's Tommy this, an' Tommy that, an' 'Tommy, go away';
    But it's 'Thank you, Mister Atkins', when the band begins to play . . .
                                (Rudyard Kipling, 'Tommy')

By the shores of Gitche Gumee,
By the shining Big-Sea-Water,
Stood the wigwam of Nokomis,
Daughter of the Moon, Nokomis . . .
                (Henry Wadsworth Longfellow, 'The Song of Hiawatha')

Metres like these make a terrible racket, making it hard to hear the meaning through their incessant noise. They make the poems seem as though they are really about themselves. Pressed to an extreme, this kind of thing becomes doggerel.

The modern idea of the 'materiality of the signifier' – that the word has its own texture, pitch and density, which poetry exploits more fully than other verbal arts – is probably best exemplified in English not by a modern poet, but by John Milton:

> . . . There was a place
> (Now not, though Sin, not Time, first wrought the change)
> Where Tigris, at the foot of Paradise,
> Into a gulf shot underground, till part
> Rose up a fountain by the Tree of Life.
> In with the river sunk and with it rose
> Satan, involved in rising mist; then sought
> Where to lie hid. Sea he had searched and land,
> From Eden over Pontus, and the pool
> Maeotis, up beyond the river Orb;
> Downward as far antarctic; and, in length,
> West from Orontes to the ocean barred
> At Darien, thence to the land where flows
> Ganges and Indus . . .
>
> (*Paradise Lost*, Book 9)

Reading lines like this is almost a physical labour, as the eye struggles to unravel the intricate syntax and negotiate a path through the bristling thicket of proper names. All the way from that 'Satan' bursting dramatically upon us as we step across from line 6 to line 7, we need to keep the sense of the lines steadily in our heads as we pursue its twists and turns through Milton's grammatical maze. The blank verse slows us down, forcing us to experience the celebrated Miltonic music in all its high-pitched rhetorical bravura. From 'Sea he had searched and land' to 'Ganges and Indus', we seem to be re-enacting Satan's wanderings in the restless shifts and turns of the syntax and laborious pile-up of clauses, no sooner sent off in one fruitless direction than reoriented to another. There is a complex interplay between metre and speaking voice, as each weaves its way in and out of the other. The speaking voice plays across the metrical scheme with the kind of extreme flexibility and variation typical of English blank verse; but the elevated tone of the piece loftily survives all these resourceful syntactical twists and turns.

Poets, then, are materialists of language. Even so, much poetry cultivates the virtues of plainness and transparency. This is particularly true of some eighteenth-century English verse, which displays the Enlightenment virtues of clarity, equipoise and exactness; but it is also true for quite different reasons of a good deal of modern and postmodern poetry. Modernism, among other things, reflects a crisis of faith in language. There is a scepticism of the extravagant metaphor and the histrionic verbal gesture in an age which has good reason to be suspicious of manipulative rhetoric, whether it stems from autocrats or advertisers. There is also a distrust of language in an age when experience seems either too intricate or too appalling to find

adequate expression. In fact, such a suspicion of language, at least in its unre-
deemed everyday condition, may well lie behind Hopkins's somewhat hectic
heightening of it. For some modernist writers, you need to wreak organised
violence on language in order to knock some truth out of it, rather as for
authoritarians you need to beat children senseless if you are to knock any
values into them.

This passage from Jonathan Swift's 'Verses on the Death of Dr. Swift', in
which the author discuses his own life's work, is a model of Enlightenment
clarity:

> Perhaps I may allow the Dean
> Had too much satire in his vein;
> And seemed determined not to starve it,
> Because no age could more deserve it.
> Yet malice never was his aim;
> He lashed the vice, but spared the name;
> No individual could resent,
> Where thousands equally were meant;
> His satire points at no defect,
> But what all mortals may correct . . .

This is poetry in its rhyme, metre, economy and pointedness of verbal effect;
but there is nothing in the least verbally self-conscious about it. Much the same
goes for a poem by one of Swift's later compatriots, Bernard O'Donoghue:

> Stumbling my fingers along the shelves,
> I observe an interesting thing: books
> I have had for more than thirty years
> Feature my name in proud fountain-pen.
> Now I'm reminded of it, I recall
> Practising on rough paper to reach
> Such a convincing dash of signature.
>
> For a while they went slantwise,
> In legible ballpoint; then anywhere,
> With any implement: rollerpoint, red even.
> Recently I am perturbed to find
> I've started to sign in pencil. HB,
> Naturally; but will the time come
> When less permanent leads will do?
> 2B, 3B, 4B . . .

> ('Pencil It In')

This has the linguistic low-keyedness of much modern poetry, enlivened by the odd, discreet alliteration ('Stumbling'/'shelves', 'Feature'/'fountain-pen'). There is the occasional verbal flourish like 'Such a convincing dash of signature', where the verse, as though in ironic homage to the self-conscious panache of the poet's youthful signature, rises briefly to the grandeur of an iambic pentameter. And 'stumbling' is a good word with which to begin a poem about ageing. Once again, however, none of this can be said to reflect a predominance of the signifier over the signified, or the texture of the language over its meaning. It is not, one is gratified to note, the kind of stuff one finds in the worst of Algernon Charles Swinburne:

> Come with bows bent and with emptying of quivers,
>   Maiden most perfect, lady of light,
> With a noise of winds and many rivers,
>   With a clamour of waters, and with might;
> Bind on thy sandals, O thou most fleet,
> Over the splendour and speed of thy feet;
> For the faint east quickens, the wan west shivers,
>   Round the feet of the day and the feet of the night.
>
> ('Atalanta in Calydon')

Nobody could deny that this is poetry, which is exactly what is amiss with it. In symbolist fashion, the narcotic music of the words works to muffle the meaning. One finds a more extreme version of this effect in nonsense poetry like Lewis Carroll's "Twas brillig, and the slithy toves', which is really a symbolist poem. Perhaps it is just as well that Swinburne blurs the meaning, since there isn't much of it on offer. That last, self-consciously 'beautiful' line is intellectually vacuous (how can day and night have feet?), and it is hard to see how you can bind on a sandal over speed. For all its reverent heavy breathing, the passage is perfectly cerebral: 'With a noise of winds and many rivers' is a fuzzy abstraction, and 'with might' a notably lame appendage. 'Faint east' and 'wan west' are merely verbal counters to shuffle around in place of genuine observation. The passage is full of florid gestures and empty of substance.

Poetry uses language in original or arresting ways; but it does not do so all the time, and in any case this is not quite the same as a steady focus on the signifier. This is overlooked by those theories of poetry for which the word 'poetic' simply means 'verbally self-conscious'. So 'verbally inventive', however vague, will have to do instead. The word 'inventive' here is meant to be factual rather than evaluative: it does not imply that a poem is always *successfully* inventive, since this would rule out the possibility of bad poetry.

We have seen that breaking up a text into lines on a page is a cue to take it as fiction. But it is also an instruction to pay particular attention to the language itself – to experience the words as material events, rather than to gaze right through them to the meaning. In most poetry, however, it is not a question of experiencing the word rather than the meaning, but of responding to both of them together, or of sensing some internal bond between the two. Being more than usually sensitive to language does not necessarily imply that the language in question is peculiarly 'foregrounded'. A poem may be verbally inventive without flamboyantly drawing attention to the fact. Poems differ, so to speak, in the ratio they establish between signifier and signified. So do whole schools of poetry, or different cultural epochs, or different works by the same author. It is this which was largely overlooked by the Russian Formalists, who were the first modern group of critics to define poetry as an excess of signifiers over signifieds, and to whom we can now turn.

Chapter 3

Formalists

3.1 Literariness

The early twentieth-century school of Russian Formalists saw poetry as language which is placed in a peculiarly self-aware relationship to itself.[1] For these audaciously avant-garde critics, the literary *enfants terribles* of their time, poems were made up not of images, ideas, symbols, social forces or the poet's intentions, but of words. They therefore took as their object of inquiry the materiality of language, or what they called 'literariness'. 'Literariness' meant language which is peculiarly conscious of itself as such – or, to put it another way, language which has been 'made strange', so that it becomes newly *perceptible* to the reader or listener. Instead of being a transparent medium through which we stare at the world, it is now a tangible object in its own right. 'Nay, but to live in the rank sweat of an enseamed bed' is poetry because to grasp what the words mean is inseparable from relishing the taste of them in our mouths. It is not like saying 'OK, but to roll round in dirty sheets!' On this theory, literariness 'foregrounds' or highlights verbal signs, so that they become newly palpable. As such, as we have seen, it fails to reckon with the fact that much of what we call poetic does not do this to any remarkable degree.

---

[1] See Victor Erlich, *Russian Formalism: History – Doctrine* (The Hague, 1955); Fredric Jameson, *The Prison-House of Language* (Princeton, NJ, 1972); L. Matejka and K. Pomorska (eds.), *Readings in Russian Poetics* (Cambridge, MA, 1971), and Tony Bennett, *Formalism and Marxism* (London, 1979).

The Formalists did not claim that this foregrounding of the sign was confined to literature. 'Literariness' is not the same as 'literature'. Literariness can crop up in jokes or riddles or advertising slogans, while in some works of literature (realist novels, for example) it is fairly rare. Some tabloid newspapers, their editor would be astonished to hear, go in for literariness far more than does George Orwell. 'Making language strange' meant deviating from a linguistic norm, and in doing so 'defamiliarising' our shopsoiled, 'automated' everyday discourse. As such, poetry is a kind of creative deformation of our practical communication. Phrases like 'Thou still unravished bride of quietness' wreak systematic violence on our ordinary speech.

It follows from this that literariness is a relative concept, since you can only spot a deviation if you can identify a norm. And linguistic norms shift around. 'Estrangement' only works against a taken-for-granted linguistic background, but one person's taken-for-granted background may be another person's estrangement. Dropping your aitches in Knightsbridge probably counts as a deviation, whereas it is normative in parts of Lancashire. Pronouncing 'aitch' as 'haitch' is normative in the Republic of Ireland but deviant in Devon. To pronounce 'bath' with a long vowel is correct in Bath but not in Seattle. 'Is it himself you're after speaking to?' may sound quaint in Brooklyn but could be everyday speech in Kerry. What looks from one viewpoint like poetry, in the sense of language intensely aware of itself, may be another person's ordinary speech. Language which is archaic often sounds poetic to us, but may well not have done so to its original users.

3.2 Estrangement

The Formalists, then, recognised that literariness, or what they called the poetic function, was not a thing in itself, eternally fixed and objectively isolable, but a relation between different kinds of discourse. The poetic is the function of a difference between kinds of language, not an immutable set of properties. It is a matter of self-referential signs; but what counts as this changes from place to place and time to time. Even so, it is not always clear with the Formalists what exactly is being estranged. Is it the word (or signifier) itself; the idea (or signified); or the object (or referent) to which the word refers? Do we come away from the poem with a refreshed sense of the phrase 'Golden Gate Bridge', or of the concept, or of the actual structure itself? The general idea, anyway, is clear: poetry is a kind of creative abnormality, an exhilarating illness of language – rather as, when we are actually ill and so cease to take our bodies for granted, we have an unwelcome opportunity to experience them afresh.

In arguing all this, the Formalists boldly offered what they saw as a universal theory of poetry; but it is a theory which clearly belongs to a certain kind of civilisation. Generally speaking, it stems from the kind of social order in which language has become excessively pragmatic and instrumental. Poetry is really a kind of spiritual therapy for those moderns whose words have withered, whose speech has become as bland and flavourless as their food, and whose experience has been drearily routinised. It is the poetics of a social order governed by utility – one in which everything appears to exist purely for the sake of something else, and in which our senses have grown calloused and anaesthetised. ('Anaesthetic', which means 'unfeeling', is the opposite of 'aesthetic', a word which originally refers not to art but to sensation and perception.) Formalism is the poetics of an alienated society – and its response to this condition, ironically, is to alienate the alienation. It estranges our automated language and experience so that we can begin to live and feel them anew. Two negatives make a positive.

It is worth noting, then, that Formalism, like so much of modernist theory, is a negative aesthetics – one that defines poetry not by any positive features it might exhibit, but by its difference or deviation from something else. The poetic is constituted by what it bounces off against, and so is dependent on the very alienated reality to which it is a response. It is not obvious what Virgil, Dante or Milton would have made of this account of what they were up to. It also implies, questionably, that creativity is nowhere to be found in everyday language and experience; it is, rather, the privileged preserve of whatever resists them. There is a smack of elitism about this doctrine, even though several of the Formalists were Bolshevik fellow travellers. This 'radical' scepticism of the common life has raised its head again in our own time, in the postmodern assumption that the creative is to be found only in margins and minorities, in the deviant and anti-consensual.

Formalist critics like Viktor Shklovsky, Boris Eichenbaum and Roman Jakobson argued that the function of estrangement was common to all literary devices. This is an astonishingly audacious claim. If it is true, then these theorists really have stumbled upon the literary equivalent of the philosopher's stone. They have achieved what no other literary critic in history has managed to do: namely, to show what rhyme and plot, repetition and dramatic irony, assonance, metaphor, narrative structure and so on all have in common. It is a marvellously imaginative notion, and the fact that it is not true should not be allowed to obscure its resourcefulness. Estrangement in Formalist hands becomes an admirably versatile notion. It succeeds in explaining, for example, what rhyme and plot parallelism have in common, or what links alliteration with the breaks in a narrative. But it is hard to see how, say, the device of the Chorus in drama, or third-person narrative, or the happy ending of comedy, or the convention of not showing a duel on stage, can be invariably classed as examples of estrangement or defamiliarisation. Like many a universal claim, it begins to unravel at the seams when pressed too far.

The Russian Formalist critic Roman Jakobson distinguishes six elements of any act of verbal communication: addresser, addressee, message, code, contact and context. Any one of these can be dominant in a specific utterance. Let us suppose that the message in question is 'Joseph Stalin was a gentle soul.' To focus on the addresser involves what Jakobson calls the *emotive* function: 'What a gentle soul was Joseph Stalin!', proclaimed in an exalted tone of voice. The *conative* function, by contrast, concerns the effect the statement is striving to have on the addressee: 'Can't you see what a gentle soul old Stalin was?' Focusing on the code, meaning the pattern of elements which makes the communication possible, involves the *metalinguistic* function: 'Do you understand what I'm trying to tell you here about the gentleness of Joe Stalin?' The *phatic* function is dominant when we attend to the contact between speaker and listener: 'Well, here we are again, jawing on about old Joe Stalin'; while to direct attention to the context is to examine the *referential* function: 'It's Joe Stalin we're talking about here.' If, however, we focus on the message itself, then the *poetic* function comes into play. In the case of this particular message, we might note the alliteration between 'Stalin' and 'soul', the way that some of the vowel sounds of 'gentle' and 'Joseph' mutually reverberate, the fact that metrically speaking the statement is a trochaic pentameter, and so on. We might also add to Jakobson's categories that of genre or register, meaning what kind of discourse this is. One answer is that it is an instance of irony.

Words refer to things in the world, but it can be argued that they do not do so in a one-to-one kind of way. 'Gentle' alludes to certain human qualities, but it does so only because it is caught up in a chain of other signs, from which it marks itself out. There could not just be one word, as there could not be one number or one human being. So any particular word faces, so to speak, two ways: towards what it denotes (its referent), and towards other signs. And one might claim that it can do the former only because of the latter. 'Parsnip' can mean a parsnip only by virtue of its location in a tangled web of signs. And this location can always be ambiguous: in the Russian language, the word for parsnip is also the name of a celebrated poet, Pasternak.

This double-reference is true of language as such; but poetry, once again, turns out to be a paradigmatic case of it. In a poem, the fact that a word is able to denote only through its complex interrelations with other words is rather more obvious than it is in a casual snatch of conversation. This is because poems are peculiarly compressed structures of language which exploit to the full the criss-crossing affinities between their various elements. It is not that they take ordinary referential signs like 'parsnip' and rid them of their denotations, so that the word 'parsnip' now doesn't mean a parsnip at all. It is rather that by putting each word into intricate play with the others, they preserve this referential function but subordinate it to the entire pattern of verbal relations which is the poem. Or, as the Prague school of structuralism might put it, the aesthetic function predominates over the communicative one. (The Prague school were the theoretical offspring of the Russian Formalists.)[2] Once again, however, it is important to note that this ratio between the aesthetic and the communicative varies from poet to poet, or from one kind of poetry to another. Symbolist poets like Mallarmé seek to purge words almost entirely of their denotative aspect, cutting them loose from their referents and floating the signifier free. An author like John Dryden or Charles Olson, by contrast, has his eye fixed firmly on the referent.

3.3   The Semiotics of Yury Lotman

The Russian semiotican Yury Lotman, another eminent descendant of the Formalists, develops this case in a highly original direction.[3] For Lotman, a poem is not just a structure or system of signs, but a 'system of systems'. The poetic text is multi-systemic, in the sense that each of its formal aspects – metre, rhythm, rhyme, meaning, sound-texture and the like – constitutes a separate system within it. We can speak of the poem's phonic, semantic, lexical, graphic, metrical, morphological systems and so on. These systems exist in dynamic interaction with each other, an interaction which includes collisions and disparities between them. And this, in effect, is in Lotman's eyes what constitutes the poem as a whole. Whether this is universally true of poetry, as Lotman seems to imagine, or whether it represents a specific-ally modern, post-Romantic theory of it, is another question. Perhaps it works better with Wallace Stevens than with Lucretius or a traditional ballad.

Another way of putting Lotman's point is to claim that poetic works are peculiarly *overcoded*. If we look at any one element within the poem – say,

---

[2]   See Paul Garvin (ed.), *A Prague School Reader* (Washington, DC, 1964).
[3]   See in particular Yury Lotman, *Analysis of the Poetic Text* (Ann Arbor, MI, 1976), and *The Structure of the Artistic Text* (Ann Arbor, MI, 1977).

an individual word or rhyme or image – it is easy to see that it occupies a place within a host of different systems. It never has simply one context. It exists at a conjuncture of contexts. We can examine a particular word in relation to the poem's semantic system, which is to see it from the standpoint of overall meaning; but we can also locate it within the work's phonic system or pattern of sounds, its metrical system, its symbolic system, and so on. In Lotman's view, what we call the aesthetic effect of the work as a whole results from the conflict or friction between all of these semi-autonomous systems. Each system deviates from or 'disrupts' the others; and it is from these tensions and collisions that what we know as 'poetic' effects spring.

Let us take an example from Ben Jonson's poem 'Inviting a Friend to Supper', chosen more or less at random:

> . . . Yet shall ye have, to rectify your palate,
> An olive, capers, or some better salad
> Ushering the mutton; with a short-legged hen,
> If we can get her, full of eggs, and then
> Lemons, and wine for sauce; to these a cony
> Is not to be despaired of, for our money.
> And, though fowl now be scarce, yet there are clerks,
> The sky not falling, think we may have larks . . .

The lines are heroic couplets, which in Lotman's terms already yields us two distinct systems: rhyme and the iambic pentameter. Yet cutting constantly across these are the much less predictable 'systems' of syntax, rhythm and so on; so that, say, the word 'hen' stands in a phonic relation to 'then', a semantic relation to 'short-legged', a metrical relation to 'Ushering the mutton, with a short-legged . . .', a syntactical relation to the whole sentence which runs from 'Yet' to 'money', a rhythmical relation to the same lines, an analogous relation to 'cony' (rabbit), a grammatical relation to 'her' and 'full of eggs' and so on. This is what is meant by 'overcoding'. Poetry, on this theory, activates the full body of the signifier. By simultaneously exploiting its sound, sense, shape, pitch, rhythm, symbolic value, and so on, it releases its richest potential. We have seen already that this does not really apply to poems which are deliberately sparse and linguistically low-key; but it is a suggestive hypothesis about how a good deal of what we call poetry operates.

This constant interference of one system with another is, in Lotman's view, vital for the effective workings of poetic language. Metre, for example, is a relatively invariant system, which left to itself would probably prove monotonous and inert. It would set up too predictable a pattern of expectations

53

on the reader's part, and would thus, in Formalist idiom, tend to 'automate' our perceptions. Rhythmical variations, however, act to disrupt this autonomisation, and so produce aesthetic effects. Poems are thus both systemic and non-predictable at the same time; and this, in Lotman's eyes, means that they generate well-nigh inexhaustible possibilities of information. A poem is both a system of rules, and a system of their violation. It establishes equivalences, but also differences. Think, for example, of rhyme, which forges a phonic (sound) equivalence between two words, but highlights their semantic difference in dong so. The same double effect can be achieved by rhythm.

Metre, too, homogenises words by pulling them into a single pattern, but in doing so creates a background against which their differences may become all the more perceptible. Metaphor asserts a kinship between items which can also be seen to differ from each other. Lotman even conjures a theory of poetic value out of this ceaseless play of difference and identity, which as it stands is merely a fact about poetry. Good poems are those in which there is a satisfying interplay between the predictable and the disruptive, system and the transgression of system; bad poems are those which are either excessively predictable or excessively random. It is an interesting claim, though perhaps too severely normative: how would so-called automatic or aleatory writing, or the unconscious flow of a Dadaist poem, fare on this account?

For an illustration of Lotman's theory, let us look at Yeats's celebrated refrain from his poem 'Easter 1916', 'A terrible beauty is born'. What makes this line so effective? To answer this question adequately, we would naturally have to return the words to their context rather than scrutinise them in splendid isolation; yet even in splendid isolation they can yield something interesting. Leaving aside the line's various meanings (i.e. the part it plays in the poem's semantic system), as well as its symbolic, figurative and other functions (it contains a semi-oxymoron or contradiction in terms, for example), let us focus purely on its phonic (or sound) and metrical values. 'A boisterous beauty is born' clearly wouldn't do, not only because it isn't clear how beauty can be boisterous, but because the over-alliteration would yield us an excess of identity and not enough difference. Such a brief line (it is a trimeter, with only three feet) can really sustain only one alliteration. The word 'Terrible' introduces a promisingly different complex of sound into the line; yet the fact that its final syllable starts with a *b* also binds it unobtrusively to the initial letters of both 'beauty' and 'born'. So there is an affinity or equivalence here; but because it involves the last syllable of a word, it is not too foregrounded, and thus not too offensive to the ear.

In a similar way, the first syllable of 'beauty' resembles the last syllable of 'terrible', but the two sounds, though close, also diverge. And the last syllable

---

Formalists

of 'beauty', as well as the _i_ of 'terrible', is echoed in the vowel-sound of the word 'is'. Then, however, as though the line is in danger of becoming too tediously uniform, we have that intrusive 'born', with its insertion of a very different vowel-sound. Even so, the _r_ of 'born' picks up on the _rr_ of 'terrible', which binds the line more tightly together. (In Yeats's Hiberno-English idiom, the _r_ sound would be accentuated more than it is in standard English.) One reason why the line works, then, is because phonically speaking it sets up a subtly modulated interplay of identity and difference. But it also pleases the ear rhythmically, consisting as it does of an iamb and two anapaests. (An iamb has one stressed and one unstressed syllable, while an anapaest consists of two unstressed syllables followed by one stressed one – _di-di-dum_.)[4] This is an interestingly complex, varied foot, neither too heavy nor too tripping; and having two of them side by side makes for a kind of balance and symmetry gratifying to the ear, as the line seems to pivot somewhere between the two.

In Lotman's view, a good literary work is one rich in information; and information is a matter of deviation. The more stable, predictable elements of a text, such as metre, belong to what one might call its dominant code. But because they are so regular, they tend also to be less perceptible. These are known to information theory as 'redundant' elements, which are necessary for conveying information but not in themselves informative. Think, for example, of the letters of the alphabet, which are meaningless in themselves but a necessary medium of meaning. The text is at its most informative when it deviates unpredictably from one of its codes, creating effects which stand out against this uniform background.

An example of this can be found in the first stanza of Robert Lowell's magnificent poem 'Mr. Edwards and the Spider':

> I saw the spiders marching through the air,
> Swimming from tree to tree that mildewed day
> In latter August when the hay
> Came creaking to the barn. But where
> The wind is westerly,
> Where gnarled November makes the spiders fly
> Into the apparitions of the sky,
> They purpose nothing but their ease and die
> Urgently beating east to sunrise and the sea . . .

[4] Though it should be said that this kind of thing is never an exact science. There are other ways of scanning the line.

55

We begin with two iambic pentameters, which sets up the expectation that this metrical form will continue; but lines 3 and 4 shift unpredictably into iambic tetrameters, lopping of a metrical foot, while line 5, an iambic trimeter, lops off yet another. Having shrunk around its waistline, so to speak, the stanza then begins to expand again into pentameters. The final line, however, is an alexandrine (six iambic feet), a traditional way of ending a stanza which provides yet another unforeseen twist to it.

Part of the surprise of the stanza is that its metre and rhyme are a good deal more formal than its language. The homely image of the hay creaking to the barn, where the imaginative masterstroke of 'creaking' redeems what might otherwise prove too banal a phrase, comes wrapped within a highly sophisticated manipulation of metre. What is creaking is presumably the wagon in which the hay is loaded; but since the poem does not actually say this, we are free to indulge the imaginative conceit that the hay itself is creaking. There is the sudden drama of an abrupt break in the line, followed by those two terse words 'But where', and then the hurried step across to the next line to sustain the sense, a line which turns out to be arrestingly short ('The wind is westerly'). It is as though form suddenly thrusts itself upon us, as we are made aware of the poet's need to conform his otherwise unostentatious language to the stringent requirements of rhyme and metre. 'Mildewed' day, a phrase in which the *d* in 'mildewed' discreetly echoes the *d* of 'day', is a particularly deft touch.

Dropping a metrical foot or two, as Lowell does in the verse, is what Lotman would describe as a 'minus device', meaning that our expectations are disrupted by something which we expect to appear but doesn't. So unpredictability can include the absence of an element as well as its presence. A rather more dramatic disruption of expectations occurs in the following limerick – one, appropriately enough, whose theme is poetic metre:

> There was a young poet of Japan
> Whose verses never would scan;
> When they asked him why, he said 'It's 'cos I
> Just can't help getting as many words into the last line as I possibly possibly can.'

Information, then, springs from deviation, and deviation requires the regularity of a code. The poetic for Lotman just is this alternation between the random and the regular carried to a point of well-nigh bottomless complexity. Indeed, in his view poetry is the most complex form of discourse imaginable. The puzzle would seem to be that a poem is the most 'semantically saturated' form of writing we have, yielding more information in a condensed space than any other kind of text; but that this in normal circumstances would run the risk of an informational overload. For information theory, too great an increase in information means a decrease in communication, as there is too much material for us to digest. Poetry, however, appears at once semantically saturated (crammed with meaning) and entirely communicable. Yet it is very low on 'redundancy', since it is the kind of text in which every element counts. How can this be so?

The answer lies in what Lotman has argued already about a poem's unique mode of organisation. A poetic text is rich in information because each of its elements, as we have seen, is located at the intersection of several overlaid systems. Each unit, if you like, is a kind of switching mechanism between a host of systems and sub-systems. It participates in several different systems simultaneously; and this is greatly complicated by the fact that every feature of a poem also leads a double life as both 'paradigmatic' and 'syntagmatic'. (The former term refers to the total pattern of the text, grasped as a spatial whole, while the latter refers to the relations set up 'laterally', as the poem moves forward line by line through time.) Each of these systems represents a norm from which the others diverge. Each system 'defamiliarises' the others, breaking up their regularity and throwing them into more vivid relief. Just as one system threatens to become too routinised and monotonous, another cuts across it to disrupt it into newly palpable presence.

It is as though a poem is a constant invasion of system by system, in which one system momentarily provides the norm and another the transgression, in a constantly shifting pattern. It involves a continual generating and violating of norms or expectations. Each system contains its own internal tensions, parallelisms, oppositions and so on, and each is constantly at work modifying the others. If, say, two words are associated by their sound, or by their place in the metrical scheme, this will also tend to yoke their meanings together; but it may also highlight their differences of meaning, so that the poem's semantic system disrupts its metrical or phonic ones. In doing so, it produces an increase in information. Since any two words in the text may be allied on some basis or another, these possibilities are effectively endless. How, we might then ask, does a poet accomplish all this without the aid of a computer? The answer is that he relies on his ear, rather as a tennis player relies not on aerodynamics but on her reflexes.

So a poem is an unfathomably complex interplay of systems. Because this interplay can never be predicted, it is rich in information; but because we are speaking of *systems* here, we are also speaking of regularity, and thus of

y. It is the overlaying and interacting of systems which pro-
nation and communication. What deviates from one system
ı; and this both produces information and preserves com-
_ation. In Lotman's eyes, it also provides a basis for evaluation. Good
poems are those rich in information. Whereas Keats claimed that truth was
beauty, Lotman maintains that information is.

Attending to the systemic nature of poems should not blind us to the fact
that they are also examples of play. This is another way in which they stand
askew to a civilisation obsessed by business. Simply by existing, poetry fulfils
a utopian function, testifying to a form of life which would be less in thrall
to labour, coercion and obligation. Poets, like infants, relish sounds for their
own sake. Poetry is a superior form of babbling. The most lofty exercises of
the imagination, as we have seen, border on the most regressive of fantasies.
A poem is a piece of semiotic sport, in which the signifier has been momentarily released from its grim communicative labours and can disport itself
disgracefully. Freed from a loveless marriage to a single meaning, it can play
the field, wax promiscuous, gambol outrageously with similar unattached
signifiers. If the guardians of conventional morality knew what scandalous
stuff they were inscribing on their tombstones, they would cease to do so
immediately.

Play is the opposite of instrumental activity, even though it performs a vital
role in our development. One problem with that development, according to
the psychoanalytical theories of Jacques Lacan, is that the small infant can
never really distinguish what is being done to it for instrumental or utilit-
arian reasons from what is not. Being fed, washed and kept warm by its
carers is in fact an act of love on their part; but for Lacan this expression of
love is experienced by the infant as troublingly ambiguous, since it can never
appear purely as itself.[5] Instead, it must inevitably be obscured by the func-
tional form it takes. What the infant demands is to be recognised in its own
right; but it can never be entirely sure how to recognise such recognition.
In Lacanian theory, it is in this gap between the demand for unconditional
recognition and the satisfaction of pragmatic need that desire, or the unconscious, first germinates. To play with infants, however, is to do nothing other
than to recognise them for what they are, with no ulterior goal in mind.
It is in play that we come into our own as human subjects. And poetry is
among other things a memory-trace of this primordial sense of being accepted
for what we are.

---

[5] For an account of Lacan's thought, see Terry Eagleton, *Literary Theory: An Introduction* (Oxford,
1983), Ch. 5.

3.4   The Incarnational Fallacy

Lotman emphasises that each system in a poem is semi-autonomous of the others; and this is a point which many critics have damagingly overlooked. Instead, they have sought for a theory of the work which sees each of its aspects as harmoniously integrated with the rest. Prominent in this kind of approach has been what we might call the 'incarnational fallacy'. On this view, form and content in poetry are entirely at one because the poem's language somehow 'incarnates' its meaning. Whereas everyday language simply points to things, poetic language actually embodies them. There is a theology lurking behind this poetics: just as the Word of God is the Father made flesh, so a poem does not simply talk about things, but in some mysterious way 'becomes' them. This sacramental view of signs is to be found, among many other places, in T. S. Eliot's *Four Quartets*, though it crops up there in bleakly negative guise: poetry, with its intolerable wrestle with words and meanings, can never attain the fullness of presence of the Incarnation. Words can never attain the status of the Word. Language can intimate truth by drawing attention to its own limits, and thus to what transcends them; or it can yield a negative insight into truth by cancelling itself out; but in a fallen world it cannot capture it in the flesh. It is a quintessentially modernist motif.

A rather eccentric example of the incarnational fallacy can be found in F. R. Leavis's comments on the phrase 'moss'd cottage trees' in Keats's ode 'To Autumn':

> The action of the packed consonants in 'moss'd cottage trees' is plain enough: there stand the trees, gnarled and sturdy in trunk and bough, their leafy entanglements thickly loaded. It is not fanciful, I think, to find that (the sense being what it is) the pronouncing of 'cottage-trees' suggests, too, the crisp bite and the flow of juice as the teeth close in the ripe apple.[6]

If this is not fanciful, it is hard to know what is. It is 'plain' to Leavis that we can see the gnarled, sturdy trees with their thickly loaded leafy entanglements, though the poem says nothing of this. This is rather like claiming that it is plain that Hamlet has freckles and a broken nose.

For Leavis, genuine poetic language is as packed and ripe as an apple, and reading becomes rather like chewing. Words are at their most authentic when

[6]   F. R. Leavis, *The Common Pursuit* (Harmondsworth, 1962), p. 16.

they are plumped with the ripe physicality of things. Pressed to an extreme, this means that the truest poet would be a greengrocer. In seeking to do homage to words, revering them as densely physical objects in their own right, the incarnational fallacy only succeeds in abolishing them. For words which 'become' what they signify cease to be words at all. At their most material, they disappear into the objects they are supposed to denote. For all its celebration of the muscularity of language, the incarnational fallacy reflects a covert distrust of it. Only when words cease to be themselves and merge into their referents can they be truly expressive. Leavis believes that English speech is naturally incarnational, whereas ill-starred foreigners like the French have to make do with an inferior kind of language altogether, one which palely reflects things rather than concretely enacts them. This linguistic Little Englandism is one of the more absurd aspects of an astonishingly courageous and pioneering critic.

Seamus Heaney's 'Digging' may illustrate the point:

> . . . The coarse boot nestled on the lug, the shaft
> Against the inside knee was levered firmly,
> He rooted out tall tops, buried the bright edge deep
> To scatter new potatoes that we picked
> Loving their cool hardness in our hands . . .
>
> The cold smell of potato mould, the squelch and slap
> Of soggy peat, the curt cuts of an edge
> Through living roots awaken in my head . . .

This intensely physical language seems the outward expression of the poem's subject matter, as form and content appear to melt into one another. The 'curt cuts' of the spade are also the curt cuts of a language which admits only two trisyllabic words, and one of these is the lowly, palpable 'potato'. Otherwise we get a chain of elemental, bluntly expressive monosyllables: 'coarse', 'lug', 'shaft', 'mould', 'squelch', 'slap', 'curt', most of them redolent of earth, mud and moisture. So the language seems to incarnate what it speaks of. Like the digger himself, it appears to be rammed right up against the coarse grains and textures of the world, rather than floating loftily above them. It is as though the words absorb into their own bodies the bitter soil and mould of which they speak, to the point where it is hard to slide even the thickness of a hair between signifier, signified and referent.

Compare these lines, then, with the first verse of Rupert Brooke's famously patriotic 'The Soldier':

If I should die, think only this of me:
   That there's some corner of a foreign field
That is for ever England. There shall be
   In that rich earth a richer dust concealed;
A dust whom England bore, shaped, made aware,
   Gave, once, her flowers to love, her ways to roam,
A body of England's, breathing English air,
   Washed by the rivers, blest by suns of home.

This, too, is about the earth, but it scarcely smacks of it. On the contrary, its fervent, edifying tone tends to obscure just how abstract and non-particularised a poem it is – as in that very notional 'her flowers to love, her ways to roam', which could have come straight from a greetings card in a way that Heaney's 'squelch and slap of soggy peat' could not. 'Earth' and 'dust' for Brooke have a purely symbolic value, which is by no means a defect in itself. Poems can be symbolically generalised, indifferent to the density of actual things, without losing anything of their persuasive force. But if dust is what we are made of, then dying can be made to sound like merging effortlessly back into our native element, and so can have the sting and messiness taken out of it. It is an understandable fantasy to indulge in for a soldier in the First World War.

Yet the difference between the two kinds of language is fundamentally a *trompe l'oeil* or illusion. It is not that Heaney's language is actually closer to reality, while the more refined diction of the Brooke poem stands further off from it. Language and reality are not two objects like bookends, with variable distances between them. The language of 'Digging' is just as conceptual as the idealising phraseology of 'The Soldier'. This is because all language is conceptual, and making it seem otherwise is just a kind of poetic sleight of hand. It may feel as though the words of the Heaney poem somehow embody the very stuff they speak of, but what looks incarnational is really associational. We associate one kind of materiality – the blunt, unmelodious, coarse-grained sounds of 'lug', 'shaft', 'squelch' and so on – with another kind of materiality: the soil, spade, mud and vegetation which constitute the poem's subject matter. But the former kind of physicality does not 'embody' the latter. The two kinds of materiality are of quite different orders. One is a matter of the way certain words feel in our mouth, while the other is a question of natural processes. (It is not fanciful, perhaps, to suggest that the two converge in our unconscious memory in the form of one of our very earliest experiences: the gratifying taste of milk in our mouths.) The language moves at one level, and the subject matter at another; but we are persuaded to see them as stitched together as closely as a jacket and its lining.

Words like 'silk', 'softness' and 'murmur' are not usually regarded as 'earthy' because they slide easily from our mouths, requiring a minimum of labour. It is words we chew, bite on or spit out which we associate with the material world, since both demand a certain amount of labour. Words which are mouth-filling or recalcitrant tend to evoke material substances, since these substances, too, resist us in their heft and density. But a lot of these associations are purely fanciful. You may imagine that the word 'dank' has a dankish feel to it, but if this is to do with the vowel sound, why is 'prank' not similarly evocative? The word 'slimy' may sound slimy, but this is only because it means slimy.

We have come to forge magical associations between words and things, seeing them as necessarily bound up with one another. This, to adopt an image from the philosopher Ludwig Wittgenstein, is rather like marvelling at the way a word on a page seems to fit the space provided for it so exactly. We come to transfer some of the qualities of an object to the word that stands for it. It is what the critic Paul de Man called the 'phenomenalisation of language', an operation he associated with the wiles of ideology.[7] But we have only to look at languages other than English to puncture this delusion. 'Cow' may sound a blunt, inelegant sort of word, rather like the animal itself; but do we feel the same about *vache*? And how do the French feel about the matter?

There are two words in the Heaney poem which really do embody what they refer to, and those are 'squelch' and 'slap'. This is because both of them are onomatopoeic. They sound like what they signify. This, however, is about the only way that poems actually do 'incarnate' their meanings. And it is a very minor part of poetic business. We have seen already that poetry involves at least two things: a certain memorable or inventive use of language, and a moral insight into human existence. But most theories of poetry have come to grief on the question of how these are interrelated. The Formalists could reconcile them after a fashion, since renewing our language also meant refreshing our experience, and this, broadly speaking, is a moral process. But making the world more 'perceptible', more palpable to our senses, is moral only in a rather fuzzy sense of the word. It is not a matter of investigating human values and activities in depth, in the manner of Homer's *Iliad* or Arthur Hugh Clough's *Amours de Voyage*.

---

[7] See Paul de Man, *The Rhetoric of Romanticism* (New York, 1984).

The truth is that these two different dimensions of a poem – its language and its moral exploration – need not be internally related at all. (I mean by 'internal' a kind of logical or necessary relationship, such that the one entails the other.) What we might call the paradigmatic case of poetry is when they do indeed come together – when the pleasing, inventive, unusual or arresting use of words suddenly yields us a fresh insight into some experience or situation. Take these well-known lines by A. E. Housman from his volume *A Shropshire Lad*:

> Into my heart an air that kills
> From yon far country blows:
> What are those blue remembered hills,
> What spires, what farms are those?

The juxtaposition of 'blue' and 'remembered' is notable because the two adjectives seem so different – the first describing a material quality, the second concerning an act of consciousness. The physical and psychological are coupled casually together, as though they were the same sort of thing. Not putting a comma between them, as one might conventionally expect, enhances this effect. There is no practical association between the two terms, since it is not as though the poet is remembering that the hills are blue. The juxtaposition suggests rather that they are remembered in the same sense that they are blue. It evokes an equivalence between the two adjectives. Squeezed up against 'blue', 'remembered' comes to sound like a quality of the hills themselves, rather than a function of the poet's mind. The hills are 'remembered' rather as they are grassy or craggy. Because the line (an iambic tetrameter) is so short, it can accommodate only about half a dozen words; so the choice of 'blue' and 'remembered', out of all the fancier epithets Housman could have opted for, stands out fairly starkly. What is important about these hills is that they are remembered, as permanently and intensely as they are blue. They are remembered all over the place, just as they are blue from one end to another.

The line estranges the words 'blue' and 'remembered' both by choosing them when we feel it could have selected so many alternatives, and by letting each word rub the other into a new kind of palpability. 'Remembered' is an ordinary sort of term; but 'remember' is more often encountered in its verbal than adjectival form, so that its impact here is more forceful and jolting than we might otherwise expect. 'Well remembered' or 'lovingly remembered' would be predictable, but 'remembered' by itself is not. And 'blue' is striking in its monosyllabic simplicity. It is almost as though the poem is daring us to complain that it is too commonplace, a waste of an opportunity for some finer epithet. But it is the blueness of the hills which is precious.

So this would be an instance of the paradigmatically poetic: of an arresting piece of language which is at the same time a fresh kind of moral insight. Not all poetry, however, works like this all of the time. If a piece of writing had no striking verbal effects at all, and no moral insights, then it is doubtful we would call it a poem. But what if it *only* had striking verbal effects, like 'Jeepers, Creepers, where d'ya get those peepers?', or 'Di-dee-diddly-doo-de-dum-dee-dah'? ('Striking', as the reader may have gathered, does not necessarily mean 'deeply impressive'.) We might call this wordplay rather than poetry proper, rather as Freud distinguishes between jokes, which have a content, and jests, which are more concerned with the play of the signifier. Or what if the work displayed some powerful moral insights but verbally speaking was as dull as an income-tax return?

The truth, surely, is that we look to poetry both for a bravura of the signifier and a depth and subtlety of the signified. But it is asking too much to expect these things always to happen precisely in terms of each other, and theories of poetry which stake themselves on such notions of unity bite off more than they can chew. Faced with Robert Frost's 'My little horse must think it queer / To stop without a farmhouse near', we reap a modest pleasure from the tripping of the metre and the rhyming of 'queer' and 'near', as we do from the idea which the lines proffer to us. It is amusing and mildly illuminating to think of a horse behaving like a taxi-driver and wondering whether his stopping is scheduled or random. But there is no sense in which the two effects, one of form and one of content, are inseparable. Frost could presumably have formulated the same idea with another rhyme. Poetic language, after all, is not as inevitable and unalterable as some commentators imagine. Nor are the kinds of satisfaction we glean from these two dimensions of the poem at all similar. There is a pleasure of the signifier and a pleasure of moral cognition, but it is excessively 'organicist' to imagine that the one always operates in terms of the other. If this is what Keats meant by claiming that beauty was truth and truth beauty, then he was, dare one suggest, mistaken.

In the last two chapters we have examined some theoretical questions about the nature of poetry. It is now time to put these to the test by looking at poetic form in action.

Chapter 4

In Pursuit of Form

4.1   The Meaning of Form

Roughly speaking, what we call content refers to what a poem says, while form refers to how it says it. Most critics would want to insist that these two aspects of the work are inseparable. In fact, this doctrine is as well-entrenched with literary critics as a belief in witches was with the Inquisition. Pushed to an extreme, it becomes mildly ridiculous, as when critics claim to hear the rustling of the silk in the hissing of the *s* sounds. This is known as the mimetic theory of form, for which the form somehow imitates the content it expresses. Alexander Pope admonishes us in his poem *An Essay on Criticism* that in poetry 'the sound must seem an echo to the sense', though some examples of this he finds rather silly. The alexandrine, for instance, 'That, like a wounded snake, drags its slow length along'.

If it is true in one sense that form and content are inseparable, it is false in another. It is true, as they say, 'existentially' – true as far as our actual experience of the poem goes. When we read John Milton's words 'Eyeless in Gaza at the mill with slaves', we do not hear or see a distinction between form and content. But we recognise a conceptual distinction between them even so, just as we recognise a conceptual distinction between the evening star and the morning star, even though they are existentially speaking one and the same (the planet Venus). This is what philosophers refer to as an analytical rather than a real distinction. Form and content may be inseparable in experience; but the very fact that we use two different terms here suggests that they are not identical. Literary forms have a history of their own; they are not just the obedient expression of content.

W. B. Yeats, with this dichotomy, among others, in mind, asked in a poem how we could tell the dancer from the dance; and it is true that this is hard to do while the dance is actually in progress. A dancer just is someone who dances, and a dance is just the way a dancer moves. Even so, Yeats's claim is truer of modern-day dancing than it is of the old-fashioned ball-room variety. It is truer of the kind of dance which you improvise on the spot than of waltzes and foxtrots, which clearly have some notional existence distinguishable from dancers themselves. If they didn't, nobody could ever learn them.

Form concerns such aspects of the poem as tone, pitch, rhythm, diction, volume, metre, pace, mood, voice, address, texture, structure, quality, syntax, register, point of view, punctuation and the like, whereas content is a matter of meaning, action, character, idea, storyline, moral vision, argument and so on. ('Form' is sometimes used in a narrow sense as synonymous with 'structure' or 'design', meaning the way the various elements of a literary work relate to one other; but there is no reason to restrict the term to this.) In one sense, these two dimensions of form and content are obviously distinct. We can speak, for example, of two poems sharing the same metre or even much the same mood. Or we can speak of them as using the same devices of assonance or alliteration, without implying that the poems in question are one and the same. What the two poems 'say' with the aid of these strategies is clearly different. We can also, for example, distinguish in fiction between narrative and narration – the former referring to the storyline, the latter meaning the way the story gets told. The same narrative can be narrated in different ways.

The distinction between form and content is notoriously leaky. Mood and tone, for example, are aspects of what we might call semantic content – of a specific pattern of meaning – from which they cannot really be dissociated. Even so, the distinction can be a useful one. You can write a history of lit-erary forms – of types of allegory, for example, or the use of the Chorus in drama, or first-person narration – which doesn't attend in exhaustive detail to the content of particular works; or you can produce a history of the bicycle in literature which cuts across works which have very different formal properties. You can discuss a piece of poetry in terms of form – say, how it handles irony or metaphor or ambiguity; or you may be more interested in the actual meanings at stake in the irony, metaphor or ambiguity, in which case you are looking at content. Discussing the character of Elizabeth Bennet in *Pride and Prejudice* is a matter of content (of 'what?'), whereas examining Jane Austen's techniques of characterisation is a question of form (or 'how?'). Some may find these fine distinctions scholastic, but then some find any fine distinctions scholastic.

Yet form and content are inseparable in this sense – that literary criticism typically involves grasping *what* is said in terms of *how* it is said. Or, to put it slightly more technically, grasping the semantic (meaning) in terms of the non-semantic (sound, rhythm, structure, typography and so on). Of course readers will sometimes want to attend more to the one, and sometimes more to the other. You may be more concerned for the moment with examining sexual passion in *Wuthering Heights*, which roughly speaking is a matter of content, than with the novel's use of so-called unreliable narrators like Lockwood and Nelly Dean, which is largely a question of form. Not every critical statement has to be a what-in-terms-of-how one. It can be claimed, however, that the *prototypical* act of criticism is just this. And this seems to be true above all of poetry – a literary genre which could almost be defined as one in which form and content are intimately interwoven. It is as though poetry above all discloses the secret truth of all literary writing: that form is *constitutive* of content and not just a reflection of it. Tone, rhythm, rhyme, syntax, assonance, grammar, punctuation and so on are actually generators of meaning, not just containers of it. To modify any of them is to modify meaning itself.

But isn't this equally true of everyday language? What's so special about literature here? The tone in which I address my 'Good morning' to you, whether frosty or fawning, can make a dramatic difference to its meaning. Whole dialogues have been composed by taking a single obscenity and repeating it a number of times, each time inflecting it in a different tone. This kind of thing may not have the grandeur of *War and Peace*, but it makes a point even so. Tone, pace, pitch and the like may help to constitute the sense of what I say in ordinary life as well as in poetry. I am telling you that it is three minutes past six in this orotund, absurdly emphatic way in order to convey the fact that I regard you as a pest who ought to have the decency to buy your own watch. An ironic or sarcastic tone can actually reverse the meaning of what I say. Making sense in everyday life is a matter of the way we use signs which are meaningless in themselves according to certain agreed conventions; and this is another way of saying that the content of our speech is determined by its form. Individual words have a purely formal existence, as is clear from the fact that 'pig' and *cochon* have the same meaning.

So there is no clean break here between literature and life. It is true that a great deal of poetry exploits the resources of language more intensively than most of our everyday speech, unless one happens to be Oscar Wilde.

(Even here, however, we should be on our guard: some poems are plain and austere, while some everyday utterances can be florid and profuse.) But poetry also puts on show what is true about our language anyway, but which goes generally unnoticed. In everyday language, too, 'content' is the product of 'form'. Or, to put it more technically, signifieds (meanings) are a product of signifiers (words). Meanings are a matter of how we use words, rather than words being a matter of conveying meanings which are formed independently of them. I could not have the idea 'Tigers should be frolicked with wherever possible' unless I had words or signs to have it in. In daily life, however, we are mostly content analysts, reading for meaning rather than form. We stare right through the signifier to what it signifies. We do not generally point out to the butcher with a cry of triumph that he has just come up with two alliterations and an anapaest.

So it is as though poetry grants us the actual experience of seeing meaning take shape as a practice, rather than handling it simply as a finished object. Or, if you like, seeing form take shape as content, a process which for most of time we mercifully don't notice. 'Mercifully', because this insensitivity to the texture and rhythm of our speech is essential to our practical lives. There is no point in shouting 'Fire!' in a cinema if the audience are simply going to linger over the delectable contrast between the violently stabbing *F* and the swooning, long-drawn-out vowel. (Those among the audience disadvantaged by an old-style literary education might even detect in this verbal performance a mimetic image of the fire itself: the *F* representing its abrupt beginnings, and the swooning vowel the rush and roll of its inexorable spreading. . . .)

Just as it looks as though the sun moves round the earth, so ordinary language seems to invert the relations between signifiers and signifieds, or words and their meanings. In everyday speech, it seems as though the word is simply the obedient transmitter of the meaning. It is as though it evaporates into it. If language did not conceal its operations in this way, we might be so enraptured by its music that, like the Lotus Eaters, we would never get anything done – rather as for Nietzsche, if we were mindful of the appalling butchery which produced civilised humanity, we would never get out of bed. Ordinary language, like history for Nietzsche or the ego for Freud, operates by a kind of salutary amnesia or repression. Poetry is the kind of writing which stands this inversion of form and content, or signifier and signified, on its feet again. It makes it hard for us to brush aside the words to get at the meanings. It makes it clear that the signified is the result of a complex play of signifiers. And in doing so, it allows us to experience the very medium of our experience.

One might put the point this way. Business executives, technologists and other practical types tend to gaze at the world through the clear window-pane of language; while poets are those strange, socially dysfunctional creatures who never cease to be fascinated by the minute warpings and convexities of the glass itself, its coolness to the forehead and slithery feel to the fingerpads. Yet the image is deceptive. There are indeed poets of this kind – formalists or symbolists for whom the point of their art is to investigate the medium rather than the meaning. This means wrenching words from their senses so that their sounds and textures can be relished more fully. If the window image is to apply to most poets, however, we would need to show how the density and refraction of the glass, its flaws and scratches, actually give shape to what they see through it. Where the window metaphor breaks down is that the objects we see 'through' the pane, however apparently solid, are actually created by it. A poem constitutes the very things it is about. In this sense, every poem curves back on itself. The word for this process is 'fiction'. Wallace Stevens speaks in *Opus Posthumous* of a poem as being 'Part of the res (thing) itself and not about it'; but it might be more exact to say that it is each in terms of the other.

Actually, language is nothing like a window – for one thing because a window clearly separates an inside from an outside, which is the last thing that language does. On the contrary, being on the 'inside' of a language is a way of being 'outside' it as well. It is a way of being among things in the world. The whole misleadingly spatial image thus breaks down. Poetry is an image of the truth that language is not what shuts us off from reality, but what yields us the deepest access to it. So it is not a choice between being fascinated with words and being preoccupied with things. It is the very essence of words to point beyond themselves; so that to grasp them as precious in themselves is also to move more deeply into the world they refer to. Not to see this is like claiming that you can't use a spade to dig with because the iron bit at the end of the handle keeps getting in the way.

Grasping the 'what' of content in terms of the 'how' of form, however, does not necessarily mean seeing the two as harmoniously united. The doctrine of the indissolubility of form and content is as sacred to some critics as a belief in the indissolubility of marriage is to the Pope. But to see form and content in terms of each other is not necessarily to see them as unified. Like married couples, form and content can be at loggerheads. Indeed, it is fortunate that they can be, since otherwise a whole range of fascinating poetic effects would be ruled out. These are the kind of effects one gets from playing the one off against the other, setting up tensions and ambiguities between the two.

4.2   Form versus Content

A particularly blatant example of form versus content is the following rather mediocre piece of dramatic dialogue, which puts the Nazis in a Shakespearian setting:

1st Politician: How fares it with the National Socialists?
2nd Politician: Like to a swollen sea, whose glutted maw,
Plucking unwary workers to its bed,
Belches their bones to heav'n. The Führer now,
Crazed with the blood of fourteen million votes,
Rages, an insatiate vampire, through the realm.
Stormtroopers, boys whose side-nicked helmets hang
Ill-fitting round their blunt and flaxen brows
Burst wide the doors of workers' hovels, rip
Infants from dugs they doubt of Marxist milk.
The proletariat is quite undone,
Its several strengths like straw stamped into earth,
Its leaders hung like dried flesh in the wind,
Spear'd on the swastika's thick-venom'd points.
Stranger and Jew, whose outer shapes are guess'd
Mere figments to belie a brutish soul
Stand stripp'd at history's stark extremity
To perish in a little puff of gas.[1]

There is a deliberate mismatch of form and content here, for some obscure reason perhaps best left unexamined.

But the same can happen with genuine poets like William Blake. Take, for example, his celebrated 'Tyger' poem:

Tyger! Tyger! burning bright
In the forests of the night,
What immortal hand or eye
Could frame thy fearful symmetry?

In what distant deeps or skies
Burnt the fire of thine eyes?
On what wings dare he aspire?
What the hand dare seize the fire?

[1]   From the play *Brecht and Company* by the present author, first performed at the Edinburgh Festival in 1979.

And what shoulder, & what art,
Could twist the sinews of thy heart?
And when thy heart began to beat,
What dread hand? & what dread feet?

What the hammer? what the chain?
In what furnace was thy brain?
What the anvil? what dread grasp
Dare its deadly terrors clasp?

When the stars threw down their spears,
And water'd heaven with their tears,
Did he smile his work to see?
Did he who made the Lamb make thee?

Tyger! Tyger! burning bright
In the forests of the night,
What immortal hand or eye
Dare frame thy fearful symmetry?

The chant-like refrain of this, its awed tone and nursery-rhyme-like quality, all contribute to a sense of childlike wonderment. But this strain of naivety is at odds with the complex imagery. Perhaps we should be put on our guard by those rather excessively repetitive questions, which after two or three stanzas become troublingly insistent, almost a compulsive ritual. It is as though the speaker is mesmerised by the mighty creature he confronts, unable to do much but blurt out one breathless query after another. He seems to be stuck fast in a single rhetorical groove. Maybe there is a strain of panic as well as reverence here, as the questions come tumbling pell-mell. The speaker might be more cowed than awestruck. Breathlessness, after all, can be a symptom of both. Are we dealing with terror rather than admiration, as these dumbfounded queries thud on each other's heels?

The poem's interrogative structure might indicate the limits of the speaker's own rather parochial mentality, rather than the sublimity of the tiger itself. One pointer to this is the dislocated grammar of the third verse ('And when thy heart began to beat, / What dread hand? & what dread feet?'), as sense-making itself threatens to break down in the face of this ferocious magnificence. In a boldly assured stoke, the poet throws up the sentence before finishing it, realising that the suggestive and unspoken might be preferable here to grammatical coherence. Language itself is beginning to buckle under the strain of conceptualising the inconceivable.

71

The speaker of the poem resorts to industrial imagery (hammer, chain, furnace, anvil) to express his sense of this formidable flourish of life; and we happen to know that this kind of imagery in Blake is almost always negative. The speaker seems able to grasp the tiger's transcendent energy only in the sort of mechanistic imagery which risks falsifying it. He can portray the process of its creation only in terms of manufacture, as though the animal was made in Manchester. He even calls the terrors of the beast 'deadly'. As one critic has remarked, there is something violent, pitiless and inhuman about the poem's language, which is largely a matter of hard labour and brutal work discipline.[2] It is in some ways as much a poem of the early Industrial Revolution as a nature poem. If there is something enthralling about the superbly flaming beast at its centre, there is also more than a touch of Frankensteinian monstrosity. Does the beast seem to be burning bright only because the speaker perceives its surroundings (the forests of the night) in such a negative way?

Some of the natural imagery the poem goes on to deploy – stars, tears, water, spears – has equally ominous connotations in Blake's view of reality. Nature to him is a realm of snares and illusions, so that imagery like this might well contain an echo of the Fall and false consciousness. The apparently harmless little query, 'Did he who made the Lamb make thee?' could be taken simply as a flattering compliment paid to the tiger: it is such a stupendous form of creation that it might be beyond even God's powers to fashion it. Perhaps it created itself. But the line may also suggest a way of seeing the world to which Blake himself would be distinctly hostile. To his mind, everything that lives is holy, and moral distinctions between good and bad are largely ideological; whereas the speaker of this poem, bemused by the sheer verve and radiance of the tiger, might be tempted by the Manichaean doctrine that there are two principles of creation, one good and one evil, and that the tiger is the creation of the latter. Perhaps as a mark of dissent from this hypothesis, Blake himself mischievously adorned the poem with an illumination of a remarkably toothless, cuddly-looking tiger – quite like a lamb, in fact. And this has puzzled commentators who assume without question that the speaker of the poem must be Blake himself.

Edward Larrissy points out that there is a kind of sublime, Old Testament strain about the pattern of questioning in the poem, but that the songlike metre of the piece detracts from this effect. So here we have a clash not between form and content, but between one aspect of form (an exalted quality of language) and another (metre). There are other poems like 'The Tyger' whose

---

[2] See Edward Larrissy, *William Blake* (Basil Blackwell, 1985), p. 58.

form leads us to expect simplicity, but which in fact conceals a complex content. Take, for example, that desperately enigmatic narrative, 'Three Blind Mice':

> Three blind mice, three blind mice,
> See how they run, see how they run.
> They all ran after the farmer's wife,
> She cut off their tails with a carving knife,
> Did you ever see such a thing in your life
> As three blind mice?

It is hard to unravel exactly what is going on here. Are the mice of the first two lines running *away* from the farmer's wife because she has cut off their tails, or are they running *after* her? Does the verse describe two actions or one? One possible chronology of events is that the farmer's wife cut off the tails of three mice who were running after her, an act which somehow blinded them (the connection here is admittedly obscure, but there are undertones of castration), thus causing them to take fright and run away from her. This would account for the shift of tense from present to past: the narrative opens with an event in the present, then backtracks to highlight its past cause.

But one could also read the verse as a single action in the present: three mice, already blind, are running after the farmer's wife, who cuts off their tails. This, admittedly, fails to account for the change of tense, and it is hard to see how the mice could run after the farmer's wife if they were blind; but otherwise it is a reasonably plausible reading. If one opts for the first interpretation, a certain ironic reversal is detectable, of which the nub is the shift from line 2 to line 3: the mice who previously scampered so gleefully in pursuit of the farmer's wife are now fleeing, panic-stricken, away from her. Nobody comes out of the piece particularly well, not least the sadistic speaker.

Some poems mean one thing by what they say, and another, perhaps contradictory thing by the way they say it. William Empson, for example, brilliantly demonstrates in his study *Some Versions of Pastoral* how a verse in Thomas Gray's 'Elegy in a Country Churchyard' involves just this sort of ambiguity:

> Full many a gem of purest ray serene
> The dark, unfathomed caves of ocean bear;
> Full many a flower is born to blush unseen
> And waste its sweetness on the desert air.

The lines are meant to illustrate the pathos of the fact that some bright people are held back by their obscure origins from attaining worldly fame. But as

Empson points out, the elegance of the verse dignifies this dire situation in a way which makes us feel reluctant to see it altered. By comparing it to a natural condition, it also makes it seem as though it could not in fact be altered. Intellectually ambitious farm labourers presumably object to the poverty which holds them back; but as Empson points out, gems do not mind being in caves, and flowers prefer not to be plucked. The imagery is askew to the argument it is meant to underpin. 'Blush', Empson speculates, carries a resonance of virginity, and so a suggestion that renunciation is desirable, including perhaps the kind of sacrifice forced upon talented people from modest social backgrounds.

There are also poems, however, in which an elaborateness of form conceals a paucity of content. Dylan Thomas's 'A Refusal to Mourn the Death, by Fire, of a Child in London' is a case in point:

> Never until the mankind making
> Bird beast and flower
> Fathering and all humbling darkness
> Tells with silence the last light breaking
> And the still hour
> Is come of the sea tumbling in harness
>
> And I must enter again the round
> Zion of the water bead
> And the synagogue of the ear of corn
> Shall I let pray the shadow of a sound
> Or sow my salt seed
> In the least valley of sackcloth to mourn
>
> The majesty and burning of the child's death.
> I shall not murder
> The mankind of her going with a grave truth
> Nor blaspheme down the stations of the breath
> With any further
> Elegy of innocence and youth.
>
> Deep with the first dead lies London's daughter,
> Robed in the long friends,
> The grains beyond age, the dark veins of her mother,
> Secret by the unmourning water
> Of the riding Thames.
> After the first death, there is no other.

This goes to extraordinary lengths to say astonishingly little. Thomas's rhetoric is impressive in its excessively high-pitched way, but if you strip away the sonorously ceremonial language, the poem falls to pieces. The pseudo-scriptural imagery, some of which is tellingly original and inventive, is really there to pad out a central emptiness, diverting attention from the fact that the poem has little to say about the burnt child, and even less sympathy for her. Its language moves at one level and its subject matter at another. The whole first half of the piece is a kind of extended metaphorical riff on the word 'Never', the imagery of which is largely at a tangent to the poem's official subject, and the whole of which concerns the poet himself (and his artistic virtuosity) rather than the dead victim.

The reader has to wait ten lines, until the arrival of the main verb 'Shall I let pray', to see what this 'Never' clause is modifying, as though the poet is so absorbed in his own metaphorical pyrotechnics that he comes near to losing track of what he was about to say. This, we shall soon learn, is because he has embarrassingly little to say in the first place. The child is a mere occasion for baroque image-spinning. It is as though the fact that she is a corpse, rather than a living individual, can be used to rationalise her purely notional status in these verses. To treat her as an impersonal symbol or mythological archetype, the poem seems to insinuate, is somehow a deeper insight than to see her as an actual person. The whole piece is flagrantly opportunistic. It is the orotund rhetoric of the clause beginning with 'Never', with all its freewheeling metaphorical fertility, which the poet invests in most deeply, not the substantive statement which it is supposed to be modifying. The poem is actually built out of this imbalance of form and content, one which it seems brazenly to flaunt.

When the piece finally gets round to the girl, which isn't until the last stanza, it manages to make indifference sound like wisdom. 'The majesty and burning of the child's death', a line meant to dignify its subject, simply succeeds in making being burnt to death sound noble. 'I shall not murder / The mankind of her going with a grave truth' sounds impressively candid and tough-minded: other may perfume this death with their moral platitudes, but Thomas himself, who is laying pontifical claim to the high moral ground here, defiantly refuses to play along with this hypocritical bombast. The only problem is that the very language in which he rejects this posturing is itself rhetorical posturing. 'Grave truth' is a cheap pun.

The 'mankind' of the child's death presumably means that death is natural to humanity, and so not an occasion for mourning (though Thomas maintains just the opposite in a poem about the death of his father). But 'mankind' is too close to 'humaneness' for comfort, and one suspects in any case that it is there largely to alliterate with the typically hyperbolic flourish of 'murder'. The last thing Thomas's language is is candid. Its *gravitas* and ornate solemnity make his refusal to mourn seem somehow profound, as though he has divined a truth beyond the shallow perceptions of others. The last stanza finally discloses that truth, which turns out to be a piece of reach-me-down Nature mysticism. Mother Earth has taken her daughter back to her bosom, and since the Thames isn't mourning, why should we? 'After the first death, there is no other', for all its grave air of prophetic insight, is uncomfortably close to 'Once you've seen one, you've seen the lot.'

There is also a use of poetic form which seems to detach it from the content in order to make an implicit comment on it. The famous seduction-of-the-typist scene in T. S. Eliot's *The Waste Land* might serve as an illustration:

> He, the young man carbuncular, arrives,
> A small house agent's clerk, with one bold stare,
> One of the low on whom assurance sits
> As a silk hat on a Bradford millionaire.
> The time is now propitious, as he guesses,
> The meal is ended, she is bored and tired,
> Endeavours to engage her in caresses
> Which still are unreproved, if undesired.
> Flushed and decided, he assaults at once;
> Exploring hands encounter no defence;
> His vanity requires no response,
> And makes a welcome of indifference . . .

The iambic pentameters fall with a kind of jaded, you-know-the-sort-of-thing sophistication, as the sordid scene unfurls itself with a kind of weary fatalism. (The famous opening line of the poem, incidentally – 'April is the cruellest month, breeding . . .' – is a kind of broken-backed pentameter, a frail ghost of what was once a robust literary form). The loveless, mechanical sex is reflected in the pat, automated stresses of the lines. The ritualised beat of the rhymes and rhythms seems to point up the squalid predictability of the whole affair. The poetry seems bored by what it is narrating, superciliously holding its nose and trying to put as much distance between itself and its own subject matter as it can. 'One of the low', 'propitious', 'As a silk hat on a Bradford millionaire': these are all phrases which rise distastefully above the scene, disdaining it in the act of observing it.

The language of the piece is nothing like the kind of idiom which the typist and the clerk would use themselves, though it has been suggested that a phrase like 'Endeavours to engage her in caresses' is the kind of bureau-cratic language the clerk might *write*. The very emotional blankness of the piece is a kind of emotional response. Those who might imagine that the sniffiness of some of this language is Eliot's own will not be pacified to learn that the observer here is in fact the ancient prophet Tiresias. As usual, Eliot is to be found lurking elusively around the edges of the poem, ventriloquis-ing his own prejudices through figures who make it appear a timeless, dis-passionate wisdom.

John Keats's poetry is celebrated for its sensuous lushness, as in this gor-geously wrought passage from 'The Eve of St. Agnes':

> A casement high and triple-arched there was,
> All garlanded with carven imag'ries
> Of fruits, and flowers, and bunches of knot-grass,
> And diamonded with panes of quaint device,
> Innumerable of stains and splendid dyes,
> As are the tiger-moth's deep-damasked wings:
> And in the midst, 'mong thousand heraldries,
> And twilight saints, and dim emblazonings,
> A shielded scutcheon blushed with blood of queens and kings.

Elsewhere in the poem, this sumptuousness is pressed to a point which some readers may find rank and cloying:

> And still she slept an azure-lidded sleep,
> In blanched linen, smooth, and lavendered,
> While he from forth the closet brought a heap
> Of candied apple, quince, and plum, and gourd;
> With jellies soother than the creamy curd,
> And lucent syrups, tinct with cinnamon;
> Manna and dates, in argosy transferred
> From Fez; and spiced dainties, every one,
> From silken Samarcand to cedared Lebanon.

It is as though beauty here has become sweetly intolerable in its intensity, so that pleasure begins to veer into distaste. Some might find this creamy, curdy, syrupy sensuous riot a touch decadent. At least one critic has been reminded of baby food. In Keats's narrative poem 'Lamia', however, there is a different kind of problem, as this sort of sensuousness has to coexist with a different rhyme pattern:

> She was a gordian shape of dazzling hue,
> Vermilion-spotted, golden, green, and blue;
> Striped like a zebra, freckled like a pard,
> Eyed like a peacock, and all crimson barr'd;
> And full of silver moons, that, as she breathed,
> Disolv'd, or brighter shone, or interwreathed
> Their lustres with the gloomier tapestries . . .

Some readers may find this effective; but others may detect a slight tension between the fast-moving metre, which is particularly well adapted to narrative, and the luscious imagery itself, which invites us to linger over it longer than we are allowed to. The metre is the iambic pentameter, the same as Keats uses in 'The Eve of St. Agnes', so in a sense the difference in pace between the two poems is an illusion. What makes the difference, however, is the rhyme scheme. Because the lines here are rhymed in pairs (technically speaking they are heroic couplets), the effect is of a more rapid, headlong movement forward. This is because heroic couplets, however superbly accomplished, can never quite avoid an echo of the jingle. Each rhyming couplet seems like a self-enclosed unit of sense, which is clinched by the second rhyme-word and instantly left behind for the next unit. It is as though the clinching rhyme gives the lines a little impetus forward. So the pace seems faster, as we nip from one trim bloc of meaning to another; and this sense of speed is enhanced by the fact that there is often less enjambement or carrying-over of the sense from one line to the other. You can do this in heroic couplets if you like, just as you can in blank verse (or unrhymed iambic pentameters); but there is a tendency to confine the sense within the couplet, which then makes the poem feel less discursive. The poetry of Alexander Pope is a case in point.

Because heroic couplets appear fast-moving, they are particularly appropriate for satire, with its rapid stingings and lashings. A good deal of Pope's poetry would illustrate the point. But it is also deployed to impressive effect in these lines from Lady Mary Wortley Montagu's 'The Small-Pox', in which a Society beauty laments her faded charms:

> As round the room I turn my weeping eyes,
> New unaffected scenes of sorrow rise.
> Far from my sight that killing picture bear,
> The face disfigure, or the canvas tear!
> That picture, which with pride I used to show,
> The lost resemblance but upbraids me now.
> And thou, my toilette, where I oft have sat,

> While hours unheeded past in deep debate,
> How curls should fall, or where a patch to place;
> If blue or scarlet best became my face;
> Now on some happier nymph your aid bestow;
> On fairer heads, ye useless jewels, glow!
> No borrowed lustre can my charms restore,
> Beauty is fled, and dress is now no more.

Montagu was herself disfigured; but the neatness and economy of the couplet form have the effect of distancing and externalising the feeling, placing it, so to speak, squarely in the public sphere, and thus fending of the perils of self-pity.

4.3 Form as Transcending Content

For another sort of discrepancy between form and content, we can turn to Cleopatra's grieving words over her lover Antony's corpse in Shakespeare's *Antony and Cleopatra*:

> The crown o' th' earth doth melt. My lord!
> O, wither'd is the garland of the war,
> The soldier's pole is fall'n! Young boys and girls
> Are level now with men. The odds is gone,
> And there is nothing left remarkable
> Beneath the visiting moon.

Nothing left remarkable, indeed, except for these ravishing lines themselves, which affirm the possibility of value even in the act of denying it. We know, of course, that it is conventional for characters in verse drama to continue to spin out complex imagery even with a knife between their ribs; but the sheer metaphorical fertility of this passage, its delicate rhythmic stops and starts, its brief, broken snatches of gorgeously inventive imagery, suggest both the distraction of sorrow and its transcendence through language. The lines even risk a discreet phallic image. One is reminded of Edgar's sagacious comment in *King Lear*: 'The worst is not / So long as we can say "This is the worst."' As long as we can give voice to our despair, there is still value of a sort. 'Visiting moon' implies that the planet's regular motion, suggestive of universal order, now has a kind of futility about it, as Antony's death has struck meaning from the cosmos as much as from Cleopatra. It is as though the moon carries on placidly, unperturbedly, even a touch obtusely, with its habitual circuit of visits, not knowing that these calls are now pointless since Antony is no longer at home. But this sense of futility cannot entirely erase the momentary genius of the adjective 'visiting'.

Tragedy does not cancel out the havoc it portrays by giving it sense and shape; but it manages to rise above it, to some degree at least, by the sheer integrity of its forms. The hero may not carry on, but the poetry does. As such, it implies an alternative source of value in the act of lending a tongue to the sense that value has disintegrated. As Bertolt Brecht once remarked: 'Lamentation by means of sounds, or better still words, is a vast liberation, because it means that the sufferer is beginning to produce something . . . he's already making something out of the utterly devastating. Observation has set in.'[3]

The sheer diversity of Cleopatra's images, as her mind slips erratically from 'crown' to 'lord' to 'garland', and from there to 'odds' and 'moon', suggests the gathering incoherence of grief. Nothing can be sustained. But these random modulations from one image to another are subtly managed, and the imagery itself is arrestingly impersonal. Cleopatra's language is not focused on Antony as an individual, even if her grief is. Instead, her words imbue him with mythological status, at the calculated risk of depersonalising him to a cosmic principle. It is the combination of formal generality and emotional intensity, captured in the phrase 'My lord!', which is most impressive. It is as though the queen is prepared to sacrifice her personal feelings about Antony to the ceremonial task of granting him what she regards as his authentic universal dignity, a status which then seems oddly to distance him from her. She does not address him by his first name, and the last three and a half lines of the quotation are not about Antony at all, but make a reflective statement about reality as a whole.

At the very moment of the Roman's death, then, Cleopatra delivers the kind of speech which one might expect to find at a memorial service. This, again, is in part a dramatic convention, but it is also a calculated rhetorical effect. We are meant to register the hyperbole or exaggeration, and see this as a symptom of Cleopatra's anguish; yet we are also meant to grasp that for her there is no clear distinction between Antony the lover and Antony the crown of the earth – that the modern distinction between public and private has little force here, and that there is thus something appropriate – something 'personal' – in speaking of one's dead partner in such grandly

[3] Bertolt Brecht, *The Mesingkauf Dialogues* (London, 1965), p. 47.

mythologising terms. In praising Antony as the crown of the earth, his lover betrays the skewing of proportion which is so often an effect of erotic passion, at the same time as she effaces herself courteously from the scene and grants her dead lover a nobility so supreme that he seems as indifferent to herself as a star.

Just as Cleopatra's words rise above the tragedy they are part of, so do the last stanzas of W. B. Yeats's poem 'Coole Park and Ballylee', as the poet mourns the passing of what he sees as his own heroic generation of poets and patricians:

> We were the last romantics – chose for theme
> Traditional sanctity and loveliness;
> Whatever's written in what poets name
> The book of the people; whatever most can bless
> The mind of man or elevate a rhyme;
> But all is changed, that high horse riderless,
> Though mounted in that saddle Homer rode
> Where the swan drifts upon a darkening flood.

The grandeur, in short, has faded; but this can scarcely be true if poetry of this distinction, with its intricate tapestry of rhyme and para-rhyme and deftly controlled syntax, is still possible. The poem, so to speak, survives the tragedy it records. The final image of the swan adrift on the darkening flood graces and ennobles what the poet sees as incipient chaos. The high horse may be lacking a rider, but it is still present on the scene. There are, to be sure, one or two dubious moves: 'Traditional sanctity and loveliness' hardly trips lightly off the tongue in a verse that sets so much store by its rhythm-ical integrity. 'Whatever's written in what poets name / The book of the people' is resonantly evocative, but its suggestiveness threatens to shade off into sheer vagueness; and the horse image is rendered a little suspect by the fact that we have no idea who Homer was, let alone whether he indulged in the occasional gallop. It is, however, a remarkably fine verse for all that, its rhythms artfully varied, its language at once simple and heightened, its tone soberly elegiac without being bitter or lachrymose.

So the verse is melancholy but not self-pitying. Gentlemen like Yeats do not whine, not even when history is showing them the door. It is the kind of poetry which is not afraid to make perilously general claims, a gesture which demands an immense degree of self-assurance. Yeats isn't afraid to risk appearing naïve, as in 'whatever most can bless / The mind of man or elevate a rhyme', which is in danger of sounding blandly platitudinous, as

well as seeming implausibly open-minded for a poet of such assertive doctrinal views. In the end, however, it is the moving simplicity of the lines that
comes through. Modern poets are not supposed to write as plainly as this,
and in an age of obscurity it takes a good deal of self-belief to do so. The
reader can feel this self-assurance in the poise and authority in the language,
even if he or she may also suspect that it is rather too easily come by, sustained by sheer force of assertion. Perhaps the poet is a mite too much on
his high horse, even though he is complaining about being knocked off it.

Yet however anxious and historically vulnerable the poet may be feeling,
his eye is steadily on the imagery, not on himself; and we have no sense that
this is an elaborate defence or displacement. Yeats quite often relates to his
own images as though they were independent of him. He can even write
poems to them from time to time. The feeling in these verses lies in the images
themselves, so to speak, not in a subjective response to them. The poem
simply tells us that 'all is changed'; and though we know that it regards this
change as pretty catastrophic, it neither tell us so nor makes a virtue out of
its own reticence. It does not risk imperilling the robustness of its texture and
coherence of its grammatical structure with an ill-natured rant (though Yeats
can sail close to such ranting elsewhere). As the last verse closes, the poet's eye
is selflessly caught by the image of the swan, not by his own dispiritedness;
and even if the former is an emblem of the latter, the lines momentarily allow
the creature its own autonomous life.

There is a similar, more poignant moment at the end of Yeats's 'The Man
and the Echo':

> O Rocky Voice,
> Shall we in that great night rejoice?
> What do we know but that we face
> One another in this place?
> But hush, for I have lost the theme,
> Its joy or night seem but a dream;
> Up there some hawk or owl has struck,
> Dropping out of sky or rock,
> A stricken rabbit is crying out,
> And its cry distracts my thoughts.

If the stricken rabbit seems a lot more real to us than the Rocky Voice, so
does it to the poet, who is honest and poetically self-possessed enough to
break off his train of thought when it catches his attention, and to do so without embarrassment, in full view of the reader. No sooner has he launched

an imposingly 'metaphysical' theme than he aborts it as a bad job before he can get into his stride, and all for the sake of a rabbit. (Not before time, perhaps: that oracular, hollowly booming phrase 'O Rocky Voice', with its portentous capitalisations, is hardly propitious.) This change of tune is, of course, an artistic device; but Yeats is a dab hand at making this kind of throw-away gesture or casual self-undercutting seem spontaneous, as when he appears not to remember a place-name in 'In Memory of Major Robert Gregory', or pads out a line of 'The Circus Animals' Desertion' with the phrase 'the Lord know what'. He will build up a complex argumentative structure only to qualify or undermine it with a single, cavalier gesture. Or he will suggest that a single pithy, proverbial-sounding image could say it all much better: 'What's water but the generated soul?'; 'And there's but common green-ness after that'; 'Old clothes upon old sticks to scare a bird'; 'Daybreak and a candle-end'. Something of this abrupt change of key, which in Yeats is a kind of calculated bathos, is happening here.

There may be a light touch of aristocratic hauteur in Yeats's sudden switch of subject. The gentleman, unlike the deferential lower middle classes, is not ashamed to do up his fly buttons in the presence of another, or abruptly change the topic of conversation if it takes his fancy. But there is an im-pressive degree of candour and moral courage here as well – qualities fore-shadowed, before the poem shifts its focus, in those almost unbearably stripped, stark lines 'What do we know but that we face / One another in this place?', which would make a far finer epitaph than the bogus, self-vaunting one Yeats eventually wrote for himself. Only wisdom could confess such ignor-ance. It is the rawness of the lines, their uncivil, unflinching directness, their blunt refusal to tart themselves up, which is so stunning. There is no time for such verbal foolery any more, as death begins to bear in.

Equally, only a prodigiously talented poet could venture such a nakedly vulnerable appeal without making it sound tremulous, plangent or embar-rassingly panic-stricken. If there is an anxious agnosticism in these words, there is also a strain of tragic stoicism, as though the point is to accept that this knowledge of our lack of knowledge is where we must start – that this itself is an answer of sorts. In this sense, the lines are as much a statement as a question – or, if you like, a rhetorical question, one expecting the answer 'noth-ing'. Perhaps the poem is reminding us of something rather than appealing to us. Maybe it is because it is not a genuine question that the poet can turn to the rather more pressing panic of the rabbit without waiting for an answer. The rabbit's cry sounds outside the poem, as it were, and the poem lets it in, as though a poem had to keep half an eye on various random events and rumblings on its edges as it went along.

Form and content also work productively against each other in the first stanza of 'Sailing to Byzantium', one of the great Irish emigration poems:

> That is no country for old men. The young
> In one another's arms, birds in the trees
> – Those dying generations – at their song,
> The salmon-falls, the mackerel-crowded seas,
> Fish, flesh, or fowl, commend all summer long
> Whatever is begotten, born, and dies.
> Caught in that sensual music, all neglect
> Monuments of unageing intellect.

The poet is telling us that he must abandon the perishable domain of human love, sexuality, death and reproduction for some more enduring kingdom, one less carnal and fugitive. Yet even though the opening demonstrative already places this perishable domain at arm's length ('That' rather than 'This'), the imagery which portrays it is tender and mutedly sensuous. And this grants the natural, human world of the dying generations a grace and preciousness which makes it hard to abandon. Yeats is refusing to make things easy for himself by setting up a convenient straw target of the fleshly world he is leaving behind – one, let's say, with something of Eliot's complex disgust with the sexual body. Instead, he pays homage to what he is repudiating. He does this, too, by rather courteously suggesting that the fault is his own and not that of the dying generations – that the place is unfit for 'old men' like himself, a self-deprecatory phrase which one can imagine costing this youth-obsessed poet a fair amount of *amour propre*. We suspect that he believes that the profane realm of the dying generations is pretty degenerate anyway, but he is in elegiac mood, and thus tactful enough not to say so outright.

Instead, in a charmingly diplomatic gesture, he discreetly tucks the phrase 'Those dying generations' as a kind of warning aside into his otherwise alluring portrait of the young, the birds and the fish. The punctuation of the first five lines of the stanza has the effect of placing all these items on the same level. This suggests an equation between the erotic young and the birds and mackerel, which is scarcely much of a compliment to the former. Once again, then, there is a delicately muted criticism: human beings are really just as helplessly caught up in an endless biological cycle as salmon, which may be one good reason to sail off to Byzantium. Even so, Byzantium does not sound all that appealing an alternative, at least at this point in the poem. That rather too contrivedly imposing line 'Monuments of unageing intellect', with its plodding stresses and surplus of solemnity, is perhaps intended to sound faintly rebarbative, in order to throw a final flattering light on the sensuality being left behind. There is also, perhaps, a slightly schoolmasterish feel to the admonition 'all neglect', as though a spot of finger-wagging is going on here. But the poem gets away with it.

Yeats is not the kind of writer who explores nature in Keatsian or Hopkinsian detail. There is nothing lavish, profuse or sensuously detailed about the birds in the trees, the salmon-falls and the mackerel-crowded seas. 'Fish, flesh, or fowl' sounds more like a grocer's terminology than a poet's. 'Mackerel-crowded' is a fine stroke, and 'mackerel' (if the pun may be forgiven) a splendidly mouth-filling word; but 'the young in one another's arms' and 'birds in the trees' are deliberately bare and notational. It is as though Yeats is just touching them in on his poetic canvas, without the least intent to lend them complex, convincing life. They are little more than emblems, like (for the most part) the swan in 'Coole Park and Ballylee'.

Yet the poem's achievement is to create the *effect* of lavishness and profuseness from these few meagre, economical items, an effect which would have taken Gerard Manley Hopkins at least another dozen lines. The stanza generates a cornucopian sense of abundance out of the sparsest of materials. And whereas one feels that Hopkins might have been carried away by this potentially inexhaustible fertility, Yeats remains rigorously in control, as the orderly syntax suggests. By about line 4, we are growing a little anxious: what are all these bits and pieces adding up to? Then, suddenly, a main verb ('commend') locks authoritatively into place in the next line, to bind these various elements together and lend them some overall thrust and coherence.

It is as though the chain of brief phrases, with its rapid, cumulative build-up, generates a sense of mounting excitement, one those young lovers might find familiar. Its grammatical open-endedness suggests that this copious piling of life-form upon life-form could in principle go on forever, creating just the sense of exuberance and prodigality that the verse is after. But that clinching main verb, not to speak of the beautifully intricate rhyme scheme, is on hand to assure us that everything is under control. It is as though Yeats's breathing-in, in preparation for the delayed arrival of the main verb, has been deep enough to allow him to voice one brief phrase after another ('the salmon-falls, the mackerel-crowded seas . . .') without things getting out of hand. So the intellect is not just in Byzantium, to be encountered on disembarking, but is already unobtrusively at work in the present. The exclamatory excitement of the lines, with their staccato rhythms, hint at the possibility of an ecstatic loss of control in the face of these fleshly delights, without ever coming remotely close to it.

In 'A Disused Shed in Co. Wexford', a later Irish poet, Derek Mahon, demonstrates a masterly dominance of form over content. Here is the final stanza or so of the poem, which daringly compares a crowd of fetid mushrooms trapped in the darkness of a shed to concentration-camp victims. The metaphor is breathtakingly bold, not least because it courts the danger of dignifying the mushrooms only at the cost of devaluing the victims:

> . . . Grown beyond nature now, soft food for worms,
> They lift frail heads in gravity and good faith.
> They are begging us, you see, in their wordless way,
> To do something, to speak on their behalf
> Or at least not to close the door again.
> Lost people of Treblinka and Pompeii!
> 'Save us, save us', they seem to say,
> 'Let the god not abandon us
> Who have come so far in darkness and in pain.
> We too had our lives to live.
> You with your light meter and relaxed itinerary,
> Let not our naïve labours have been in vain!'

The build-up to this last stanza is full of grotesque, nightmarish imagery, as the 'web-throated' mushrooms, racked by draught, groan piteously for their deliverance. Yet just as the agony grows well-nigh intolerable, that formal, scrupulously well-turned line 'They lift frail heads in gravity and good faith' intervenes with its double alliteration, so that what follows is not a panic-stricken scramble of rotting mushrooms but a dignified, sombrely eloquent appeal. The poem, too, asserts its control, calmly refusing to lose its head. As the door swings open to reveal this almost unbearable pathos, the speaker needs to retain his poise because this is now the moment when he must speak out on behalf of these wordless creatures, ventriloquising their agony through his own verse. He is not shocked spectator but interpreter, rather like the interpreters whom those who liberated the Nazi death camps would no doubt have had in tow. It devolves on the poet to explain to those too traumatised or distraught to grasp this horror precisely what is going on, inserting an almost pedantic 'you see' into his commentary like a conscientious guide.

In the teeth of this appalling spectacle, the poem continues in its unruffled way to analyse and qualify: note that 'Or *at least* not to close the door again', and the complex verb of the final line. This is not the kind of thing that the mushrooms themselves could say, but there is a kind of courteous pretence that they could ('they *seem* to say'), one which restores to them some of their lost dignity. 'Who have come so far in darkness and in pain' is not only an iambic pentameter but is meant to be perceptible to us as such. Even in this state of extremity, language continues to rebuff silence, to the point where the verse can venture what could almost be a piece of elegant, Audenesque wit or irony: 'You with your light meter and relaxed itinerary'. The studied, self-conscious artifice of this line is far beyond the capability of the tormented mushrooms themselves; but once more the poem hands it to them, so to speak, as a kind of gift, lending them something its own poise and eloquence.

Note, finally, that line 'Lost people of Treblinka and Pompeii!', which seems to hang by itself in the stanza. It has no grammatical link to anything around it, occurring as it does as a single interpolated sentence. It is presumably uttered by the speaker, not by the mushrooms, since it is not in quotation marks, but despite this it gives off a certain air of anonymity. It does not actually assert that the mushrooms are like the lost people, a simile which would tie it into its surrounding context; it is simply a brief, exclamatory utterance, possibly by the speaker or possibly not. The force of this is to prevent the poem from making too explicit an analogy between the mushrooms and the camp victims. The analogy is certainly implied; but to spell it out might risk robbing the mushrooms of their own specificity, reducing them to a mere symbol of something else. This might in turn imply that they deserved our sympathy only because they reminded us of the human condition, which would be unduly anthropocentric. The poem refuses to spell out the analogy, then, in order to preserve a tactful balance between attending to these fungi in their own right, and allowing a deeper human dimension to emerge obliquely from their plight.

The power of poetic form to rise above the materials with which it deals is also observable in this passage from Alexander Pope's mock-heroic poem *The Dunciad*, as the goddess Dullness ascends her throne to blot out reason and order from the world:

> Now flamed the dog-star's unpropitious ray,
> Smote every brain, and withered every bay;
> Sick was the sun, the owl forsook his bower,
> The moon-struck prophet felt the maddening hour:
> Then rose the seed of Chaos, and of Night,
> To blot out order and extinguish light,
> Of dull and venal a new world to mould,
> And bring Saturnian days of lead and gold.
> She mounts the throne: her head a cloud concealed,
> In broad effulgence all below revealed,

('Tis thus aspiring Dulness ever shines)
Soft on her lap her laureate son reclines.
Beneath her foot-stool, *Science* groans in chains,
And *Wit* dreads exile, penalties and pains.
There foamed rebellious *Logic*, gagged and bound,
There, stript, fair *Rhetoric* languished on the ground . . .

One might say that Pope's own riposte to this carnival of unreason is the literary form in which he portrays it. There is a balance and symmetry about these heroic couplets which reflect the reason, order and logic flouted by the apostles of Dullness. The couplet works by equipoise, antithesis and fine discrimination, whereas Dullness merges all distinctions into an amorphous sludge. Its polished trimness suggests an elegance beyond the reach of the poetic hacks whom Pope is lambasting here. Its clinching rhymes lend it an air of logic and precision, and the drastic economy of the form, distilling so much information in so brief a compass, demands the virtues of wit, exactness and lucidity. Each couplet forms a little enclosed world of relations and affinities, and as such becomes a microcosm of an orderly cosmos. The form of the poem itself, then, offers some resistance to the tedious long-windedness of those it is sending up.

4.4   Poetry and Performance

This kind of tension between form and content, of the kind we find in the mock-heroic of *The Dunciad*, is sometimes known to students of language as a performative contradiction. Roughly speaking, this means saying one thing while doing something which runs counter to it, like preaching the virtues of humility in a hectoring tone. In this sense, irony is a kind of performative contradiction. Male conference participants who rise to deliver lengthy, hotly indignant speeches about why no woman is contributing to the discussion, thus ensuring that no woman is able do so, are caught in such a bind. A performative contradiction is a useful concept because it reminds us that poems are performances, not simply objects on the page. We can think of a poem as a pattern of sound or meaning; but we can also see it as a strategy which aims to get something done. Or, indeed, a number of different, perhaps mutually incompatible things at the same time. To achieve this, the poem mobilises its army of formal devices; but this isn't to suggest that they always work harmoniously together. They may always pull in different directions.

There is, however, a paradox at stake here. Poetry is language organised in such a way as to generate certain effects, and to this extent it has much in common with everyday speech. One difference, as we have seen, is that everyday utterances usually skim over the flavour and texture of words in order to achieve their ends; whereas in poetry, one of these ends is precisely the exploration of words in themselves. This is how poetry can be rhetorical without being crudely instrumental. Part of the purpose for which it organises words is to reveal the nature of words. This, to be sure, is not its only function: it has a semantic dimension as well, which is to say that it is concerned with meaning as well as with investigating its own verbal materials. Or, as the aestheticians might say, the sign in poetry is at once communicative and autonomous. And though these two aspects of a poem do not always slide neatly together, as we shall see later, they have to be taken in terms of each other.

A poem, then, is a rhetorical performance, but (unlike most rhetorical exercises) not typically an instrumental one. It does things to us, though not usually so that we can get something done. Even so, there are forms of poetry which are written with the explicit intention of praising, cursing, consoling, inspiring, blessing, commemorating, denouncing, offering moral counsel and so on. Because the modern age is neurotically suspicious of the didactic, with its curious assumption that to be taught must be invariably unpleasant, it tends to imagine that poems which seek to do this must be inferior modes of writing. They are to be relegated to the lowly status of the pragmatic, along with bus tickets and 'No Entry' signs. But the didactic, a word which simply means 'teaching' and originally carried no pejorative overtones, is the purpose of one of the finest of all traditional literary genres, the sermon. Virgil's *Georgics*, as we have seen, includes technical advice to farmers (though they would be ill-advised to take it too seriously). Many an accomplished poem has been written with an immediate end in view. It is only the prejudice of the modern critic, for whom the practical is generally rather a vulgar affair, which obscures this fact. Some poems may be aesthetically poor but pragmatically rich, like the verses written by parents in memory of a dead child. Most modern critics revolt at the word 'dogma', too, but a great many traditional poems are dogmatic, in the original, non-derogatory sense of adhering to a system of belief. Dante and Milton, for example. It is a mistake to hold with some modern critics that too much belief, like too much salt, is invariably bad for you. It depends on the kind of belief in question. And the critics are of course usually thinking of other people's beliefs rather than their own. My beliefs are supremely flexible, while yours are absurdly arthritic.

Even so, poems are clearly not slices of propaganda. (This is another much-abused term, by the way: it originally meant simply the dissemination of information.) As W. H. Auden famously put the point:

> . . . For poetry makes nothing happen: it survives
> In the valley of its making where executives
> Would never want to tamper . . .
> ('In Memory of W. B. Yeats')

Yet this is only one side of the story. What poetry can make happen is a kind of constructive non-happening. By refraining from an immediate intervention in human affairs, it can allow truth and beauty to come about, in ways which may then make things happen.

The notion of strategy or performance reminds us that words have force as well as meaning. 'Force' means the effect or intended impact of a piece of language, which may not be at one with its meaning. What she actually said was 'It's getting awfully late', but the force of her statement was 'Why don't you leave this minute?' Poems do things to us as well as say things to us; they are social events as well as verbal artefacts. And the notion of a verbal event – of language as a practical activity – was known to the ancients as rhetoric, as we have seen already. Rhetoric means language organised in such a way as to achieve certain determinate ends, and this involves taking account of a whole number of considerations: the material nature of language itself; the way its various formal devices typically operate; the nature and capacities of its audience; and the social situation in which all this takes place. One modern term for this is 'discourse', which means language grasped as a concrete social occurrence inseparable from its context. It is language seen as a transaction between human subjects, rather than viewed formally or abstractly. All poetry has palpable designs on us, whatever John Keats may have considered. It is a matter of design in more senses than one. Poems are material events and fields of force, not simply verbal communications. Or rather, they are the latter only in terms of the former – which brings us once again to the question of form and content.

We can ask, then, what a piece of poetry is trying to do, as well as what it is trying to say. A relevant example might be the first two verses of T. S. Eliot's 'Mr Eliot's Sunday Morning Service':

> Polyphiloprogenitive
> The sapient sutlers of the Lord
> Drift across the window-panes.
> In the beginning was the Word.

In the beginning was the Word.
Superfetation of τὸἐν,
And at the mensual turn of time
Produced enervate Origen.

The reader's first response is one of blind panic. What on earth is going on here? Dutifully reaching for the dictionary proves only of limited help: we discover that 'sapient' means wise, or perhaps pretending to wisdom; that a sutler is someone who sells provisions to an army; that 'superfetation' means the fertilisation of the same ovum by different kinds of pollen, or a second conception during pregnancy which gives rise to embryos of different ages in the uterus. 'Polyphiloprogenitive' presumably means something like 'enjoying multiple reproduction'. (The dictionary will not help us here, just as it will not enlighten us as to why there is that curious full stop after the second 'In the beginning was the Word'.) 'Enervate' means deprived of vigour or vitality, which in this context (since Origen emasculated himself) may serve as a euphemism for 'castrated'. One scholar informs us that there is no such word as 'mensual', which may be a slip for 'menstrual', and that the Greek phrase contains a trifling error.[4] As we read on in the poem, the wild suspicion begins to dawn on us that the piece is actually about *bees*.

But none of this will get us very far. What we should have done was to trust our first impressions. This kind of writing is surely *meant* to baffle us. What it does is at least as important as what it says. Nobody fills a whole first line with the ridiculously tongue-twisting 'Polyphiloprogenitive' without some slyly mischievous intent. The esoteric diction and arcane allusions deliberately prevent us from reading for 'content'. Instead, we are held firmly at the level of the signifier, rammed helplessly up against its thickness and opacity. We are made to experience language itself, not what it points to. The language of the piece is so rebarbative, so bristling with pitfalls and enigmas, that we are forced to abandon trying to peer through it to the underlying meaning. And this, one imagines, is part of the effect which the poet is after. What the piece says, among other things, is 'This is modernism.' It proclaims itself as a type of literature which is impossible to consume. In fact, it represents a calculated guerrilla assault on the very idea of poetry. Or at least on the conception of poetry that the reader in 1920 might well have brought to these outrageously avant-garde verses.

Note, however, that the poem is not at all outrageous in metrical form. Instead, its metrical trimness leads us to expect a transparency of meaning

---

[4]   See F. W. Bateson, 'The Poetry of Learning', in Graham Martin (ed.), *Eliot in Perspective* (London, 1970), p. 36.

which we are craftily denied by its language. And this metrical economy also lends it an impersonal air, one which allows it to get away to some extent with its shamelessly (or is it ironically?) self-flaunting display of erudition. It is a scandalously 'coterie' piece, accessible only to the cognoscenti; but because the poem's 'voice' seems purged of much distinctive personality, it is hard for us to feel that this is a matter of personal superiority. Eliot is often seen as an intellectually difficult, fearfully elitist writer, and so in some ways he was. But he was also the kind of poet who put little store by erudite allusions, and professed himself quite content to have his poetry read by those who had exceedingly little idea of what it meant. This should be deeply gratifying to us all. It was form – the material stuff of language itself, its archaic resonances and tentacular roots – which mattered most to him. In fact, he once claimed to have enjoyed reading Dante in the original even before he could understand Italian, which is perhaps pushing the centrality of poetic form a little too far.

This is one reason why the perversely misleading Notes to *The Waste Land* are largely spoof. In some ways, a semi-literate would have been Eliot's ideal reader. He was more of a primitivist than a sophisticate. He was interested in what a poem did, not what it said – in the resonance of the signifier, the lures of its music, the hauntings of its grains and textures, the subterranean workings of what one can only call the poem's unconscious. Eliot's poems are full of ghosts, even though his character Gerontion denies that he has any. Poetry sets up rhythms and resonances which in Eliot's view penetrate far beneath the intellect, infiltrating the visceral depths of the body and its secret psychical domains. It throws us the odd fragment of meaning, but only to keep us distracted while it goes to work upon us in stealthier, more devious ways.

The celebrated opening image of 'The Love-Song of J. Alfred Prufrock' is another case in point:

> Let us go then, you and I,
> When the evening is spread out against the sky
> Like a patient etherised upon a table . . .

The allusion to the evening and the sky sets up a conventionally Romantic expectation, which the following line casually or callously deflates. There is an equal baffling of expectations in the irregular rhythms of these three lines, which seem deliberately maladroit. The last two of them are rather dishevelled iambic pentameters. The lines lurch rather than glide, and the fact that the first two of them rhyme simply helps to throw their clumsily contrasting rhythms into relief. Their language is deliberately spiky and unlovely, more like the bleached bureaucratese of a form you might pick up in the post office than what we have come to expect from poetry.

How, the reader wonders, can the evening look like an anaesthetised body? Yet the point surely lies as much in the force of this bizarre image as in its meaning. We are in a modern world in which settled correspondences or traditional affinities between things have broken down. In the arbitrary flux of modern experience, the whole idea of representation – of one thing predictably standing for another – has been plunged into crisis; and this strikingly dislocated image, one which more or less ushers in 'modern' poetry with a rebellious flourish, is a symptom of this bleak condition. The point is not to ask how the evening can resemble an etherised patient, but what kind of alienated consciousness could make such an arbitrary, eccentric connection. It is a send-up of a simile.

It is the kind of question we might also ask about John Donne's 'Metaphysical' conceits, which are self-preening, virtuoso performances rather than plausible descriptions of reality. One of the most quoted passages in English poetry may demonstrate the point:

> Our two souls therefore, which are one,
>   Though I must go, endure not yet
> A breach, but an expansion,
>   Like gold to airy thinness beat.
>
> If they be two, they are two so
>   As stiff twin compasses are two;
> Thy soul, the fixed foot, makes no show
>   To move, but doth, if th'other do.
>
> And though it in the centre sit,
>   Yet when the other far doth roam,
> It leans and hearkens after it,
>   And grows erect, as that comes home.
>   ('A Valediction Forbidding Mourning')

We admire the appositeness of the compasses image at the same time as we feel the full force of its arbitrariness. If we did not sense the coerced nature of the conceit so keenly, the way it is wrenched wilfully into place by such perverse ingenuity, we would appreciate its skill a good deal less. What we watch is less the lovers than the sheer brio by which the poet manages to pull various ill-assorted bits and pieces of the world together, apparently against the odds. The poem tries to convince us that the lovers really are like a pair of compasses, at the same time as it rubs the disparity between them impudently in our faces and so persuades us into admiring its own deviously opportunistic wit.

Look, for another example, at the last two lines of George Herbert's poem 'Love', in which the poet is speaking to Christ:

> 'You must sit down', says Love, 'and taste my meat'.
> So I did sit and eat.

The sudden modulation in tone and metre here, from the formal courtesy of the first line to the quiet, throwaway matter-of-factness of the second, is a rhetorical effect. It is its impact on the reader which matters, not just its meaning. The full stop after 'meat' makes the last line a single unit, thus emphasising its terseness and flatness. A comma would have been fatal to the effect.

A much more abrupt transition than Herbert's can be found in T. S. Eliot's poem 'Burbank with a Baedeker: Bleistein with a Cigar':

> Princess Volupine extends
>   A meagre, blue-nailed, phthisic hand
> To climb the waterstair. Lights, lights,
>   She entertains Sir Ferdinand
>
> Klein. Who clipped the lion's wings
>   And flea'd his rump and pared his claws? . . .

'Klein', which means 'small' in German, is literally a comedown from the noble-sounding 'Sir Ferdinand', suggesting that this upstart Jew (Klein is also a Jewish surname) has been clipped of his bogus grandeur rather as the lion's wings are clipped. The poem actually performs a violent act of diminishing, even of humiliating, rather than simply speaking of it.

Or think of the opening lines of Book 2 of *Paradise Lost*, in which Milton introduces us to Satan on his kingly throne:

> High on a throne of royal state, which far
> Outshone the wealth of Ormus and of Ind,
> Or where the gorgeous East with richest hand
> Show'rs on her kings barbaric pearls and gold,
> Satan exalted sat . . .

The appearance of Satan is deferred to the fifth line, as with some florid introduction to a mighty personage which concludes by dramatically whisking back the curtain on him. The first four lines serve as a kind of flourish of trumpets to the devil's verbal entry into the poem. Presenting him amid this regal pomp makes it clear enough that Milton, a revolutionary republican, is definitely not of his party.

Or take the edgy exchange of challenges which opens *Hamlet*, as the sentry Francisco stands at his post on the castle battlements and his colleague Bernando arrives to relieve him:

Bernardo: Who's there?
Francisco: Nay, answer me. Stand and unfold yourself.

This terse snatch of dialogue is enough to tell us that nerves are not as steely as they might be in Hamlet's Elsinore. As scholars have pointed out, it is the soldier coming on sentry duty who barks out the traditional challenge, and the guard already on duty who responds. Francisco, his authority a mite flouted, presumably snarls 'Answer *me*.' We can detect the tonal emphasis from the social context. The force of the words, then, is distinct from their meaning; we cannot register it fully without some sense of context.

As far as the performative effects of poetry go, think also of Othello's grandiloquent first line as he comes marching on: 'Keep up your bright swords, for the dew will rust them.' This is, precisely, a grandiloquent first line, of the kind we imagine he might have been meticulously rehearsing for ten minutes in the wings. What the line says is 'Put away your swords', but its force is 'Here I am at last before your expectant gaze, the tragic hero with his rotund, dramatically arresting opening line.' It is almost as though the line, with its stately self-consciousness and sudden soaring of poetic temperature, is a quotation – in fact it caries a faint resonance of Christ in the Garden of Gethsemane. Othello, as usual, is performing himself magnificently – unlike Hamlet, who finds it hard to live up to himself, Macbeth, who performs himself as badly as a third-rate actor, and Lear, who hasn't a clue who he is.

The most renowned of all twentieth-century poems, T. S. Eliot's *The Waste Land*, betrays a different kind of discrepancy between form and content. The poem itself is a mighty collage of quotations, allusions, fractured phrases, spectral figures and listless snatches of memory. As such, it seems no more than a heap of fragments from a collapsed civilisation, of the kind that some archaeologist from the distant future might stumble across. Yet all this is being secretly woven, behind the reader's back, so to speak, into a dense tapestry of cross-references, symbols and archetypes, all of which holds at least some of these materials together. The result is an imposingly panoramic vision of decay and futility. But if such an authoritative overview is still possible, can civilisation really be all that fragmented after all?

Or to put it another way: how can the poem itself be possible, if what it says is true? Where does its structural unity spring from? Where is the poet himself standing?

4.5   Two American Examples

For a different illustration of this contrast, look at Robert Frost's much-loved 'Stopping by Woods on a Snowy Evening':

> Whose woods these are I think I know.
> His house is in the village though;
> He will not see me stopping here
> To watch his woods fill up with snow.
>
> My little horse must think it queer
> To stop without a farmhouse near
> Between the woods and frozen lake
> The darkest evening of the year.
>
> He gives his harness bell a shake
> To ask if there is some mistake.
> The only other sound's the sweep
> Of easy wind and downy flake.
>
> The woods are lovely, dark and deep,
> But I have promises to keep,
> And miles to go before I sleep,
> And miles to go before I sleep.

What is striking about these lines is the tension they set up between the every-dayness of the event portrayed, which is reflected in the homespun, even quaint quality of the language, and the elaborate rhyme scheme which frames it. If the experience is about Nature, the intricate rhyming pattern, along with the odd well-honed phrase ('easy wind and downy flake') reminds us insistently that this is art. The event itself is low-key, while the closely packed rhymes thud as portentously as a heartbeat, made all the more obtrusive by the short-ness of the lines.

The rhymes also stand out as they do because there is not much enjambe-ment in the poem, which means, as we have seen, letting the sense run over from one line to another. When this happens, our eye tends to skim over the rhyme in its pursuit of the meaning from one line to the next. Here, however, many of the lines are units of meaning complete in themselves ('His house is in the village though' . . . 'The woods are lovely, dark and deep'), which allows us to savour the rhyming words to the full. The unvaried metre, with its regular, metronome-like tapping, contributes to this air of artifice; and all this is at odds with the naturalness of the content (the snow, woods and horse), and the sheer chanciness and spontaneity of the actual event. One might even describe this contrast as a kind of irony.

The rhyme scheme gives the appearance of moving forward only to keep curving back on itself: 'know', 'though', 'here', 'snow', 'queer', 'near', 'shake', 'mistake' and so on. We inch forward a shade only to find that we are also thrown back a pace or two. There is much recurrence and repetition in this *aaba / bbcb* rhyming pattern, which brings with it a curious sense of stasis. By the time the last verse arrives, we have the mesmeric, incantatory repetition of a single rhyme ('deep' . . . 'keep' . . . 'sleep'). There is no longer any progress or modulation in the rhyme scheme, even though the speaker is now reminding himself to move on. The effect is rather like someone trying to shake himself out of the paralysis of sleep with the thought that he should get up. Perhaps we can relate this sense of arrested motion to the death which we sense lurking in the shadow of these final lines. If death is part of what sleep and the woods symbolise, then the poem seems to find it both alluring and foreboding; and something similar can be said of its own rhyme scheme, which is beautifully managed yet also faintly ominous in its bell-like tolling. If the second 'And miles to go before I sleep' refers to the poet's death, then the fact that it is so distant should seem like a good thing; but the dying fall of the repetition make it sound more regrettable than reassuring. The poet has had a glimpse of a seductive stasis he is reluctant to abandon. It is a glimpse he has almost literally stolen from the owner of the woods, who, he assures himself rather guiltily, will not see him stopping here to take a look at his trees, rather as he would not see him furtively helping himself to some firewood.

This rather static form, which seems to revolve upon itself rather than move purposefully forward, thus reflects the suspended moment in the woods itself, where the poet's progress has been arbitrarily halted by the vision of the falling snow. The rhyme scheme moves in a kind of arrested motion, like a waterfall; and this is mirrored by the fact that what flickerings of life there are in the forest – the wind, the snow falling, the horse shaking its harness bells – are contained within a more general stillness. In this sense, form and content match one another as well as being at odds. It is as though the poem, like the speaker, is trying to forge ahead, but keeps being held back.

In another sense, however, form and content move at different levels. The poem's ritualised rhyming pattern, with its sober, almost fatalistic drumbeat, lends it a sense of inevitability; but there is nothing in the situation it depicts which would seem to warrant this. The situation itself is random, down-to-earth and open-ended, whereas the form is taut, closed and ceremonial. The horse shakes its bell to ask if there is some mistake – if stopping to watch the snow silently falling is a chance deviation from the regular course of events, which presumably it is. But the form of the poem could be seen as intimating otherwise. Its formal patterning, along with that reference to 'The darkest evening of the year', might be taken to hint that this fleeting experience in the woods is somehow 'meant' – that it is a kind of epiphany or revelation – at the same time as the language used to describe it suggests, quite to the contrary, that it is simply a natural, casual occurrence. The very fact that this is a poem, not an entry from a country diary, reinforces the sense of trembling on the brink of some obscure revelation. It is as though the form has a meaning which is at odds with the content. Perhaps the poet is being tempted to extract a meaning out of something which he suspects does not have one, and this is part of the poem's meaning. Perhaps all poetry is a sort of *trompe l'oeil* or illusion, plucking meaning out of materials which are senseless in themselves.

There is an unembellished, casually conversational feel to the poem's language, though the piece, ironically, is a monologue. The phrase 'fill up with snow', for example, is both delicately suggestive and entirely commonplace. So any too-obtrusive symbolism would risk overloading the verses. Perhaps this is one reason for the repetition in the last lines, which hints at a deeper, more 'metaphysical' meaning, but does so obliquely rather than explicitly. What the repetition does is to suddenly make the first 'And miles to go before I sleep', which we had taken literally, appear both literal and symbolic. It is as though the line has suddenly realised that it means more than it had imagined, and registers this by repeating itself. Poetry is not supposed to be just a bare record of experience; as we have seen, it is also expected to draw deeper or wider implications from what it observes. So perhaps Frost needs that final, portentous repetition, which implies in its muted way that the experience in the snow-filled woods points to more than itself.

In one sense, a repetition like this is a kind of clinching gambit, allowing us a sense of closure like the final, repeated chords of a classical symphony. Yet the closure is uneasy, since repetition can in principle go on forever, making the conclusion as open-ended in one sense as it is rounded off in another. Does the poem wrap itself up or simply trail off? Is the final line indeed a dying fall or exhausted murmur, or a slight turning up of volume and emotional intensity? The line wearily gets nothing new said; but saying nothing new may also suggest that there is nothing more to be said, thus giving the sense of an achieved conclusion.

This ominous intimation comes right at the end of the piece, which means that the poem cannot follow it up. In any case, we cannot be sure that it is an ominous gesture; it might just be a tired trailing off. If the poem prevents itself from pursuing its own intimation, however, given that it has just come to an end, it may be because of its respect for the integrity of the everyday world it describes. To move into a more visionary or metaphysical mode might risk undercutting its faith in ordinary things, a faith reflected in its idiomatic, scrupulously unshowy language. So the poem teeters on the brink of being 'symbolic', without quite taking the plunge. There is something elusive at the heart of this experience, yet the experience itself must not be devalued by being reduced to a mere symbol of whatever it is. Modern poets like Frost still want to make 'deep' statements; but they are also more sceptical of such high-sounding generalities than many of their forebears. So, rather like T. S. Eliot's *The Waste Land*, they gesture enigmatically to such profundities while at the same time being nervous of committing themselves to them. If this is true of the Frost poem, then the poem becomes to some extent an allegory of the dilemmas of modern poetry – which is to say, an allegory of itself.

There is another sense in which the poem might be seen as an allegory of poetry. The speaker is caught between continuing on his way in businesslike fashion, and staying put to relish the sight of the snow; and this represents a conflict between the pragmatic and the non-pragmatic. If the unpoetic, briskly commonsensical horse tugs him in one direction, the darkly mysterious woods draw him in another. Perhaps it is not surprising that Frost, who was both a poet and a farmer, should feel a tension between an aesthetic and an instru-mental attitude to nature. The poem may be about how he would like simply to be a poet, savouring the sounds and textures of things, but can't afford to do so. So this prospect, like the prospect of death, is both seductive and unsettling. Looking too closely into things, exploring too adventurously beyond the familiar, may have its dangers, not least the danger of detaching you from the kind of common wisdom which the poem's language reflects. There may be something undemocratic about it. In the end, then, the poet throws in his lot with conventional morality ('But I have promises to keep') and the conservatively minded horse, who is a creature of habit as easily disturbed by innovation as the middlebrow reading public. But this option is not without it perils either. Anyway, Frost has produced a poem out of the tension between poetry and practicality, which should be enough for the present.

Contrast Frost's poem now with this one by Emily Dickinson:

> Because I could not stop for Death –
> He kindly stopped for me –
> The Carriage held but just Ourselves –
> And Immortality.
>
> We slowly drove – He knew no haste
> And I had put away
> My labor and my leisure too,
> For His Civility –
>
> We passed the School, where Children strove
> At Recess – in the Ring –
> We passed the Fields of Gazing Grain –
> We passed the Setting Sun –
>
> Or rather – He passed us –
> The Dews drew quivering and Chill –
> For only Gossamer, my Gown –
> My Tippet – only Tulle –
>
> We paused before a House that seemed
> A Swelling of the Ground –
> The Roof was scarcely visible –
> The Cornice – in the Ground –
>
> Since then – 'tis Centuries – and yet
> Feels shorter than the Day
> I first surmised the Horses' Heads
> Were toward Eternity –

The metre of this is more varied than in the Frost poem, as lines of four stresses alternate for the most part with lines of three. This gives the piece a more jaunty, less solemnly measured air than 'Stopping By Woods'. In fact, if you press this kind of rhythm far enough you end up with a sort of jingle. (It has been noted that almost all of Emily Dickinson's poems can be sung to the tune of 'The Yellow Rose of Texas'.) And this sprightliness is ironically at odds with those mournful, momentous allegorical figures of Death, Immortality and Eternity. The metre takes the sting out of these fearful abstractions, just as it does by setting them in as humdrum a context as a ride in a carriage. Yet the effect, far from being one of domesticating the unknown, is of a surreal strangeness, which the everyday imagery only sharpens. The whole scene is at once luminously etched and eerily unreal, as in a dream. As in some dreams, the speaker seems oddly unperturbed by the outlandish situation in which she finds herself. Somehow, the poem's very casualness about Death and Immortality – the sense that these figures are as familiar as old friends – adds to its uncanniness.

In this chapter, we have examined a number of poems in some detail, with particular attention to the way that form and content may work productively against one another. Part of the point of this exercise has been to challenge the piety that the two always form a harmonious whole. But there is an objection to the kind of close analysis we have been conducting, which we should tackle before we carry on.

Chapter 5

How to Read a Poem

5.1 Is Criticism Just Subjective?

There is an argument against the close analysis of literary form that goes
something like this. Establishing what a poem literally says, or what metre
it may use, or whether it rhymes, are objective matters on which critics can
concur. (Punctuation also used to be ranked among these things, in the age
before the owners of pubs began unwittingly casting doubt on the genuine-
ness of their own products by advertising 'real' ale.) But talk of tone, mood,
pace, dramatic gesture and the like is purely subjective. What I hear as ran-
corous you may hear as jubilant. You read as garrulous what strikes me as
eloquent. Tone in a poem is not a matter of F major or B minor. Ironically,
only a few features of form – metre and rhyme, for example – can actually
be formalised. Form in poetry is mostly unformalisable. There can be no
consensus on these questions, so it would be better to drop such fanciful
talk altogether and concentrate on what we can be sure of.

There is something in this allegation. There is no exact science of these
matters, and there is indeed a good deal of room for disagreement in discussing poems. But we may note to begin with that being able to disagree
over an issue does not necessarily imply pure subjectivism. We might clash
over whether torture is permissible or not, yet there may still be a right and
wrong to the question, whatever our dissensions. We might disagree over
whether someone is waving or drowning, but it is unlikely that he is doing
both. Unless the swimmer has a remarkably nonchalant attitude to his
death, one of us is almost bound to be wrong. Opinions we advance in purely

conjectural style may later turn out to be cast-iron certainties, as more evidence becomes available.

As far as literary arguments go, take, for example, Robert Browning's darkly Gothic poem 'Porphyria's Lover', in which the speaker, possibly a psychopath, describes how he coolly decided to strangle his mistress:

> . . . I found
> A thing to do, and all her hair
> In one long yellow string I wound
> Three times her little throat around,
> And strangled her . . .
> And thus we sit together now,
> And all night long we have not stirred,
> And yet God has not said a word!

The offhandedness of that 'thing to do', as though the speaker might equally well have chosen to trim his moustache, is especially chilling. But how is one to read the last line? The most obvious interpretation is surely as a cry of (perhaps slightly manic) triumph: the lover has deliberately tempted God by this dreadful deed into revealing himself, and God has remained silent. So perhaps the whole grisly murder was an experiment in demonstrating the truth of atheism. Yet I have heard the line delivered by an actor in a tone of sullen resentment. For this reader, no doubt, the speaker is not a jubilant atheist but a would-be believer, who has sacrificed his lover in an attempt to force God into revealing his hand, and is now bitterly downcast by the Almighty's obdurate silence. He has, so to speak, lost his Maker and his mistress at the same time, and all for nothing.

There is no foolproof way of deciding between such competing interpretations. We cannot appeal to Browning, and even if we could it might well not settle the question. This is not only because poets can be peculiarly obtuse about the meaning of their own work. T. S. Eliot, for example, once described *The Waste Land* as just a kind of rhythmic grousing, though he was probably being disingenuous. It is also because when Browning was once asked what one of his poems meant, he replied that at the time of writing it, 'God and Robert Browning knew; now, God knows.' Yet those who feel that these questions are too chancy and subjective, in contrast with 'what the poem says', might care to note that 'what the poem says' is not always that well-founded either. Take, for example, Browning's title. We know that Porphyria is the name of the murdered woman, since the poem makes this clear. Which means that the lover must be the male speaker. But why do we assume that the speaker is male? There is nothing in the text to indicate this. It is simply a hypothesis we bring to the piece in order to make sense of it. Perhaps the speaker is also a woman, and this is a lesbian relationship gone horribly awry. No doubt it would be rather brazen to adduce the phrase 'tonight's gay feast' in support of this hypothesis. It is also the case that the vast majority of murderers are men, not least those killers driven by sadistic sexual motives. The arrogant sexual possessiveness of the speaker is much more stereotypically masculine than feminine. And the odds against an eminent Victorian poet writing a piece about lesbian sexuality, however cunningly he concealed it, are positively astronomical. Titles are part of poems, and we may note that this title, significantly, refers to the murderer and not his victim. So even the title reflects a morbid self-obsession which, stereotypically speaking, is arguably more masculine than feminine. (Actually, one suspects that Browning put the lover rather than the victim in the title to place some distance between himself and his protagonist, treating him as a pathological case.) Even so, we cannot absolutely rule out a lesbian reading. One of the apparently most self-evident facts about the poem turns out to be contestable.

Questions of tone crop up again in these celebrated lines from Andrew Marvell's 'To His Coy Mistress':

> But at my back I always hear
> Time's wingèd chariot hurrying near:
> And yonder all before us lie
> Deserts of vast eternity.
> Thy beauty shall no more be found;
> Nor, in thy marble vault, shall sound
> My echoing song: then worms shall try
> That long-preserved virginity,
> And turn your quaint honour to dust,
> And into ashes all my lust.
> The grave's a fine and private place,
> But none, I think, do there embrace.

As with a lot of so-called Metaphysical poetry, the speaker seems sportive and serious at the same time, so that a good actor delivering these lines would need to convey their urbane sophistry (the speaker is really just trying to get her into bed with a lot of high-toned metaphysics), along with their undertow of urgency and anxiety (he really is worried about decay and death). It is possible that he is being both debonair and deadly earnest, and to suppose this makes the piece more interesting and ambiguous. The tone of the last two lines, depending on how you judge the overall ratio between erotic teasing and ontological anxiety, could be anything from roguish to playfully sardonic to cuttingly sarcastic. You could deliver them to reveal a real impatience and irascibility beginning to peep through the cavalier wit, or as impishly bantering, or as a piece of hard-boiled flippancy.

Tone, mood and the like may be matters of interpretation over which critics can conflict; but this is not the same as their being purely subjective. As we have just seen, we can conflict over meaning as well. But there are usually limits to such contentions. It is just possible that Porphyria's lover is a woman, in the sense that you can adopt this hypothesis and still make sense of the work; but nobody would suggest that the lover is a giraffe. This is not just because Victorian writers did not generally go in for poems about bestiality, but because the textual evidence simply would not support it. Giraffes do not wind people's hair three times around their throat and strangle them. Their hearts do not swell at the thought that they are worshipped by a woman. Nor do they entertain thoughts about God, atheistic or otherwise. If someone asked us how we know that giraffes do not spend their time feverishly brooding on metaphysical questions, it would be enough to reply: by looking at what they do. We do not have to get inside their brains to be reasonably sure of this, just as I do not have to get inside your brain to know that when I see you rolling at my feet with your hair on fire emitting strange noises, you are clearly not happy.

Something of the same is true of more elusive questions like mood, address, implication, connotation, symbolism, sensibility, rhetorical effect and the like. There can be serious divergences of opinion about these things, but there are also constraints on how deeply these may run, at least for those who share the same culture. This is because tones and feelings are quite as much social matters as meaning. It is not that meaning is public whereas feeling is private. It is only a disreputable philosophical tradition which persuades us to think this way. On this theory, my feelings are something private and subjective. I know them inwardly, intuitively, simply by looking inside myself. But if this is so, it is hard to see how I can ever misidentify what I am feeling. It becomes difficult to say things like 'I don't know whether I'm afraid of her or not', or 'I thought at the time that I cared for him, but looking back I realise that I didn't care for him in the least.' In any case, when I look into myself, how do I identify what I find there? How do I know that what I am feeling is envy and not disgust? Only because I already have the concept of envy to help me identify this feeling among the whole welter of emotions and sensations I discover when I reflect on myself. And I learnt this concept by being introduced into a language as a child. If I did not have language I would still have feelings, but I would not know what they were. And some feelings which I have now I would not have at all.

Bertolt Brecht puts the point well:

One easily forgets that human education proceeds along highly theatrical lines. In a quite theatrical manner the child is taught how to behave; logical arguments only come later. When such-and-such occurs, it is told (or sees), one must laugh. It joins in when there is laughter, without knowing why; if asked why it is laughing it is wholly confused. In the same way it joins in shedding tears, not only weeping because the grown-ups do so but also feeling genuine sorrow. This can be seen at funerals, whose meaning escapes children entirely. These are theatrical events which form the character. The human being copies gestures, miming, tones of voice. And weeping arises from sorrow, but sorrow also arises from weeping.[1]

Brecht's case is rather too 'culturalist': very small babies laugh, for example, long before they have grasped the social institution of laughter. They also cry and smile, activities which have a biological basis. Even so, Brecht is on to something vitally important, which he has learnt not 'philosophically' but through his practical activity as a playwright and theatre director. Emotion in the theatre is clearly a public affair, which is not so obviously the case in the bedroom. Brecht spent much of his life watching actors *learn* modes of feeling, and the kinds of speech and behaviour which seemed appropriate to them. The theatre could show him something about real life which real life tended to conceal. He was able to extend what he found in theatre rehearsals to human emotions in general, and their 'mimetic' or imitative character. Being brought up in a culture is a matter of learning appropriate forms of feeling as much as particular ways of thinking. And all of these are sedimented in that culture's language and behaviour, so that to share a language is to share a form of life. To imagine that this means that our feelings are never sincere would be like thinking that I can never use the words 'I love you' and mean them because millions of people have used them before.

In a culture which lacked the concept and institution of private property, for example, one could not conceive a burning desire to become a billionaire entrepreneur. This is not to claim that such a culture would be without feelings of greed or ambition, simply without these specific forms of them. People do not generally feel revolted by the very sight of their second cousin if they do not inhabit cultures in which there are strong taboos on their marrying them. What we can feel is to some extent determined by the kinds of

---

[1] *Brecht on Theatre: The Development of an Aesthetic* (London, 1964), p. 152. See also Terry Eagleton, 'Brecht and Rhetoric' in Eagleton, *Against the Grain: Essays 1975–1985* (London, 1986).

material animals we are. But what we might call styles of feeling are shaped by our cultural institutions. And both of these are public affairs.

Children, then, observe various kinds of behaviour around them, and learn to grasp this as *expressive* behaviour. Their understanding of emotions is thus bound up with the kind of material things people do, and with their own growing participation in such practical forms of life. Like actors (though not, in fact, Brechtian actors), they sometimes begin by miming styles of emotion and end up by feeling them for real. In cultures like our own, they then usually go on to be taught that feelings are private, natural, internal and universal. But this is just how our kind of culture feels about feelings. There are indeed natural, universal feelings, such as grief at the death of a loved one, which we have because we are the kind of creatures we are; but what we make of that grief is a cultural affair. And there are other emotions, such as feeling embarrassed about using the wrong cutlery at a formal dinner party, which might be unintelligible to some other cultures.

It is also hard to see why we should think of our emotions as being 'inside' us, and so shut off from public view. It seems strange to say of someone who is busy smashing up the furniture and tearing out great clumps of his hair that his anger is inside him. We can conceal or dissemble our emotions, of course, but they are not hidden by nature; and concealing them is a complex social practice which we have to learn. Infants, unfortunately, have not yet got the hang of it. One sees what it means to say that someone who is behaving maliciously has malice 'inside' her, since malice is among other things a matter of feelings, and feelings are not part of the public world in the same way that pool tables are. In another sense, however, to say this is as odd as to say that someone who is singing has the notes inside her. It is simply a misleading way of saying that it is *she* who is singing or feeling malice, not someone else. Emotions are not private affairs which we can occasionally choose to put on display, not even for the English. This is as false as the idea that meaning is a private process in our heads.

An example of a falsely subjective approach to feeling can be found in the singer Van Morrison's versions of some Irish songs. What is amiss with Morrison's performances, at least for some of us devotees of traditional Irish music, is that they seem to regard emotion as something to be superadded to the tunes and lyrics. This is why Morrison engages in so much florid, 'feelingful' improvisation when singing them, inserting a wailing repetition here or a choked bit of sobbing there. It is as though he does not trust his material enough to appreciate that the feelings are, so to speak, already *there* in the songs, inseparable from their words and music. The tunes and lyrics are as they are because they express or embody certain patterns of feeling in their

107

actual materials; so that if these materials were different, the emotional patterns would be different too. Listening to Morrison, one is tempted to adapt a line by Wallace Stevens about another singer: 'But it was he and not the song we heard.'

It is as if Morrison's performances in this field reflect a flawed epistemology, surprised though he would doubtless be to hear it. If only he would stop indulging in sudden snatches of 'passion' and heartfelt heavy breathing, he might come to see that he does not need to add his own 'subjective' feelings to the songs. All he has to do, like a *sean-nós* (traditional) Irish singer, is to articulate them by letting them flow through him, rather than to stamp his 'personality' all over them. Such an articulation is 'subjective' in the sense that every singer or musician does things in his or her own way; but it is not 'subjective' in the sense that the meaning and emotional power of these pieces are purely in the gift of the performer. This is one reason why Irish musicians have been known to perform with their backs to the audience.

To regard feeling as subjectively superadded is also to see the songs themselves as so much inert material waiting for life to be breathed into them by the performer. The other side of subjectivism is objectivism. The songs are just brutely there, senseless and emotionless in themselves, to be stirred into expressive meaning at the touch of a human subject. It is a view which subtly devalues everything but human consciousness, and is thus, for all its pious cult of feeling, a typical piece of humanistic arrogance.

5.2   Meaning and Subjectivity

Just the same view can be taken of language. For one kind of theorist, poems are just meaningless black marks on a page, and it is the reader who constructs them into sense. This is true in one sense and false in another. We may note first of all that to speak of 'meaningless black marks' already involves us in meanings. It is notoriously hard to get back behind meaning altogether, for much the same reasons as it is impossible to imagine ourselves dead. We may also note that to regard words as black marks is an abstraction from what we actually see on a page. And this is an operation which already requires a good deal of interpretative labour. Every now and then, we see a row of black marks and then realise that what we are seeing is words, just as every now and then we see a large grey patch and then realise that we are looking at an elephant. Most of the time, however, we see words and elephants, not black marks and grey patches. Someone who keeps seeing grey patches where he ought to be seeing elephants should pay a visit either to his optician or his psychiatrist.

It is true, even so, that all we literally have are words on a page. Reading these words as a poem means restoring to them something of their lost material body. It involves grasping them as tonal, rhythmical, metrical, emotional, intentional, expressive of meaning, and so on. In a face-to-face dialogue, the material body of language is as solidly present as its meanings are, and this acts as a control on interpretation. We know that the tone is despairing because the other person is clutching a sodden handkerchief and tottering on a very high window ledge. Or we can ask a speaker whether he is being sarcastic, and adjust our understanding of his words accordingly. Or we know that she does not intend 'Let us put continents between us!' metaphorically because she is handing us our air ticket to Sydney as she speaks. Poetry is language which comes without these contextual clues, and which therefore has to be reconstructed by the reader in the light of a context which will make sense of it. And such contexts are in embarrassingly plentiful supply. Yet they are not just arbitrary either: on the contrary, they are shaped in turn by the cultural contexts by which the reader makes sense of the world in general.

So in one sense none of the formal features we have been examining is actually 'there' on the page. But neither are they just arbitrarily implanted by the reader. If this were so, then the reader could make a particular pattern of black marks mean anything she chose, which would be to strip her of her culture. Belonging to a culture means that not everything is up for grabs all of the time, as it might be for a cultureless being like God. It means that the world comes to us not as brute fact or raw material, but as already signifying. And this applies as much to the words on a page as to a *coup d'état* or a telegraph pole. Being part of a culture also entails that we are not inexorably bound by these built-in interpretations, as we can imagine a crocodile being constrained by its biology to interpret certain kinds of stuff as edible. Some cultural versions of the world (the assumption that eating boot polish is excellent for your health, for example) are fairly free-floating, and thus quite easy not to be coerced by. But because a lot of interpretations are actually built in to our form of life, resisting them (if that seems the right thing to do) involves us in a struggle. And there are some solidly entrenched assumptions and investments built into our culture which we probably could not even imagine being without, like the assumption that there are other people.

We can make the cluster of black marks 'syrup' mean 'historicism', given enough context. But we cannot do it just by deciding to do it, since this would be a meaningless ceremony. We would not be able to make the new meaning stick. It would simply have no force within our social life. Since meanings are deeply bound up with our cultural behaviour, we cannot change language radically without transforming a lot of what we actually get up to. To think otherwise, to adopt an image of Wittgenstein's, would be like a man passing money from one of his hands to the other and thinking that he had made a financial transaction.[2] All the same, one could imagine a situation in which 'syrup' plausibly meant 'historicism'. Perhaps the more traditionalist members of an English department wish to conceal their contempt for historicism from their more avant-garde colleagues, and adopt this code in order to do so. But doing this means being aware of what 'syrup' commonly means, or at least being aware that it is not commonly regarded as a synonym for 'historicism'. Opting for a new meaning involves being conscious of the culturally agreed one. In any case, one could not even have the concept of 'new meaning' unless one already had a language.

Take, for example, the question of connotation. It is characteristic of poetic language that it gives us not simply the denotation of a word (what it refers to), but a whole cluster of connotations or associated meanings. It differs in this respect from legal or scientific language, which seeks to pare away surplus connotations in the name of rigorous denotation. By and large, legal and scientific language aims to constrict meaning, whereas poetic language seeks to proliferate it. This is not a value judgement: there are times when the rigorous definition of a word is just what we need (it may come in handy, for example, when we are up in court on a treason charge), and there are other times when it is pleasant to cut the signifier free from its anchorage in a single sense and let it interbreed with other bits of sense.

Connotations are less controllable than denotations, which is one reason why lawyers, scientists and bureaucrats are nervous of them. But doesn't this then pose a problem for poets? If connotation is a kind of free associating, how can a poem ever come to mean anything definite? What if Shakespeare's line 'Shall I compare thee to a summer's day?' reminds me irresistibly of fried bananas? The brief answer to this is that meaning is not a matter of psychological associations. Indeed, there is a sense in which it is not a 'psychological' matter at all. Meaning is not an arbitrary process in our heads, but a rule-governed social practice; and unless the line 'Shall I compare thee to a summer's day?' could plausibly, in principle, suggest fried bananas to other readers as well, it cannot be part of its meaning.

It may be that Shakespeare's Cordelia reminds me of a cross-dressed version of my uncle Arthur; but I am aware that this is not the case for those

---

[2] All references in this work to Wittgenstein are taken from his *Philosophical Investigations* (Oxford, 1953).

readers who have not had the pleasure of meeting my uncle Arthur; and that Shakespeare, for all his prescience and preternatural insight, was unlikely to have had my uncle Arthur in mind when he wrote *King Lear*. There are, to be sure, all kinds of situations in which the line between the private and public connotations of words is uncertain. But unless a connotation can plausibly exist for someone else, it cannot exist as a meaning for me either. The stray personal associations which drift in and out of our heads when we are reading *Lear* are of interest to our psychotherapist, not to the literary critic. Meaning is not a matter of having pictures in your head. You can enjoy Blake or Rilke with no pictures in your head at all.

So meanings are neither randomly bestowed by readers, nor objectively there on the page in the sense that a watermark is. The same goes for value judgements. Value judgements are not objective in the sense that mahogany cocktail cabinets are, but this does not mean that they are simply a matter of private whim. In any culture, there are certain complex sets of criteria as to what counts as good or bad poetry; and although there can be an enormous amount of disagreement over how these criteria are to be applied, or whether they are valid in the first place, their application is far from just a subjective affair. People may wrangle over whether a particular patch of colour counts as green, but this does not mean that 'green' is a purely subjective judgement. It is possible to see that a poem is a fine achievement yet dislike it intensely, just as you can love a poem you regard as aesthetically atrocious; and this suggests that value judgements are not the same as private tastes. 'I do like a good bad poem' is not an unintelligible statement. Much the same goes for such matters as mood, register, pitch, pause, and so on, upon which overall value judgements are built. If these are not just arbitrary, it is partly because they are so closely bound up with meaning, and meaning is not something that we simply legislate. A poem does not instruct us that it is meant to be melancholic; but this mood, even so, may be in some sense built into its language.

Take, as an illustration of melancholy, the first verse of Tennyson's poem 'Mariana':

> With blackest moss the flower-plots
> Were thickly crusted, one and all:
> The rusted nails fell from the knots
> That held the pear to the gable-wall.
> The broken sheds looked sad and strange:
> Unlifted was the clinking latch;
> Weeded and worn the ancient thatch

Upon the lonely moated grange.
She only said, 'My life is dreary,
He cometh not,' she said.
She said, 'I am aweary, aweary,
I would that I were dead!'

There is nothing in principle to stop us from reading this aloud as though it were intended to be uproariously funny, gasping with giggles and chortling uncontrollably. Many a high-toned poem from the past seems hilarious to us in the present. But we do not usually assume that these works were *intended* to be hilarious. There is something mildly comic about the iron predictability of the word 'dead' in the last line of this stanza, but the effect is clearly unwitting. There is no obvious signal that the poem is sadistically sending up its protagonist, winking roguishly at us over her head at the sight of her dejection. How do we know that the mood of this verse is supposed to be gloomy? It would be enough to say that we spoke English. Words and phrasings like 'I am aweary, aweary, / I would that I were dead!' have a certain kind of sensibility or emotional value built into them. People do not tend to say this sort of thing when they have just been bequeathed a fine old Tudor farmhouse along with several thousand acres of fertile land.

What is amiss with the piece, in fact, is that it is all too obvious what mood it intends to nurture. The emotional climate of the piece is far too coherent. Almost every word, sound and image is remorselessly dragooned into the overall atmospheric effect, in an absurdly homogenising way. A useful adjective to describe this is *voulu*, which means 'willed' in French and which suggests too contrived, self-conscious an effort. The piece lacks the faintest flicker of spontaneity. Nothing in this windless enclosure is allowed to have a life of its own, or to kick back against the stifling climate of woe in which it is shrouded. Even the nails fall obediently from the wall, dutifully performing their minor role in the whole over-orchestrated scene.

The piece is meticulously overwrought. Despite its technical adeptness, it succeeds only in being inert about inertia. It is thus an illustration of what is sometimes called the mimetic fallacy, whereby poets try to justify the fact that their works are dishevelled or unbelievably boring by claiming that messiness or boredom is what they are about. Even the rhyme scheme is pressed into the service of this stagnant oppressiveness, with that 'strange'/'latch'/ 'thatch'/'grange' pattern in the middle lines. This *abba* style of rhyming, which Tennyson also puts to work in his most celebrated poem 'In Memoriam', has a curiously haunting, plangent effect, as well as creating a sense of revolving solemnly in a circle. It is a suitable sort of rhyme for a poem in which the heroine's existence has been frozen into a single, sluggish moment of time.

It is not for us, then, just to decide on what mood is at stake here. In a similar way, it is not just up to us to determine what sort of feeling someone's behaviour is expressing. We have noted already that people may dissemble their feelings, but this is not to deny that there is an internal relation between what they feel and what they do. If there were not, they would not need to dissemble. Besides, poets, like goldfish, are incapable of dissembling. This is not because they are searingly honest, but because whether authors of fiction really did experience an emotion they write about is not the point. As we have seen, the word 'fiction' cues us not to ask such irrelevant questions. We can ask whether a piece of poetry sounds sincere or insincere, but we cannot determine this by finding out whether the poet actually had the experience she is portraying. The author may have done so and still sound insincere. The fact that you really have been abducted by aliens on numerous occasions does not automatically make your account of it convincing. Shakespeare did not need to experience sexual jealousy in order to create Othello. When he penned some of Hamlet's most magnificently distraught speeches, perhaps all he was feeling was whether the imagery sounded suitably diseased.

Sincerity and insincerity in poetry are qualities of language, not (at least for literary critics) moral virtues. In his embarrassing poem 'Chicago', Carl Sandburg praises the city in these terms:

Come and show me another city with lifted head singing so proud to be alive
    and coarse and strong and cunning.
Flinging magnetic curses amid the toil of piling job on job, here is a tall bold
    slugger set vivid against the little soft cities;
Fierce as a dog with tongue lapping for action, cunning as a savage pitted against
    the wilderness . . .

Sandburg may genuinely have had these feelings, but the slapdash language (*magnetic* curses?), limply stereotypical phrases ('cunning as a savage') and macho swagger suggest that the feelings themselves are bogus. We cannot establish whether a piece of language is sincere simply by consulting the speaker or writer. Someone may imagine that they are deriving a mystical experience from an appalling bit of doggerel, but they must surely be mistaken. They may be having a profound experience for some other reason (perhaps they are sipping vintage claret while they are reading, or thrusting red-hot needles into an effigy of Donald Trump), but the poem itself could not be the reason for their emotion. A poem can be the *occasion* for an emotion, as when those who are grieving the loss of a child find comfort in some lushly sentimental verses. But 'literary' feelings are *responses* to poems, not just states of emotion which occur in their presence. And for a feeling to count as a response, there must be some internal relation between it and the poem itself.

Our actions are expressive of feelings in the same way that words are expressive of meanings. There can be all sorts of ambiguities about what someone is feeling, just as there can be about what they are meaning. We speak of the feeling 'behind' someone's actions, just as we speak of the meaning 'behind' someone's words; but this spatial metaphor is surely misleading. When Cleopatra says that she wore Mark Antony's sword, the fact that her meaning is unclear (does she mean this literally, or is it sexual symbolism?) is not because it lies 'behind' her words, as though it is too remote to gain access to. This would be like thinking that not being certain whether a painting is of a storm at sea or the wild white locks of an elderly lunatic is because its subject matter lies 'behind' the painted shapes on the canvas. When someone is cowering and gibbering with fear, their fear is present in their bodily activity in the same way that a meaning is present in a word. But this does not mean that we could not misinterpret their fear as rage or shame.

5.3   Tone, Mood and Pitch

So we can misinterpret, say, the tone of a poem. But this is not because the tone lies 'behind' the words, or because the reader arbitrarily assigns a tone to words which are toneless in themselves. Let us look, for example, at the final stanza of W. B. Yeats's 'A Dialogue of Self and Soul':

> I am content to follow to its source
> Every event in action or in thought;
> Measure the lot; forgive myself the lot!
> When such as I cast out remorse
> So great a sweetness flows into the breast
> We must laugh and we must sing,
> We are blest by everything,
> Everything we look upon is blest.

Most readers will hear a defiantly exultant tone here, though some may also discern a touch of bravado and some may not. It might be thought that 'Measure the lot; forgive myself the lot!' is rather too self-satisfied a gesture, with just a hint of virile bluster; but some may simply hear it as a rather agreeable kind of gusto. Some readers may query that phrase 'When such

as I . . .', which might be taken to insinuate that especially momentous consequences will flow from the poet's casting out of remorse since he is a good
deal more morally conscientious than the average run of folk. In fact, the
grammar of the lines that follow, with the shift of preposition from 'I' to 'we',
implies that the speaker's act of self-acceptance has a transfigurative effect
not just upon himself but on everyone else as well. He has managed to relieve
not only his own guilt but that of the whole human race, an achievement
previously regarded as confined to Jesus Christ.

Yet there is also something moving, as often with Yeats, about the bold,
apparently artless directness of the lines and their jubilant, chant-like refrain
('We must laugh and we must sing, / We are blest by everything'). It is though
the lines risk a certain naivety, trusting as they do to a deeper wisdom. 'So
great a sweetness flows into the breast' could only be a line by Yeats, with
its boldly self-assured stress on a single, simple word ('sweetness') rather than
some more complex term or phrase. Whereas Keats goes in for compound
epithets like 'cool-rooted', Yeats tends to prefer simple, elemental words like
'great', 'beat', 'stone', 'fool', 'bread', 'trod', 'glitter'. 'Sweet' and 'sweetness'
figure among these. If he wants to suggest human squalor he writes something like 'foul ditch'; and these stock words and phrases, used recurrently,
come to assume the status of a kind of code, accruing complex meanings
which do not need to be spelled out but which seem communicable at a glance.
Yeats has a most unmodernist faith in his verbal medium, one inherited in
part from the Irish oral tradition. He does not appear to feel that words need
to be skewed, telescoped or overpacked in order to have an effect. If something in his poetry is ambiguous, it is probably a mistake.

'Everything we look upon is blest' is a questionable enough claim, but the
reader probably lets Yeats get away with it since his ecstatic triumph, seen
in the context of the poem as a whole, seems dearly enough won. He has
paid for it in bitter experience, rather than bought it on the cheap. Compare
those lines, then, with these from his poem 'The Tower':

> And I declare my faith:
> I mock Plotinus' thought
> And cry in Plato's teeth,
> Death and life were not
> Till man made up the whole,
> Made lock, stock and barrel
> Out of his bitter soul,
> Aye, sun and moon and star, all,
> And further add to that

That, being dead, we rise,
Dream and so create
Translunar Paradise. . . .

If the first passage is a matter of defiant exultation, this, surely, is one of pompous self-indulgence. The booming, bombastic tone, which seems to hold the lines together by sheer bull-headed assertion, is of a piece with the doctrinal arrogance of 'Death and life were not / Till man made up the whole'. The fact that this statement is palpably untrue does nothing to intensify its poetic force. Something seems to have gone momentarily awry with the iambic trimeter in that line 'Aye, sun and moon and star, all', which compels us to gabble 'sun and moon and star' if we are to keep the stresses regular, while 'And further add to that' sounds more like a solicitor dictating to his secretary than a sage about to divulge a mystical secret. The terseness of the lines is perhaps meant to have a vatic effect, but come through as merely sententious. 'Translunar Paradise' is not made any less bogus or unbelievable by those thrustingly assertive capital letters. There are, however, some strikingly inventive para-rhymes: 'faith'/'teeth', 'thought'/'were not', 'that'/'create' and (much less felicitously) 'barrel'/'star, all'.

Tone means a modulation of the voice expressing a particular mood or feeling. It is one of the places where signs and emotions intersect. So tones can be arch, abrupt, dandyish, lugubrious, rakish, obsequious, urbane, exhilarated, imperious and so on. But it is not easy to distinguish tone in poetry from mood, which the dictionary defines as a state of mind or feeling. Perhaps we could say that the mood of 'Mariana' is melancholic, while the tone is doleful or lugubrious. Then there is timbre, which means the distinctive character of a voice or musical note, apart from its pitch and intensity. Timbre in the Tennyson piece could be taken to denote its uniquely Tennysonian quality, one that would be unmistakable to anyone who has read a fair amount of his poetry. We are speaking here of a poet's distinctive hallmark or signature. Robert Lowell's verses are very Lowellish, while nothing is more Plath-like than a Sylvia Plath poem. Swinburne, alas, never ceases to be Swinburnian.

We can speak, too, of the pitch of a poetic voice, meaning whether it sounds high, low or middle-ranging. One might imagine the pitch of the last line of 'Porphyria's Lover' – 'And yet God has not said a word!' – as either a high-spirited whoop or a low growl, depending on how one interprets its meaning. Like most other aspect of form, pitch is bound up with what sense we make of the words. One can even talk of a poem's volume, meaning how loud or soft it sounds. Nobody could read these lines of George Herbert as a hushed whisper:

I struck the board and cried, 'No more;
  I will abroad!
What? Shall I ever sigh and pine?
My lines and life are free, free as the road,
  Loose as the wind, as large as store.
  Shall I be still in suit?'

                                        ('The Collar')

We know that the poet is shouting here because he tells us so. We can feel his anger and frustration in the abrupt, quick-fire shifts of rhythm, the help-lessly broken phrases, the way the lines deliberately fail to cohere into a shapely semantic pattern despite their graphological shapeliness on the page. Similarly, John Donne's line 'For God's sake hold your tongue, and let me love', with its air of jocular impatience, is presumably not meant to be deliv-ered in a blandly self-effacing voice. Nor is this feminist clarion call from Anna Laetitia Barbauld:

Yes, injured Woman! rise, assert thy right!
Woman! too long degraded, scorned, oppressed;
O born to rule in partial Law's despite,
Resume thy native empire o'er the breast!

                                  ('The Rights of Woman')

Barbauld overdoes the exclamation marks, but there is no other piece of punc-tuation designed to stress a rise of volume or intensity. They are the most expressive of punctuation marks, if also the most unsubtle.

  Some poems, however, are so deathly quiet that we have to strain our ears to catch what they are saying. Another piece of Tennyson, this time from 'In Memoriam', may serve as an example:

Be near me when my light is low,
  When the blood creeps, and the nerves prick
  And tingle; and the heart is sick,
And all the wheels of Being slow . . .

Be near me when I fade away,
  To point the term of human strife,
  And on the low dark verge of life
The twilight of eternal day.

This sounds rather like the hoarse, whispered words of a terminally ill patient, so that we have to lean in close to the pillow to hear what is being

117

murmured. It would be incongruous to deliver it in a raucous bellow, as it wouldn't be to bawl out the immortal opening lines of Tennyson's 'Charge of the Light Brigade': 'Half a league, half a league, / Half a league onward . . .'. How do we know this? We pick it up as we pick up the fact that twilight comes at the end of the day. It is part of our cultural behaviour.

5.4   Intensity and Pace

Intensity is another category of poetic feeling, distinct from tone, pitch and volume. There are muted intensities as well as full-blooded ones. This extract from a sonnet by Elizabeth Barrett Browning could not be read as flippant:

> How do I love thee? Let me count the ways.
> I love thee to the depth and breadth and height
> My soul can reach, when feeling out of sight
> For the ends of Being and ideal Grace.
> I love thee to the level of every day's
> Most quiet need, by sun and candlelight.
> I love thee freely, as men strive for Right.
> I love thee purely, as they turn from Praise . . .

This is too earnest and high-minded for modern taste. 'For the ends of Being and ideal Grace' is gauche and too much of a mouthful, while 'to the level of' sounds an oddly prosaic note. We also tend to be put off by weighty capitalised abstractions like 'Right' and 'Praise'. But the Victorians would presumably not have found the poem excessively intense. The poem uses the rhyme form Milton tended to favour in his sonnets, one which in the first eight lines (or octave) employs an *abba* scheme twice. This is also typical of Petrarch's sonnets. Another Victorian woman, Christina Rossetti, handles this double *abba* rhyme scheme more adroitly:

> Remember me when I am gone away,
>   Gone far away into that silent land;
>   When you can no more hold me by the hand,
> Nor I half turn to go yet turning stay.
> Remember me when no more day by day
>   You tell me of our future that you planned:
>   Only remember me; you understand
> It will be late to counsel then or pray . . .

The rhymes here, tolling like a bell, are vital to the mournful mood. As often in Victorian verse, the *abba* is emphasised graphically as well, by indenting the two middle lines. Some readers may find Rossetti's tone rather too tremulous for comfort, skating a little close to self-pity; but the lines are nonetheless impressive in their sad dignity. The last line is forced by the exigencies of the metre into altering the more predictable 'too late' into 'late', which has a slightly curious effect: it surely won't just be *late* for him to give her advice after she is dead, unless he is an accomplished table rapper. And it is hard to see how he could not understand this, unless he is of exceedingly low intelligence.

Another, somewhat neglected formal category is pace. Some poems creep, some jog sedately along, while others hurtle hectically forward. A piece like Browning's 'How They Brought the Good News from Ghent to Aix' moves so rapidly that it is hard to keep up with it:

> I sprang to the stirrup, and Joris, and he;
> I galloped, Dirck galloped, we galloped all three;
> 'Good speed!' cried the watch, as the gate-bolts undrew;
> 'Speed!' echoed the wall to us galloping through . . .

Percy Bysshe Shelley's 'Ode to the West Wind' swirls like wind itself:

> O wild West Wind, thou breath of Autumn's being,
> Thou, from whose unseen presence the leaves dead
> Are driven, like ghosts from an enchanter fleeing,
>
> Yellow, and black, and pale, and hectic red,
> Pestilence-stricken multitudes: O thou,
> Who chariotest to their dark wintry bed
>
> The wingèd seeds, where they lie cold and low . . .

The enjambement between the stanzas is needed to keep the wind gusting without even the briefest lull. And this single whirlwind of a sentence is sustained over more than five stanzas, as the sub-clauses sweep restively hither and thither.

Compare this, then, with the mesmerically slow pace of Tennyson's 'The Lotus Eaters':

> 'Courage!' he said, and pointed toward the land,
> 'This mounting wave will roll us shoreward soon'.
> In the afternoon they came unto a land

In which it seemed always afternoon.
All round the coast the languid air did swoon,
Breathing like one that hath a weary dream.
Full-faced above the valley stood the moon;
And, like a downward smoke, the slender stream
Along the cliff to fall and pause and fall did seem.

This tries rather too wilfully to create a mood of lethargy, all the way from the repetition of 'afternoon', with its effect of stasis and sterile circularity, to the languid alexandrine of the last line (always a risky kind of metre in English). The close-packed, sonorously recurrent rhymes (*ababbcbcc*) contribute to the sense of getting nowhere, if delectably so. No sooner do the rhymes creep forward an inch than they seem to lapse listlessly back upon themselves.

5.5 Texture

Tennyson's stanza also provides a convenient example of what we might call texture. 'Texture', which the dictionary defines as the feel or appearance of a surface or substance, is a matter of how a poem weaves its various sounds into palpable patterns. True to its indolent mood, this stanza from 'The Lotus Eaters' generally avoids sharp consonants (apart from 'pointed' and 'pause', the *p* sound of which is known as a plosive) in favour of softer, more sibilant sounds, along with a high vowel count. You can read the lines aloud without an inordinate amount of lip-work, thus re-enacting the somnolent state they portray.

Or look at the final, superb stanza of Yeats's 'Among School Children':

Labour is blossoming or dancing where
The body is not bruised to pleasure soul,
Nor beauty born out of its own despair,
Nor blear-eyed wisdom out of midnight oil.
O chestnut-tree, great-rooted blossomer,
Are you the leaf, the blossom or the bole?
O body swayed to music, O brightening glance,
How can we know the dancer from the dance?

Unlike 'The Lotus Eaters', there is a great deal of busy consonantal activity going on in this opulent tapestry of sound, not least an extraordinarily numerous set of *b* sounds ('blossoming', 'body', 'bruised', 'beauty', 'born', 'blear-eyed', 'blossomer', 'bole', 'brightening'). Yet they are not particularly obtrusive, as though the poetry is innocently unaware of them; and this is partly because they are subtly interwoven with a variety of other sounds, as in that marvellous line 'Nor blear-eyed wisdom out of midnight oil'. 'Blear' picks up the sound of 'nor', but with a pleasurable difference, while 'night' reflects the vowel sound of 'eyed'. There are also some finely accomplished semi-rhymes – 'soul' / 'oil' / 'bole', 'despair' / 'blossomer'.

Texture is also an important aspect of Thomas Hardy's poetry, as in the first verse of 'The Darkling Thrush':

> I leaned upon a coppice gate
>   When Frost was spectre-grey,
> And Winter's dregs made desolate
>   The weakening eye of day.
> The tangled bine-stems scored the sky
>   Like strings of broken lyres,
> And all mankind that haunted nigh
>   Had sought their household fires.

Even without close analysis, it is surely clear how close-packed or densely woven the sound texture is here, with every syllable in this lean verse being encouraged to work overtime. The whole stanza, highly compressed yet utterly lucid, is without an ounce of surplus fat. In the third and fourth lines, for example, the alliteration of 'Winter's' and 'weakening', and 'dregs' and 'desolate' is counterpointed by the less intrusive assonance of 'made' and 'day', along with the semi-assonance of the last syllable of 'Winter's' and the 're' sound of 'dregs'. That unmelodious 'tangled bine-stems' is chock-full of muscular syllables rammed haphazardly up against each other, a cluster of sharply diverse sounds which the reader has to work especially hard at before being rewarded with the more easily consumable consorting of 'scored' and 'sky'. The whole passage is remarkable for its tight interweaving of abstract allegory and keenly observed naturalistic detail.

5.6 Syntax, Grammar and Punctuation

A good many poetic effects are achieved through syntax. Like grammar, this has the advantage of being more 'objective' than tone or mood, and thus more easily demonstrable in its workings. Consider the opening lines of Edward Thomas's 'Old Man':

Old Man, or Lad's-love – in the name there's nothing
To one that knows not Lad's-love, or Old Man,
The hoar-green feathery herb, almost a tree,
Growing with rosemary and lavender.
Even to one that knows it well, the names
Half decorate, half perplex, the thing it is:
At least, what that is clings not to the names
In spite of time. And yet I like the names.

The herb itself I like not, but for certain
I love it, as some day the child will love it
Who plucks a feather from the door-side bush
Whenever she goes in or out of the house. . . .

One striking feature of these lines is the way they are so courageously prepared to sacrifice elegance to honesty. The jagged, knotted syntax struggles
to unpack the poet's constantly swerving thoughts about the plant he is con-
templating. As it does so, its hesitations, stops and starts and doublings-back
act out something of the convolutions and self-qualifications of his response
to the herb. Syntax is pressed into the service of a tenacious commitment to
truth, as each proposition threatens to cancel out the previous claim in a dogged
struggle to pin down just what the speaker feels. A plain exactitude is all: the
herb is 'almost' a tree, but not quite; the names 'half' decorate and 'half'
perplex, but not entirely so. 'At least' then instantly qualifies that statement,
and the stumbling, unmelodious monosyllables of the line in which it occurs
– 'At least what that is clings not to the names' – are ready to risk clumsi-
ness for the sake of a rigorous truthfulness.

This statement, in turn, is then immediately qualified by 'And yet . . .'
The poet, with the perversity of his trade, likes the names but not the
herb itself, we learn to our bemusement as we step across that break in the
lines; and this is so abrupt a turnaround that it comes through as a mildly
dramatic *élan*, a kind of mischievous pulling-out of the carpet from under
the too-credulous reader. Punctuation co-operates in this ceaseless, unstable
revision of response, as the first few lines of the poem seem positively over-
loaded with commas, one of which rather redundantly backs up a dash. The
poet simply isn't certain enough of how he feels about the herb to produce
a smoothly unfractured sentence about it. Instead, one scrupulously qualifying sub-clause tumbles hard on the heels of another. It is the candour of the
passage which is part of its attraction – the way that the poet lets us see his
doubts, shifts of viewpoint and sudden modulations of feeling as they occur
to him, without feeling the need to smooth this ungainly process into an

integrated pattern. It is as though he has left the untidy stitches on his
tapestry visible.

Yeats, once again, may serve as another illustration of the adroit use of syntax:

> Under my window-ledge the waters race,
> Otters below and moor-hens on the top,
> Run for a mile undimmed in Heaven's face
> Then darkening through 'dark' Raftery's 'cellar' drop,
> Run underground, rise in a rocky place
> In Coole demesne, and there to finish up
> Spread to a lake and drop into a hole.
> What's water but the generated soul?
>
> ('Coole Park and Ballylee, 1931')

The verse, as polished as Thomas's lines are irregular, almost deliberately
provokes us into belletristic waffle about how beautifully the sinuous curving
of the syntax mimes the flow of the stream. In a magisterial sweep, Yeats pro-
pels a single sentence around the corners and through the syntactical thickets
of seven lines of poetry, pausing fractionally to register the quotation marks
around 'dark' and 'cellar', without for a moment losing his poise. The last
line, with its artful change of key, is a kind of final flourish to this masterly
performance, with its look-no-hands bravura. It is as though the line is there to
show that the poet has some breath left in him even after this virtuoso display.

We might, however, feel disconcerted by the calculated dramatic shift
in the last line from the topographical to the metaphysical. One obvious riposte
to that rather cavalier rhetorical question 'What's water but the generated
soul?' has just been provided by the poem itself, in the shape of a detailed
description of a landscape. Are we now supposed to imagine that all this was
merely symbolic? The last line risks a certain glibness, a too-easy conversion
of reality to allegory. It is purely assertive. We might also feel that the whole
tour de force of the stanza is excessively deft – that it subdues this tumultuous
flow rather too effortlessly to a single shapely narrative. But it is syntactical
structure put to superb poetic use.

Grammar is part of the scaffolding of a poem, but it can also function as
a poetic device in its own right. The first verse of T. S. Eliot's 'Whispers of
Immortality' provides a convenient example:

> Webster was much possessed by death
> And saw the skull beneath the skin;
> And breastless creatures underground
> Leaned backward with a lipless grin.

Critics have argued the toss over the significance of that 'leaned'.[3] Does the meaning of the verse fall into two halves, so that we learn first that Webster was much possessed by death and saw the skull beneath the skin, and then, as a separate piece of information, that breastless creatures underground leaned backward with a lipless grin? This would make 'leaned' the past tense of 'lean'. This reading of the poem is reinforced by the presence of the semicolon at the end of line 2, which would seem to mark the one idea off from the other. But it makes for a slight strain as well, since there doesn't seem to any grammatical relation between the two ideas, even if that 'And' in the third line leads us to expect one. It would be rather like saying: 'My grandmother was a career criminal, and a bumble bee settled on my nose.'

So we could read the verse instead as a single unit of meaning: perhaps 'breastless creatures underground' is the object of 'saw', just as 'the skull beneath the skin' is. Maybe Webster saw them both. But what then do we make of 'leaned'? One suggestion is that this is not the past tense of 'lean' but the past participle, as in 'The broom was leaned against the fridge.' The breastless creatures are leaned backward, rather than engaging in the act of leaning backward. But then it is harder to make sense of the semicolon. If the creatures do not lean back by their own motion, this might very slightly diminish the horror of this macabre image, since then they appear not so nightmarishly alive. One wonders, incidentally, what is so horrific about the creatures lacking breasts, since men and children lack breasts, too, at least of the adult female kind. Is the gruesome point that they are females who have had their breasts lopped off?

5.7   Ambiguity

There is perhaps an ambiguity in this verse, then; and such ambiguity is built into the nature of poetry. This is partly because, as we have seen already, poems do not come readily equipped with material contexts to help delimit their possibilities of meaning. But it is also because, being 'semantically saturated', their meanings are often highly compressed, which may make them more difficult to unravel. An example can be found in Gerard Manley Hopkins's beautiful little lyric 'Spring and Fall', which is about a young girl weeping over the transience of human existence. The speaker tells her, by way of rather

[3]   I am indebted for some of this discussion of the word to William Empson, *Seven Types of Ambiguity* (Harmondsworth, 1961), pp. 78–9.

backhanded consolation, that she will be less sensitive to such matters when she grows up, and then adds: 'And yet you *will* weep and know why'. William Empson, following his mentor I. A. Richards, points out that this line can have a whole number of meanings, some of which can be laid out here:

And yet you insist on weeping, and you know why you do.
And yet you insist on weeping, and you also insist on knowing why.
And yet you insist on weeping, and know why! (Listen, I'm about to tell you!)
And yet you will weep in the future, and you know why you will.
And yet you will weep in the future, and you will know then why you do.
And yet you will weep in the future, and know why! (Let me tell you!)

Empson discerns other possibilities, too.[4] I think the line actually means 'And yet you insist on weeping, and you also insist on knowing why.' The fact that the first 'will' is in italics makes one of the first three options more likely than any of the last three. Yet there is nothing to rule out any of these alternative readings.

It is worth noticing the difference between ambiguity and ambivalence. Ambivalence happens when we have two meanings, both of which are determinate but which differ from one another. Ambiguity happens when two or more senses of a word merge into each other to the point where the meaning itself becomes indeterminate. Alexander Pope uses the word 'port' jokingly at one point in his poetry to mean both 'harbour' and an alcoholic drink, which as a simple pun is an example of ambivalence. James Joyce's *Finnegans Wake*, by contrast, is full of words which conflate different meanings to the point of indeterminacy, as in 'the firewaterloover returted with such a vinesmelling fortytudor ages rawdownhams tanyouhide as would the latten stomach even of a tumass equinous', the meaning of which is not entirely clear.

An example of ambiguity can be found in Philip Larkin's 'Days':

What are days for?
Days are where we live.
They come, they waken us
Time and time over.
They are to be happy in:
Where can we live but days?

<hr>

4   See ibid., p. 148.

> Ah, solving that question
> Brings the priest and the doctor
> In their long gowns
> Running over the fields.

There is an implicit play here on the idea of time and space. Days are slices of time, but we live in them as we might inhabit a space. And running across a field is a matter of speeding up time in order to shrink space. The second verse is a masterpiece of bare suggestiveness, pivoting so much on a single spare image which is nevertheless compellingly visualisable. Without rubbing its spareness in our faces, the verse gets away with as little as it decently can, while somehow managing to make that pregnant phrase 'in their long gowns' resonant of a lot more than itself. But are the priest and the doctor running to bring comfort and counsel to this metaphysical questioner, or are they oppressive, Blakeian figures rushing to bind him into a straitjacket? The phrase 'running over the fields' has faintly sinister undertones: we do not associate respectable, long-gowned figures with such unseemly scampering. Is there an implication of panic here, as the middle-class guardians of ortho-doxy are pitched into crisis? The rural fields and the long gowns perhaps hint at a traditional, pre-modern community, for which such meaning-of-life inquiries may appear impious. So we do not know in what tone to read the last verse, whether grim or equable.

A particularly fine ambiguity occurs in the opening lines of Shakespeare's 138th sonnet:

> When my love swears that she is made of truth
> I do believe her, though I know she lies . . .

Apart from its obvious meaning, this could also mean 'When my love swears that she is truly a maid (virgin), I do believe her, though I know she lies (has sexual intercourse).'

There is also the celebrated ambiguity of Shakespeare's 94th sonnet. Here is the poem in full:

> They that have power to hurt and will do none,
> That do not do the thing they most do show,
> Who, moving others, are themselves as stone,
> Unmoved, cold, and to temptation slow,
> They rightly do inherit Heaven's graces,
> And husband nature's riches from expense;
> They are the lords and owners of their faces,

Others but stewards of their excellence.
The summer's flow'r is to the summer sweet
Though to itself it only live and die;
But if that flow'r with base infection meet,
The basest weed outbraves his dignity:
    For sweetest things turn sourest by their deeds;
    Lilies that fester smell far worse than weeds.

Reading through the sonnet, we begin to wonder whether the speaker is praising the person he is addressing, or censuring him, or both. The root of the
ambiguity is surely that the speaker is trying to turn what could well be
seen as vices in his lover (if that is who he is talking about) into virtues.
Conversely, what might sound like virtues could be vices. The Macbeth witches'
'Fair is foul and foul is fair' might thus serve as the sonnet's slogan. Having
the power to hurt yet not hurting sounds admirable; but if commending this
also means congratulating people who do not do the thing they most do show,
it seems to involve paying tribute to hypocrisy. Men and women who are
slow to temptation sound praiseworthy, but we are troubled by that 'stone'
and 'cold', as well as by the feeling that there is something exploitative about
stirring others' feelings while remaining imperturbable oneself.

    Likewise, inheriting Heaven's graces and husbanding nature's riches from
expense seem positive attainments; but if this makes you a lord and owner
of your face, a kind of proprietor or entrepreneur of your self, we are
suddenly not so convinced that it is entirely estimable. If we have read much
Shakespeare, we might be aware that he seems generally to disapprove of
this new-fangled, bourgeois idea of self-proprietorship or possessive individualism, in which it is 'as if a man were author of himself / And knew no
other kin' (Coriolanus). Shakespeare usually regards this fantasy of self-
authorship, in which one sunders all blood ties and communal affiliations,
as deeply destructive. Ulysses in Troilus and Cressida remarks to Achilles that
'no man is the lord of anything . . . Till he communicate his parts to others',
a claim which would seem to make identity without relationship a kind of
cipher. It is good to know that the summer's flower is sweet to the summer,
though rather more disquieting to hear that it lives and dies only to itself,
which makes it sound rather unpleasantly self-absorbed.

    The trouble is that we cannot simply balance positive against negative
here, since we have the uneasy suspicion that the two are sides of the same
coin. If this is so, then the sonnet's vision is (in an exact rather than sloppy
sense of the word) dialectical. It seems as though the flower is sweet to the
summer not in spite of living only for itself, but because of it; and that for

it to break out of this narcissistic condition, which would appear a valuable emancipation in itself, might well involve its becoming infected. Relating to others makes you vulnerable to moral contamination, or even to some less comfortably abstract form of defilement like venereal disease; and this means that you might end up worse off than if you had stuck to your frigid self-enclosedness. Indeed, you might well end up worse off than most people would in the same circumstances, since the fact that you are so aloof and self-absorbed means that you don't have much experience of relationships, and are therefore more likely to be exploited or end up in an emotional mess than those who do. Lilies that fester smell far worse than weeds. The high-minded, if they take a tumble, are likely to make a greater splash than those without such moral pretensions.

So the speaker is arguing that a split between how you are and how you appear, which is usually regarded as a moral defect, may in fact be a virtue. Those, for example, who are sexually attractive but don't capitalise on the fact, are creditable versions of hypocrites. In any case, they are not really responsible for the desire they arouse in others, even though it may be precisely their standoffishness which provokes it. And emotional frigidity is not as reprehensible as it might seem if the consequence of it is to keep you out of temptation. Even a repellent sort of vanity or self-love may at least prevent you from injuring others. And though narcissism is sterile, other people may get something out of it (the summer's flower is sweet to the summer), so that it is not quite as worthless as it might appear.

Even so, it seems a touch hyperbolic to describe people like this as inheriting Heaven's graces, and 'husband(ing) nature's riches from expense'. Shakespeare likes the idea of good husbandry or stewardship because it involves preserving and expending in judicious measure, as opposed to being profligate with oneself, as some of his characters are, or jealously hoarding oneself, as other of his figures do. If you are spendthrift with your self then you give it away so recklessly that you end up with no self to bestow; whereas if you hoard yourself you also end up without an identity, since Shakespeare seems to agree with Ulysses that human identity is a relational affair. The icily self-possessed men and women he is portraying here sound as though they belong firmly to the second category; but the verse, perversely intent on idealising certain deficiencies, makes it appear as though they fall into the category of judicious stewards.

'Other but stewards of their excellence' now shifts the role of steward, which lurks unstated behind the verb 'husband', to the colleagues of the frigid brigade. But there is an ambiguity here: does 'their' excellence mean that of the emotionally autistic people, or that of those around them? The line could mean that whereas the frigid people are fully in command of their own resources, those around them merely benefit from these resources in a second-hand, mediated sort of way. They cannot own the self-possessed people as these individuals own themselves, and so are reduced to the rank of servants or stewards in relation to them. Perhaps they bathe in their reflected glory, and thus make use of their talents without being proprietors of them, as a steward might. Or perhaps the line means that whereas stonily unmoved people appear to own themselves, other people relate to themselves like stewards, tapping into their own powers and talents but without, so to speak, actually having the title deeds to them. This, one would gather from the rest of Shakespeare's writing, is the sort of condition of which he would approve; but here, once more, the sonnet sounds less in two minds about this way of living than we suspect that its author might actually be. There are some definite hints of disingenuousness. The piece is like a guileful speech for the defence by a counsel who knows that his client is guilty.

Why does the poet seem to be intent on making the best of a bad job? We might speculate that the sonnet is written about his lover, and meant to be read by him or her, so that it is really an indirect form of address. Perhaps, as William Empson conjectures, the lover is in some kind of danger, and the speaker is rather desperately trying to prevent him from some foolhardy involvement by praising his imperfections. This might be a more persuasive tactic than appealing to his virtues, which may be in embarrassingly scant supply. The lover should realise that his narcissism is a strength and refuse to compromise it. Or perhaps the distraught poet is trying forlornly to rationalise to himself his lover's airy indifference. In this case, it is as though he himself is being thrust into the ignoble position of a bad steward, squandering his self-possession, and thus may be implicitly contrasting his lover's coolness with the grovelling, weed-like condition to which this haughtiness has reduced him.

Maybe the lover is being tempted to go off with someone else, and the sonnet is the speaker's sophistical strategy for arguing him out of it. He may contract a moral or physical disease if he does so, thus losing the chilly self-possession which is his most alluring feature. To act would be to undo himself, ruining the very qualities which make him so easy on the eye. This is why he would resemble a festering lily. The speaker may be letting his partner know in a flagrantly self-interested sort of way (though it may also be the truth) that only by not yielding himself to his new lover will he be able to keep that lover on the hook. He may even be hoping that his partner will be so impressed by this commendation of what seems most defective about him that he will abandon his new lover and fall back into bed with his old partner. The poet is cloaking his amorous self-interest in just the kind of noble altruism which might turn his lover on. Or perhaps there is no such rhetorical situation at stake, and the sonnet is simply remarking on the irony by which even our vices can turn out to be perversely virtuous.

If the lover has been in some way trifling with the poet's affections, something similar may be said of the poem's relation to the reader. Its technique is to keep the reader guessing, catch her on the hop, refuse to sediment into a single, unequivocal attitude. And this seems a kind of poetic equivalent to erotic teasing, no sooner offering us a crumb of comfort than swapping it for a poisoned barb. We are uncertain where the poet actually stands, but this may not be because the poem is exactly ironic. It may be investigating what we might call an 'objective' irony, but it does not follow that it does not mean what it says. Maybe Shakespeare is perfectly sincere in believing that to be lord and owner of oneself may be to diminish the degree of human damage one might wreak. It is just that he also probably believes – outside the confines of the poem, so to speak – that there is also much that is undesirable about such self-lordship. But there is no reason why he has to say that here, even if the phrase 'are themselves as stone' hints at it almost too heavily. Nobody, not even Shakespeare, has to say everything at once.

5.8 Punctuation

One of the most neglected formal techniques is punctuation. It is puzzling, for example, why there should be an exclamation mark after the lines from Eliot's 'Whispers of Immortality' which read: 'Daffodil bulbs instead of balls / Stared from the sockets of the eyes!' Exclamation marks are clumsy markers of emotion for such a suavely adept poet as Eliot. They are naive, usually superfluous, and almost always overemphatic. So one suspects that this one is somehow ironic, though it is hard to see how. It is, so to speak, in quotation marks. There is a tender lyric by e. e. cummings which ends with this verse:

> (i do not know what it is about you that closes
> and opens;only something in me understands
> the voice of your eyes is deeper than all roses)
> nobody,not even the rain, has such small hands
>   ('somewhere I have never travelled, gladly beyond')

cummings often leaves out punctuation marks altogether, or, as here, squeezes them between words as though he wants them to be as unobtrusive as possible. (This actually makes them more obtrusive.) One can see why he doesn't want a full stop after 'roses' or 'hands': it would be too forceful, definitive a gesture for such delicate, gossamer-like verse, which may also be one reason why the poet avoids capital letters. (A less reputable reason may be the assumption that 'onion' is democratic whereas 'Onion' is elitist.) Full stops would chop up into discrete units of meaning what is intended as a series of fragile, tentative statements. They would end-stop his feelings. But in that case he might have been better off without those commas in the last line, leaving it to the reader to introduce the pauses. The title of the poem is also its first line, and one sees why it needs that comma: without it, it might sound as though he means 'somewhere I have never travelled gladly', which given the meaning of the poem's first lines would be something of a slap in the face for his lover. But it is a pity, all the same, that the comma should have to intrude.

cummings also uses colons, semicolons and commas in the body of the poem that could have been omitted. (Colons, incidentally, have today almost passed out of existence, along with string vests and sideburns.) If you want an effect of perpetual open-endedness you can leave the line-endings to do the work of pausing, rather than full-stop them. The verse puts its first three lines in parenthesis, as though they are a kind of musing aside; and this also has the added bonus of throwing that poignant final line into relief, since it is the only unbracketed one in the stanza. The synaesthesia of 'the voice of your eyes is deeper than all roses' is not quite as accomplished: eyes deeper than all roses is an imaginative conceit, or even a voice deeper than all roses, though that is rather too literal to be quite as effective; but 'the voice of your eyes' is surely just incongruous.

5.9 Rhyme

Rhyme is one of the most familiar of all technical devices, and we have seen a good deal of it so far. Perhaps it reflects the fact that we take a childlike delight in doublings, mirror images and affinities, which have something magical (but also something disquieting and uncanny) about them. There is pleasure to be reaped from repetition: small children tend to go on repeating well beyond the point that most adults find tolerable. In its predictability, repetition may yield us a sense of security. For Freudians, it reflects the natural indolence of the psyche – the fact that left to ourselves, without the goad of economic necessity, we would simply lounge around the place all day in various scandalous states of *jouissance*. We do not like to expend too much libidinal energy, and repetition is one way in we can 'bind' such energy and thus avoid an excess of expenditure. It is true that too much repetition is tedious, but rhyme can overcome this danger because it is a unity of identity and difference. We hear 'dragon' and 'wagon' as akin, but also as dissimilar.

Perhaps because modern life is felt to be somehow dissonant, a good many poets begin to abandon the use of rhyme as we enter the modern age. Or, like the First World War poet Wilfred Owen, they compromise by using para-rhyme, words which almost chime in unison but don't quite:

> Happy are men who yet before they are killed
> Can let their veins run cold.
> Whom no compassion fleers
> Or makes their feet
> Sore on the alleys cobbled with their brothers.
> The front line withers.
> But they are troops who fade, not flowers,
> For poet's tearful fooling:
> Men, gaps for filling:
> Losses, who might have fought
> Longer: but no one bothers.
>   ('Insensibility')

There is a mourning, haunting, almost eerie quality to these superbly inventive para-rhymes: 'killed'/'cold', 'fleers'/'flowers', 'feet'/'fought', 'fooling'/'filling', 'brothers'/'withers'/'bothers'. Everything is discomfortingly awry, off-key, out of kilter, as one might expect from a writer living through unimaginable human carnage. One imagines that full-blooded rhyme would seem a kind of false harmony to a poet like this, who has been reduced by the horrors of war to actually commending insensitivity and the conscious blunting of compassion. One can imagine the scandalised reaction of many a Victorian to this humane counsel.

'Cobbled' is brutal in its dehumanising force, its impact intensified by the fact that it is a sudden image in lines which have been so far fairly free of them. But the casual savagery of the term has to be held in tension with 'brothers'. It is not that the soldiers are not as much brothers as ever, just that they cannot afford the kind of sentimentality which would say so. Feeling can kill: any too-powerful emotion is likely to make the soldiers more vulnerable to their situation, and thus to intensify its dreadfulness. It is callousness here which is compassionate. This applies to 'Insensibility' as well as to the troops: one can sense its deep-seated anger, but also the icy control which throttles it back so that the poem can take place.

'Insensibility' even lip-curlingly denies its own status as poetry, which in these conditions can be no more than tearful fooling. As a piece of stony-hearted anti-poetry, it is in conflict with itself (though it is also meticulously crafted). It goes out of its way to take a smack at metaphor, even though 'cobbled with their brothers' is precisely that. Its language, for such a sensuous poet as Owen, is ascetic and austere. The line 'The front line withers' stands starkly isolated and end-stopped, four laconic words marooned at the verse's centre. It is as though any attempt to elaborate this bald fact would be a lie. If the rhymes are off-key, so is the metre, which shifts between lines of varying numbers of feet. The final phrase of the verse – 'but no one bothers' – contrasts the unavoidable anaesthesia of those plunged in the thick of warfare with the rather more culpable insensitivity of those kicking their heels comfortably at home, not least perhaps the politicians who sent the soldiers there. Insensibility applies to both groups, but for quite different reasons.

While we are on the subject of war poetry, it is worth contrasting Owen's poem with John McCrae's 'In Flanders Fields':

> In Flanders fields the poppies blow
> Between the crosses, row on row,
>   That mark our place; and in the sky
>   The larks, still bravely singing, fly
> Scarce heard amid the guns below.
>
> We are the Dead. Short days ago
> We lived, felt dawn, saw sunset glow,
>   Loved and were loved, and now we lie,
>   In Flanders fields.
>
> Take up our quarrel with the foe:
> To you from failing hands we throw
>   The torch; be yours to hold it high.
>   If ye break faith with us who die
> We shall not sleep, though poppies grow
>   In Flanders fields.

Perhaps this is the kind of war poem Owen had in his sights, though it is hardly tearful fooling. There is a jauntiness about the metre (an iambic tetrameter) which is at odds with the tragedy of the war, though perhaps not so much at odds with the martial clarion-call of the final verse. Far from exploiting the dissonance of para-rhyme, the piece (if one leaves aside the refrain) rings changes on only two rhyming sounds, thus generating a peculiarly close-knit rhyme scheme. This creates a faintly chant-like effect – one which again seems askew to the sombre feeling, but which fits well enough with the poem's rousing last lines.

What the lines say is that the dead will only feel vindicated if those left alive create even more corpses, a bloodthirsty demand for such a noble-spirited elegy. It is hard to square the piece's high-minded mournfulness with its call to arms, which is too close to vengeance for comfort. It is not the kind of sentiment one can imagine Wilfred Owen easily endorsing; indeed, it sounds like that of a non-combatant safely ensconced behind the lines. But McCrae was in fact a Canadian soldier who survived some of the bloodiest episodes of the war. It is not clear why the dead soldiers might not sleep even though poppies grow above them, unless the allusion is to the poppies' opiate effect. But it seems incongruous and undignified to suggest that the dead warriors are sleeping because they are doped.

Finally, it is worth glancing at the Second-World War author John Pudney's celebrated piece 'For Johnny', with its tight *aa/bb* rhyme scheme:

> Do not despair
> For Johnny-head-in-air;
> He sleeps as sound
> As Johnny underground.
>
> Fetch out no shroud
> For Johnny-in-the-cloud;
> And keep your tears
> For him in after years.
>
> Better by far
> For Johnny-the-bright-star,
> To keep your head,
> And see his children fed.

These terse lines, to be delivered with an officer-like crispness of accent, struggle so hard to avoid sentimentality that they lapse right into it, in a bravely-choking-back-emotion sort of way. And the rhyme scheme is among other things a way of mastering the emotion. Throttling back feeling can be a perverse way of stimulating it, as with the Dickensian type of rough-diamond sentimentalist who reaps a secret *frisson* from pretending to be gruff. It is the very tight-lipped disowning of feeling here which comes through as a lump in the throat. Yet the poem is impressive in a kitschy kind of way. It is a fair specimen of a disreputable species, hovering between genuine emotional power and barely-suppressed sentimentality. It is also an example of pragmatically effective verse: no doubt it consoled a good many families who had lost sons and husbands in the war. It is saddening, even so, to learn that the author of this gem, which Laurence Oliver read on wartime radio and Michael Redgrave quoted in a patriotic film, was also the author of *The Smallest Room*, a history of the lavatory.

5.10   Rhythm and Metre

Rhythm in poetry is not the same as metre. Metre is a regular pattern of stressed and unstressed syllables, whereas rhythm is less formalised. It means the irregular sway and flow of the verse, its ripplings and undulations as it follows the flexing of the speaking voice. Much of the effect of English-language poetry comes from playing the one off against the other. Shylock's line in Shakespeare's *The Merchant of Venice* –

How like a fawning publican he looks!

– is an iambic pentameter, with the following pattern of stresses (the syllables in bold type being the stressed ones):

How **like** a **fawn**ing **pub**lican he **looks**!

An actor who delivered the line like this, however, would no doubt receive a less than rapturous response from the audience. Instead, he might articulate it like this:

How like a fawning **pub**lican he **looks**!

which clings to the curve of the speaking voice. But the metre leaves open various possibilities. Its beat can be heard as a dim throbbing behind the actual delivery, forming a stable background against which the freestyle acrobatics of the voice can stand out. It is as though metre supplies the score on which rhythm improvises.

Rhythm is one of the most 'primordial' of poetic features. It can be a simple matter of tripping and lilting, or it can well up from a much deeper psychic level, as a pattern of motion and impulse which is inherited from our earliest years, which has tenacious somatic and psychological roots, and which is imprinted in the folds and textures of the self. A baby of six months cannot talk, but scientists have established that it can detect subtle variations in the complex rhythmic patterns of Balkan folk-dance tunes. And it can do so even if it is born in Boston.

A poem by Walter Raleigh shows just how beautifully sinuous and flexible poetic rhythm can be:

> As you came from the holy land
> of Walsinghame
> Mett you not with my true love
> by the way as you came
> How shall I know your trew love
> That has met many one
> As I went to the holy lande
> That have come, that have gone . . .
>
> ('As You Came from the Holy Land')

That delicately lilting second line, consisting as it does of just two words, comes as a wonderfully subtle rhythmical modulation after the more conventional metre of the first line. As we shift from line to line, we move in a kind of fine surprise from one set of cunningly varied rhythmic impulses to another. If the sense is continuous, the rhythmic units which go to make it up are delightfully diverse and unpredictable.

Something similar can be said of Stevie Smith's legendary 'Not Waving But Drowning':

> Nobody heard him, the dead man,
> But still he lay moaning:
> I was much further out than you thought
> And not waving but drowning.
>
> Poor chap, he always loved larking
> And now he's dead
> It must have been too cold for him his heart gave way,
> They said.
>
> Oh, no no no, it was too cold always
> (Still the dead one lay moaning)
> I was much too far out all my life
> And not waving but drowning.

The first stanza alternates lines of three stresses with lines of two, a pattern which the second two stanzas sustain in a more irregular way. The effect of this is a kind of rise and fall, or a shift from a major to a minor key, as the more expansive line is followed up by the more downbeat, diminished one. A sense of bathos lurks behind this device, one which informs the poem as a whole: from the tragedy of drowning to the triviality of waving is a mere nuance of perception. The two keywords, 'waving' and 'drowning', are dissonant but vaguely reminiscent of each other, as though from a distance one could mistake the one for the other, just as from the beach one can confuse the actual gestures.

The first two lines of the second stanza conform to the metrical pattern of the first, as bathos breaks out again with that comically matter-of-fact 'And now he's dead'; but with 'It must have been too cold for him his heart gave way, / They said' the rhythm goes grotesquely awry. One would expect this clumsily lurching line to be broken up into two neatly balanced ones ('It must have been too cold for him, / His heart gave way, they said'), but Smith wants to get a sense of the dead man's companions' flurried, disorganised chatter. Like a breathless snatch of gossip, the line lacks punctuation. It has the clumping lack of symmetry of everyday speech. Smith also wants to create a ridiculous effect, deflating the high drama of the drowning by ineptly crowding this cack-handed line with too many words, as though the stanza has suddenly bucked out of her control. Then, after this ridiculously gauche line, one which captures the *faux-naïf* quality of the poem as a whole, we have bathos once more, with the lame trailing-off of 'They said' being incongruously allotted a whole line to itself. The swimmer even muffs the big moment of his death, unable to rise to the grandeur of the tragic; and the verse follows suit by disastrously losing its sense of rhythm.

The final stanza is spoken by the drowned man himself (there are three interweaving voices in this brief poem), and devalues his death even further by suggesting that it is really not much different from his life. His explanation, however, has come too late: nobody hears him in death, just as nobody heard him in life. Perhaps this is not entirely the fault of the friends: perhaps he really did lark about, as a way of proudly concealing the fact that he was in trouble, and so is partly responsible for the farcical misinterpretation which was his existence. The poem beautifully blends comedy and poignancy.

Let us look finally at a poem by a distinguished, unduly neglected poet of eighteenth-century Ireland, William Dunkin. Dunkin's finest piece is entitled 'The Parson's Revels', and is couched in a very rare stanza form:[5]

> His voice was brazen, deep, and such,
> As well-accorded with High-dutch,
> Or Attic Irish, and his touch
> Was pliant;

[5] It is, however, to be found in a bawdy poem called 'The Ramble' by the English Restoration poet Alexander Radcliffe, which rhymes 'clitoris' with 'Tell stories'.

Dubourgh to him was but a fool;
He played melodious without rule,
And sung the feats of Fin McCool,
The giant . . .

The rhyme scheme in the poem is a kind of comic ritual in itself. Dunkin uses some deliberately inept rhymes ('scurvy'/'topsy-turvy', 'from it'/ 'vomit', 'dead aunt'/'pedant'), but the real comic effect is reaped from the way the first three lines of each verse (which are iambic tetrameters) set up a rhythm which is suddenly disrupted by the final, lamely tacked-on phrase. These final phrases come after a slight pause, during which the reader just has time to wonder what monstrously over-ingenious rhyme is about to be perpetrated. The final phrase, with its brief trisyllabic lilt, is inevitably bathetic:

Each blithesome damsel shews her shape,
Enough to burst her stays and tape,
And bangs the boards: the fiddlers scrape
Their cat-guts:

Brave C–, foe to popish dogs,
In boots, as cumbersome as clogs,
Displays his parts, and B—jogs
His fat guts.

The final phrases, almost afterthoughts, are too laconic to bear the emphasis which the verse throws on them, and this itself is a comic effect. The phrases are necessary to round off the sense of each stanza, yet rhythmically speaking they seem like feebly superfluous gestures. Each stanza thus seems to end on an embarrassing anti-climax, as the speaking voice trails away. It is as though the sense needs these phrases but the metre does not, since it and its trim, triple rhyme are already complete in themselves. This tension between feeling that the phrases are internal to the verses, yet also pointlessly external to them, is a kind of wit.

5.11 Imagery

Finally, a word about imagery. Just as rhyme, metre and texture involve an interplay of difference and identity, so do most images. Similes and metaphors insist on affinities between elements which we also acknowledge to be different; and the more we attend to the kinship between the terms, the larger the differences may loom. Metonymy links elements in a contiguous way (bird/sky, for example), thus also creating an equivalence between things which we recognise to be disparate. Synecdoche substitutes a part for a whole (wing for bird, for example, or crown for monarch), and parts and wholes are both different and allied.

The term 'image' is in some ways misleading, since it suggests the visual, and not all imagery is of this kind. Auden, for example, is famous for images which yoke together the concrete and the abstract: 'Anxiety receives them like a Grand Hotel'; 'And lie apart like epochs from each other'. Part of the point of similes like this, which belong to an era in which the whole idea of representation is in crisis, is that they baffle any attempt to visualise them. But this is true in a sense of all such equating of one thing with another. We speak of similes and metaphors as images; but both of them are forms of comparison, and it is hard to see how a comparison can be a picture.[6] We can describe jealousy as a green-eyed monster, but this tends to mean that we picture a green-eyed monster rather than jealousy. You can take a photograph of a goat, but not of lechery. You can hold the two parts of the comparison together in language, just as in language you can have a purple-coloured pain, a grin without a cat, a square circle, a person who is both dead and alive, or a cathedral which is built entirely out of stone but also entirely out of jelly. But it is not easy to portray any of these phenomena visually. What image does 'My love is like a red, red rose' bring to mind? A rose with well-plucked eyebrows and dainty legs? It is language's lack of visualisability which confers such enviable freedom upon it. Seeing language as no more than an image or representation of reality is a way of restricting its liberty. In literary history, the words for such policing of the signifier are realism and naturalism – movements which, despite their exclusiveness, have been immensely fertile and productive.

It is true that there are kinds of imagery which do not involve visualisation. We speak, for example, of aural or tactile imagery. Yet the word remains more deceptive than illuminating. For some eighteenth-century critics, imagery referred to the power of poetry to make us 'see' objects, to feel as if we were in their actual presence; but this implied, oddly, that the function of poetic language was to efface itself before what it represented. Language makes things vividly present to us, but to do so adequately it must cease to interpose its own ungainly bulk between us and them. So poetic language

---

[6] A point made by P. N. Furbank in his *Reflections on the Word 'Image'* (London, 1970), p. 1.

attains its pitch of perfection when it ceases to be language at all. At its peak, it transcends itself.

Images, on this theory, are representations so lucid that they cease to be representations at all, and instead merge with the real thing. Which means, logically speaking, that we are no longer dealing with poetry at all, which is nothing if not a verbal phenomenon. F. R. Leavis writes of the kind of verse which 'has such life and body that we hardly seem to be reading arrangements of words . . . The total effect is as if words as words withdrew themselves from the focus of our attention and we were directly aware of a tissue of feelings and perceptions.'[7] It is ironic that on this view, poetry can create the impression of real things more powerfully than the visual arts. When we gaze at a painting of a landscape, we know that what we are seeing is not the landscape itself, precisely because the painting is itself a visual object, one which distinguishes itself from what it depicts in the very act of being faithful to it. But when the medium of representation is not itself visual, as with poetry, this is not so obvious.

The idea of the 'image', which first emerges in its modern sense in the late seventeenth century, arises from the suspicion of rhetoric felt by an Age of Reason.[8] Words are not to act as slippery figures of speech, but to behave as 'images' or clear representations of things. It is ironic, then, that in some later criticism 'imagery' and 'figures of speech' come to be more or less synonymous. Modern movements like Imagism inherited this belief in clear representations, as poets like H. D. and Ezra Pound, alarmed by a commercial and bureaucratic language which seemed out of touch with concrete reality, sought to yoke words and things more tightly together. The idea of the concrete springs to the fore when reality itself seems to have become abstract. 'No ideas but in things' became William Carlos Williams's programmatic slogan. Language on this view is at its most trustworthy when it is thing-like, and thus not language at all. At its most authentic, it flips over into something else.

Imagery, then, did not originally mean such devices as metaphor and simile. In fact, it meant almost the opposite of them. The word harboured a marked hostility to figurative language, rather than denoting certain familiar uses of it. It was only with the Romantic movement, when it was accepted that even the clearest perception of the world involves the creative imagination,

[7] F. R. Leavis, 'Imagery and Movement: Notes in the Analysis of Poetry', *Scrutiny*, September 1945, p. 124.
[8] See R. Frazer, 'The Origin of the Word "Image"', in *English Literary History*, vol. xxvii, pp. 149–61.

that the two notions began to coalesce. What had started out as a matter of clear representations now touched on the very essence of the poetic imagination, which combines, distinguishes, unifies and transforms. Moreover, if our knowledge of reality involved the imagination, then imagery was cognitive, not merely decorative. It could no longer be dismissed as so much superfluous embellishment. Instead, it lay at the very heart of the poetic. Rhetoric and reality were no longer at daggers drawn. Metaphor was now more or less equivalent to the poetic as such. It was a supremely privileged activity of the human spirit, not just a rhetorical device.

By the middle of the nineteenth century, 'imagery' had come to mean pretty much what it means for us today. Yet what exactly *does* it mean? Some dictionaries inform us that the term means 'figurative language', in the sense of language which is non-literal. But similes are surely literal enough. There is nothing figurative in claiming that your boyfriend looks like a toad, as opposed to claiming that he *is* a toad. It is true that the word 'literal' is much abused these days, as in 'I literally fell through the floor in amazement', where the word 'literal' is itself figurative. But similes are quite literally literal. Nor is everything we call a figure of speech a non-literal use of language. This is true enough of hyperbole (exaggeration), litotes (understatement), irony, personification and so on; but what of a figure like chiasmus, in which a pattern of words is repeated in reverse order? The *Oxford English Dictionary* tells us that chiasmus is a figure, yet defines 'figure of speech' as a non-literal use of words. Are imagery and figures of speech the same thing, or is the former confined to simile and metaphor?

The theory of imagery, then, is in something of a mess. One critic informs us that 'Imagery is a form of metaphor or figurative speech, a kind of picture language.'[9] Yet on some theories, metaphor, figurative speech and picture language are either distinct or mutually incompatible. Another commentator, seeking perhaps to square the circle, defines imagery as any concrete as opposed to abstract representation in poetry, whether literal or figurative.[10] One reason why the idea of the image looms so large in the post-Romantic era is because of literature's evolving love affair with the concrete. As we have seen already, the cult of the concrete particular dates largely from this period; and images are thought to be peculiarly solid, vivid and specific. Yet this is a mistaken assumption. There are lots of similes and metaphors, not least in, say, Elizabethan poetry, which are not at all sensuously particular.

[9]   Paul Haeffner, quoted in Furbank, *Reflections*, p. 56.
[10]   See Chris Baldick, *The Concise Oxford Dictionary of Literary Terms* (Oxford and New York, 1990), p. 106. Baldick's book is an excellent guide to its subject.

You can have hazy general images as well as grippingly specific ones. In any case, as we saw in discussing Seamus Heaney, the idea that some uses of language are more concrete than others needs to be handled with care. It is true that an elaborately detailed verbal portrait of a green-eyed monster is less abstract than the concept of jealousy; but the *words* 'green-eyed monster' are not less abstract than the word 'jealousy'. No word – as opposed to an idea – is more concrete or abstract than any other.

In any case, it is a mistake to equate concreteness with things. An individual object is the unique phenomenon it is because it is caught up in a mesh of relations with other objects. It is this web of relations and interactions, if you like, which is 'concrete', while the object considered in isolation is purely abstract. In his *Grundrisse*, Karl Marx sees the abstract not as a lofty, esoteric notion, but as a kind of rough sketch of a thing. The notion of money, for example, is abstract because it is no more than a bare, preliminary outline of the actual reality. It is only when we reinsert the idea of money into its complex social context, examining its relations to commodities, exchange, production and the like, that we can construct a 'concrete' concept of it, one which is adequate to its manifold substance. The Anglo-Saxon empiricist tradition, by contrast, makes the mistake of supposing that the concrete is simple and the abstract is complex. In a similar way, a poem for Yury Lotman is concrete precisely because it is the product of many interacting systems. Like Imagist poetry, you can suppress a number of these systems (grammar, syntax, metre and so on) to leave the imagery standing proudly alone; but this is actually an abstraction of the imagery from its context, not the concretion it appears to be. In modern poetics, the word 'concrete' has done far more harm than good.

But enough of theory for the moment. It is time now to turn back to the poems themselves, in a final analysis of some well-known English verses.

Chapter 6

Four Nature Poems

6.1 William Collins, 'Ode to Evening'

In this final chapter, I want to examine some English Nature poems as a further exercise in close critical analysis. There is no particular rhyme or reason in the selection of these pieces, no obvious connections between them, and no special significance in the fact that they are all about Nature. They simply provide convenient texts to scrutinise.

The first is an extract from the eighteenth-century poet William Collins's 'Ode to Evening':

> . . . Then lead, calm votaress, where some sheety lake
> Cheers the lone heath, or some time-hallowed pile
>   Or uplands fallows gray
>   Reflect its last cool gleam.
> But when chill blustering winds, or driving rain
> Forbid my willing feet, be mine the hut
>   That from the mountain's side
>   Views wilds, and swelling floods,
> And hamlets brown, and dim-discovered spires,
> And hears their simple bell, and marks o'er all
>   Thy dewy fingers draw
>   The gradual dusky veil.

It would be hard to find a style of poetry more alien to the modern sensibility. A modern reader who can enjoy this kind of stuff has developed a genuinely catholic taste. Two aspects of this magnificent poem are immediately unattractive to the typical modern reader: its elaborately formal diction, and its solemnly elevated tone. Diction means the kind of vocabulary conventionally considered suitable for poetry; and the point about modern poetry is that there isn't one. Most modern poetry uses what we might roughly call everyday speech. It is the effects it conjures from this speech which are 'poetic', not the fact that it uses a special idiom set apart from ordinary language. Neoclassical poetry, by contrast, as the critic Donald Davie observes in his study *Purity of Diction in English Verse*, achieves some of its peculiar effects by seeming to fend off certain terms which can be felt hovering on its margins but which it would be indecorous to allow in.

Shakespeare is not constrained by diction either, plundering any sort of vocabulary that comes to hand. This is no doubt one reason why many readers today find it easier to thrill to his language than to the language of, say, John Milton. There is a feeling abroad in some quarters that the native genius of the English language is to be informal and colloquial, and that any more formalised speech is more suitable to high-toned nations like the French. This belief is sometimes accompanied by an interest in Morris dancing and flagons of warm cider.

But there are other cultural situations in which if you did not employ a quasi-technical language for poetry, what you produced would not really be counted as a poem. A great many terms would be regarded as inappropriate for poetry, perhaps because they are too 'low'. This censorship extended into the twentieth century: plenty of Georgian poets would not have contemplated using words like 'steam engine' or 'telegraph' in their work. There are, to be sure, much plainer eighteenth-century poems than 'Ode to Evening'; Collins is especially enamoured of ornate poetic figures. But these figures are by and large the kind of thing that an eighteenth-century reader would have expected from his or her volumes of verse.

The other unappealing aspect of the lines to some modern readers is their tone, which seems equally removed from everyday life. Odes like this are expected to sound reasonably exalted. We may note that this noble or dignified tone is relatively uniform: it does not modulate much in accordance with whatever it is the poem is observing, nor is it intended to. Thus, when the poet makes tracks for the humble hut to shelter from the rain, we might expect some major shift of tone, but we don't get it. Instead, we get the kind of tension between form and content that we have investigated previously. If the hut is humble, the poem's language is not. It records the 'simple' bell of the hamlets or villages in fairly lofty terms. Just as the language of the poem seems to view things from an Olympian vantage point, without detailed close-ups, so the poet makes use of his refuge in the hut for a panoramic surveillance of the landscape around him, sweeping from the sublime (mountains and swelling floods) to the modest domesticity of the hamlets (or small villages). The high and the low are also combined in the image of the church spires, which are mysteriously 'dim-discovered' yet furnished with 'simple' bells. The grandeur of this spectacle is at odds with the work-aday place from which it is observed. And this, for an eighteenth-century readership as well as for many of us today, is perfectly appropriate and acceptable.

The poet is not really part of the landscape he contemplates, and this, again, is part of its poetic decorum. It is true that he dips into the scene briefly by indulging in the fiction of being driven to seek shelter from the rain, as though to account for how he gets from one part of the terrain to another; but the device of the hut is then abandoned. For the poem is not about the poet and his wanderings, which might seem distastefully subjectivist to a neoclass-ical author like Collins. It is about Evening itself. What holds its various experiences together is not the fact that they all occur to one William Collins, which would indeed be a Romantic sort of gambit, but the fact that they are all part of a conveniently wide-ranging abstraction known as Evening. And Evening, once it has arrived, covers just about everything.

This, then, allows Collins to meander around in an apparently desultory fashion, inspecting this or that at his leisure, while ensuring, as a good neo-classical author should, that all of this adds up to a harmonious totality. He allows himself a Romantic latitude within a classical whole. These particular lines of the poem are in fact the only part of it in which the author himself puts in a personal appearance. It would be poetic bad manners to centre every-thing on himself. He does not even view the landscape himself; instead, this activity is delegated to the hut, which seems to do his viewing for him. From 'The gradual dusky veil' to the end of the poem, he effaces himself from view and disappears entirely into the poem's language, which turns in impersonal fashion to a personification of the various seasons of the year.

The ode, then, is not at all to do with the poet's unique experience of the world, as a poem by Keats might be. Nor is it meant to be. We hear very little about how the poet feels about what he observes. We are not dealing with 'consciousness' here, as we might be with Wordsworth or Thomas Hardy. Wordsworth is on the whole less concerned to give us a detailed image of Nature than a detailed map of his mind. The living, breathing, active subject of Collins's poem is not the poet but Evening, on to whom subjectivity, so to speak, is displaced. But if the poem is not particularly concerned with the human subject, neither in a sense is it to do with the natural object.

Everything its author sees is mediated by elaborate literary codes, as is clear from some earlier lines of the work:

> . . . O nymph reserved, while now the bright-haired sun
> Sits in yon western tent, whose cloudy skirts,
>   With brede ethereal wove,
>   O'erhang his wavy bed . . .

There is no direct perception here at all, and no call for it. Collins is not actually looking at anything. He does not need to peer out of his study window to call the sun bright-haired, to portray clouds as skirts, or to speak of the sea as a wavy bed. This is not the kind of verse which puts any great store by meticulous observation. We post-Romantics tend to regard this as a deficiency, but for Collins it would not have seemed so, nor need it seem so to us. He might well have considered it eccentric and indecorous to think up strikingly specific phrases which sought to capture the exact tints and surgings of the ocean.

For the greatest English eighteenth-century critic, Samuel Johnson, this would be an idle distraction from the poet's proper business of conveying general truths. It is a measure of the gulf between pre-Romantics like Johnson and post-Romantics like ourselves that Johnson found generalities deeply interesting and particularities rather pointless. Scientists might want to investigate the sun in greater detail than 'bright-haired', but there is no call for poets and moralists to do so. And this applies to the study of humanity as well: what is important are the few great things that human beings share in common, not their arbitrary deviations from this uniform nature. The specialist scrutiny of individual cases obscures the few fundamental facts about them that we need to know in order to assess their place in the great scheme of things. So terms like 'bright-haired', which seem to us a kind of poetic jargon, are also ways of avoiding jargon, in the sense of specialist language. 'Bright-haired' and 'wavy bed' tell us as much as we need to know. Conventional terms are more informative than freakishly new-fangled ones. But even these terms must not be *stalely* conventional; they must involve some degree of inventiveness on the poet's part. Later in the poem a forest becomes a 'sylvan shed', which is inventive enough.

The poem, then, is really about neither human subject nor natural object, but the medium in which they commingle, which is language itself. It is an intricate, highly artificial rhetorical exercise, even though its subject matter is supposedly Nature. The work is not meant to be 'true to Nature'; instead, Nature is made to be true to it by being recast in terms of symbol, allegory, mythology, stock literary epithets and the like. Nature itself becomes a text or aesthetic object. There is nothing very natural about it. When the poet implies that he is attracted to the simple life by heading for the hut, this is as much a poetic convention as referring to Evening's dewy fingers drawing a dusky veil. It is not that the ode is insincere: terms like 'sincere' and 'insincere' are no more applicable to it than they are to a duck's quacking, or to the carpentering of a rosewood dining table.

It has become fashionable to talk of poems as being about themselves, but in much of Collins's ode this is literally true. Almost the entire first half of the work consists of the poet appealing to Evening to teach him how to sing her praises – which means that almost half the poem is about the act of writing the poem itself. In the process of this appeal, the poem waxes lyrical about Evening, so that it does what it asks to do in the act of asking to do it. All this occurs in a single sentence of considerable syntactical complexity which stretches for twenty lines:

> If ought of oaten stop, or pastoral song,
> May hope, chaste Eve, to soothe thy modest ear,
>   Like thy own solemn springs,
>   Thy springs and dying gales,
> O nymph reserved, while now the bright-haired sun
> Sits in yon western tent, whose cloudy skirts,
>   With brede ethereal wove,
>   O'erhangs his wavy bed:
> Now air is hushed, save where the weak-eyed bat,
> With short shrill shriek flits by on leathern wing,
>   Or where the beetle winds
>   His small but sullen horn,
> As oft he rises 'midst the twilight path,
> Against the pilgrim borne in heedless hum:
>   Now teach me, maid composed,
>   To breathe some softened strain,
> Whose numbers, stealing through thy darkening vale,
> May not unseemly with its stillness suit,
>   As, musing slow, I hail
>   Thy genial loved return!

What this says in bare grammatical outline is: If you would like a song, Evening, teach me one yourself. But in saying this, the poem digresses and elaborates so much, taking a circuitous route through one sub-clause after another, that it becomes the song which it is asking to sing. The form of the poem – the performative act by which it is requesting inspiration – becomes its content. This, to be sure, involves some grammatical sleight of hand: there is a slightly awkward transition, for example, from 'O'erhangs his wavy bed' to 'Now air is hushed'. Everything up to 'wavy bed' can be read without grammatical strain as part of the poet's address to Evening, but 'Now air is hushed' shifts to a descriptive passage which really stands on its own and can't easily be folded into the act of addressing Evening. It is not clear by what logic the poem slides from the performative to the descriptive. The act of addressing Evening is taken up again in 'Now teach me, maid composed', as the poem regains its rhetorical stride after this deviation into descriptiveness.

Even so, the verbal quality of that description can be related to the self-referential act which is the poem itself. Lines like 'With short shrill shriek flits by on leathern wing' and 'His small but sullen horn' betray a high degree of linguistic self-consciousness, as though the poet has his eye on the phrase rather than the object. 'Small but sullen' is a little too fastidiously qualifying, while 'short shrill shriek' overdoes the alliteration. The ostentatious artifice of these phrases signals a self-conscious distance between the poem's language and its objects, or between art and Nature. We are reminded insistently of that art, too, in the metre's constant alternation of pentameters and trimeters, lines of five stresses and lines of three. Just as the poem curves back on itself structurally, by being about the song which is itself, so some of its more local verbal effects are peculiarly self-regarding. We are perpetually aware of the gap between the 'mind' of the poem, as expressed in its form and language, and the natural world of which it speaks. In other hands – Thomas Hardy's, for example – this gap can become the stuff of tragedy; but 'Ode to Evening' is not a tragic poem, even if its blitheness of spirit feels at times a little laboured, weighed down as it is with all that top-heavy imagery.

When the poet talks about visiting a lake on the heath, or taking refuge in a hut, he is not describing actual events, and we are not meant to imagine that he is. He is talking in a general kind of way. These are the sort of things one might typically do, not necessarily things that one actually has done or will do. Only in one or two places does Collins seem to be speaking about realities actually present to his eyes, as when he writes of the sun 'now' sitting in the sky, and then, a few lines later:

> Now air is hushed, save where the weak-eyed bat,
> With short shrill shriek flits by on leathern wing,
>   Or where the beetle winds
>   His small but sullen horn,
> As oft he rises 'midst the twilight path . . .

No sooner do we seem to occupy an actual time and place than we take leave of it again. The beetle winds his horn in the present, as 'oft' he rises on the path. What seems actual turns out to be typical or general. Collins is interested in the kind of thing beetles tend to do, not in any individual beetle. And in this he is in accord with neoclassical doctrine and decorum. His ode is to Evening, not to a specific evening.

6.2 William Wordsworth, 'The Solitary Reaper'

Our next poem is William Wordsworth's 'The Solitary Reaper':

> Behold her, single in the field,
> Yon solitary Highland Lass!
> Reaping and singing by herself;
> Stop here, or gently pass!
> Alone she cuts and binds the grain,
> And sings a melancholy strain;
> O listen! for the Vale profound
> Is overflowing with the sound.
>
> No Nightingale did ever chaunt
> More welcome notes to weary bands
> Of travellers in some shady haunt,
> Among Arabian sands:
> A voice so thrilling ne'er was heard
> In spring-time from the Cuckoo bird,
> Breaking the silence of the seas
> Among the farthest Hebrides.
>
> Will no one tell me what she sings?
> Perhaps the plaintive numbers flow
> For old, unhappy, far-off things,
> And battles long ago:
> Or is it some more humble lay,
> Familiar matter of today?
> Some natural sorrow, loss, or pain,
> That has been, and may be again?
>
> Whate'er the theme, the maiden sang
> As if her song could have no ending;

> I saw her singing at her work,
> And o'er the sickle bending;
> I listened till I had my fill:
> And as I mounted up the hill,
> The music in my heart I bore,
> Long after it was heard no more.

The first verse appears rather more excited than seems appropriate. Furnished with no less than three exclamation marks, it is almost as much about the observer as the woman he is looking at. 'Behold her . . . Stop here, or gently pass! . . . O listen!': there is an insistent, exclamatory buttonholing of an imaginary spectator (who might also be the reader), as though he or she might otherwise miss the significance of an apparently unremarkable scene. It is the woman's song which seems to entrance the poet, more than her appearance and certainly more than the work she is at. He tells us that the vale is 'overflowing with the sound' of her voice, which seems a bit hyperbolic. Is she really singing at full volume, or is this a perception stirred by something in the music which is more than the music? Anyway, the comment seems as excessive as the overflowing of the woman's voice, and we are in the dark as to why this might be so.

The next verse compares the woman's voice to the nightingale and the cuckoo, but in a structurally odd kind of way. What the poem says is that this human voice is far more soothing and thrilling than the chirping of these birds; but grammatically speaking it says it in such a way as to throw all the poetic emphasis upon the birds themselves – that is to say, on what is formally being dismissed as inferior. And this creates a certain disproportion in the verse, though one that it carries off without any notable strain. If you want to praise a woman's musical talent, you do not generally claim that her voice is more alluring than the sound of a cuckoo heard in springtime in the far-flung Hebrides where it seems to break the silence of the seas. Or that it is more welcome than the sound of a nightingale chanting to weary bands of travellers in a shady haunt in the sands of Arabia. By the time the eye arrives at the end of these clauses, the reader is in danger of forgetting that all this is something that the Highland lass's voice is superior to, and has begun to focus on the images as autonomous entities. Images which offer to illustrate end up by distracting.

This, in fact, is a quite common device in poetry. A version of it can be found in the line 'No star is o'er the lake, its pale watch keeping', where we are first told there is no star and then, contradictorily, that it is keeping its pale watch. What the line means is that there is no star, of the kind which customarily keeps its pale watch, over the lake; but the effect, as in the Wordsworth verse, is to dismiss the star and conjure it into presence at the same time. This also happens in T. S. Eliot's 'Gerontion':

> I was neither at the hot gates
> Nor fought in the warm rain
> Nor knee deep in the salt marsh, heaving a cutlass,
> Bitten by flies, fought.

All this is what the speaker *didn't* do. The gates he wasn't at were hot; the rain in which he didn't fight was warm; the salt marsh he didn't stand in came up to his knees; and the flies didn't bite him at the moment he wasn't swinging a cutlass.

The secret of this imbalance in Wordsworth's verse is probably that he is not particularly interested in the Highland lass herself. He is interested, rather, in the kind of thoughts and images she inspires in him, even if these images are formally offered as less precious than the woman herself. The fact that the third word of the piece is 'single' may be significant here: stark, solitary figures marooned in bleak landscapes are peculiarly evocative for Wordsworth, but they generally serve the purpose of pointing, like symbols, beyond themselves. It is the deeper imaginative dimension they evoke which really matters to him. The wanderers, small farmers and blind beggars who inspire him in this way rarely have much substance in themselves, and the same goes for the solitary reaper. It is her lonely self-absorption which seems to fascinate the speaker, who perhaps sees in it a reflection of his own poetic solitude. Not only a reflection, in fact, but an inspiration: her very enigmatic presence is a source of 'exotic' imagery for him. There may be a sense in which he is pointing excitedly to an image of himself. An idealised image, perhaps, since the woman seems to have a composure and autonomy about her which the poet himself might feel that he lacks. She does not seem to be anxious about being alone, and if she has spotted this poetically aroused English tourist lurking near her field she is clearly unperturbed by him.

It is the first line of the third verse which delivers the surprise punch: 'Will no one tell me what she sings?' Only now do we realise with a jolt that the speaker can't actually understand what the woman is singing about, presumably because she is singing in Scottish Gaelic. This, however, proves to be no great loss. On the contrary, it provides the poet with yet another flight of fancy, this time about what the lass *might* be singing about. The subjunctive mood trumps the indicative. Because he does not know the theme of her actual song, the speaker can treat it as a blank text on to which to project his own poetic fantasies. In fact, one suspects that query 'Will know one tell me what she sings?' is a purely rhetorical one – that he would really rather not know, since such determinacy of meaning would diminish the scope of his own musings. Because the song means nothing definite to him, it can mean more or less anything, or at least anything suitably melancholic. Wordsworth is in something like the situation of John Keats before the Grecian Urn, posing a series of breathless questions to it ('What men or gods are these? What maidens loath?') which are all the more gratifying because no very precise answers are available.

In the final verse, the speaker tells us that he listened to the woman until 'I had my fill'. He has reaped what gratification he wants from her, without even knowing who she is, and now he is ready to travel on. In a sense, then, it is he who is the solitary reaper. As he does pass on, he bears the music in his heart long after the woman herself is out of sight. But in a sense she was out of sight all along, as no more than a convenient figure around which to organise his own flights of fancy. He remembers the lass's music, but the experience seemed a kind of memory even when he was having it. He relates to her rather as a modern tourist relates to a medieval castle through a camera lens, content to know nothing of its history but assured of having garnered an image of it as a souvenir for the future.

So Wordsworth has had his momentous encounter with a symbolist poet – with a discourse in which he savours the signifier all the more keenly because the signified or meaning is obscure to him. One strength of the poem, as with much of Wordsworth's work, is that he does not seem to grasp exactly why the experience is so haunting and arresting, any more than he understands what the woman is singing. It is as though the impenetrability of her song, rather than its sweetness and certainly rather than the singer herself, touches in him a kind of obscurity too deep to articulate. One can see how this might be an alarming experience, as it can be elsewhere in Wordsworth: one stumbles upon an alien, solitary figure, absorbed in its own strange despondency, which seems to turn its back enigmatically on the poet himself. But the mood of the poem is not troubled or fearful, though it is part of its complex effect that we can glimpse how it might be.

Instead, the speaker draws a reflective pleasure from the sadness of the reaper's song; indeed, sadness in Wordsworth is often more consoling than distressing. Perhaps she is offering him a lesson in how to overcome sorrow by transforming it into art; so that his own poem, while partly on the subject of grief, is nevertheless tranquil and self-possessed. In this sense, the poem doubles what the reaper does. Whether this achievement is somehow bought at her expense is one of the questions the reader is left to ponder. The woman sings in a mournful way of what may well be tragic events (though they may well not be either); but it does not follow that she is downcast herself, and the fact that she carries on working while she is singing suggests that she isn't. The song is perhaps more a work ritual than personally expressive, so that it is gloomy but she is not. And this, too, might be something that Wordsworth learns from the experience. One can see how this might be a source of comfort to a poet given to fits of glumness. 'Melancholy' suggests a tempered kind of dejection, one which is far from distraught. Wordsworth might also draw a lesson from the fact that in certain circumstances, such as a labour chant, poetry can have a pragmatic value, which was scarcely obvious to most Romantic poets.

Rather than feeling threatened by the autonomy and anonymity of the reaper, the speaker seems anxious to preserve these qualities. This, perhaps, is the point of 'Stop here, or gently pass': he does not want to call attention to his presence because this would turn the woman from an observed object to a perceiving subject, thus ruining what is most evocative about her. In another version of the work, 'I listened till I had my fill' becomes the tautological 'I listened, motionless and still', like a man with a pair of binoculars who is trying not to scare off a rare but skittish bird. Anyhow, whatever it is which the experience touches in the poet, he is shrewd enough not to moralise it away. It is when Wordsworth tries to spell out the moral significance of these mute, cryptic, disorientating encounters that he is at his most tedious.

6.3   Gerard Manley Hopkins, 'God's Grandeur'

For our third Nature poem, we move to the other end of the nineteenth century and Gerard Manley Hopkins's 'God's Grandeur':

> The world is charged with the grandeur of God.
>   It will flame out, like shining from shook foil;
>   It gathers to a greatness, like the ooze of oil
> Crushed. Why do men then now not reck his rod?
> Generations have trod, have trod, have trod;
>   And all is seared with trade; bleared, smeared with toil;
>   And wears man's smudge and shares man's smell: the soil
> Is bare now, nor can foot feel, being shod.

And for all this, nature is never spent;
    There lives the dearest freshness deep down things;
    And though the last lights off the black West went
    Oh, morning, at the brown brink eastward, springs –
Because the Holy Ghost over the bent
    World broods with warm breast and with ah! bright wings.

There is an ambiguity running through this poem which does not instantly spring to the eye. Hopkins was a Roman Catholic priest, and Roman Catholics are officially free to believe either that Nature was involved in the Fall along with humanity, or that only humanity is fallen. This is more than just an academic issue, since if Nature is fallen then it cannot easily act as a medium of divine grace for human beings; whereas if it remains unfallen, it can provide post-lapsarian beings with just such a taste of innocence and joy.

'God's Grandeur' is perhaps most interestingly read as equivocating between these two positions. We are told to begin with, in an authoritative flourish, that 'The world is charged with the grandeur of God', and that this grace seems readily available: 'It will flame out like shining from shook foil'. But the foil in this finely wrought image has to be shaken in order to shine, which suggests that divine grace is not as readily available in Nature as all that. A certain effort (that of shaking the foil) is necessary to come by it. Nature is charged with grace, but it does not release it spontaneously. Hopkins, then, is able to avoid what for him would be two heretical extremes: on the one hand, the radical Protestant view that grace and Nature are absolutely at odds with one another, and on the other hand what is known as the Pelagian heresy, for which grace is natural to us. The poem needs to tread a fine line between denigrating Nature, which would be to forget that it is God's creation, and elevating it to divine status in a way which would run the risk of pantheism. The Catholic position here is that Nature, including human nature, has the potential for grace – it is, so to speak, predisposed to share in God's life – but that this sharing in the life of infinite love nevertheless requires a laborious self-transformation. Nature needs to go beyond itself to become truly itself; but it has the built-in capacity to do so, which radical Protestantism would deny. Grace is not spontaneous, but neither is it arbitrary. It does not already suffuse the world, but it is not alien to it either.

The same delicate tension is sustained in the next image: 'It gathers to a greatness, like the ooze of oil / Crushed'. 'Gathers to a greatness' suggests an organic, spontaneous process; but that 'Crushed' abruptly intervenes as we step across the line-ending to insist, once again, that human agency is involved here. The shift from one line to another is also a shift of perspective.

In a prefiguring of modern environmentalism, Hopkins then laments the way that Nature has been polluted by humanity. If the first lines of the poem emphasised the need for active human participation in the business of grace, we are now grimly reminded of how predatory such human activity can actually be. 'Generations have trod, have trod, have trod' is a touch too onomatopoeic, rather too obviously inviting us to hear the plodding of polluting feet in its sound and rhythm; but the packed sound-pattern of the next two lines, with their complex criss-crossing of assonance and alliteration, are richly expressive of human alienation from the natural world. The prejudice against shoes, though ('nor can foot feel, being shod'), is surely rather excessive. Is Hopkins really recommending a mass reversion to barefootedness?

The foot image, however, is in a sense consoling. It suggests that the problem is with us, not with Nature. Nature may still be as charged with grace as ever; it is just that we have insulated ourselves from it by our modern technologies. The same goes for words like 'smeared', 'bleared' and 'smudge', which suggests a purely surface contamination. Smearings, blearings and smudgings you can wipe off. 'Seared with trade' is rather more troubling, since to sear is to scorch, and scorch marks cannot be rubbed off; but the general impression created by the imagery is of a Nature only superficially tainted by its most rapacious inhabitant. As the poem laments, then, its imagery simultaneously qualifies that lamentation. Nature cannot be seen as too deeply infected by humanity, since this might appear to question one's belief in its divine goodness, as well as to allot humanity itself too much cosmic significance. Surely men and women can't seriously despoil what God has created?

This sanguine view is then reinforced by the opening lines of the second stanza:

> And for all this, nature is never spent;
> There lives the dearest freshness deep down things . . .

('For' here means 'despite'.) Humanity may do its worst, but Nature's resources are inexhaustible. There is a play on words here with 'spent' and 'dearest', terms which have financial overtones. The commercialism which the poem has just been denouncing ('trade') now provides it unobtrusively with a source of imagery. Nature has the munificence of a benevolent billionaire, and will never go bankrupt. Yet in case we grow too complacent about its opulence, 'deep down' puts us on the alert. The freshness which lives in things is deep down, and thus, so the implication runs, not spontaneously available. We are back to shook foil and crushed oil. Hopkins must not play up the commonness of grace to the point where he plays down original sin. Perhaps it is just as well that Nature's treasures are so deeply stored, since then we are less able to defile them; but what keeps them secure is also what makes them hard to gain access to.

The poem's final, extraordinary image maintains this tension to the end:

> And though the last lights off the black West went
> Oh, morning, at the brown brink eastward, springs –
> Because the Holy Ghost over the bent
> World broods with warm breast and with ah! bright wings.

First we have the sanguine viewpoint again: Nature's freshness may seem to have vanished, but this is no more an irretrievable loss than the sun going down. The sun goes down (or, as the modern theory has it, the earth turns up) only to spring back up again in the morning. Grace would seem as universally available as light. Yet the last two lines of the poem implicitly rebuff this assumption. The coming and going of the light as the earth turns is itself the work of the Holy Spirit. It is because he sits like a brooding hen on the great egg of the globe that the light is hatched out of it each dawn. Daylight is not as natural and spontaneous as it seems. Like the shining of the foil and the gathering of the oil, it is the result of a labour. The world is 'bent', meaning both literally curved and morally corrupt; and only God's constant agency can conjure something beneficial from it. Hopkins has thus neatly avoided both pantheism, the doctrine which would see God and Nature as identical, and Pelagianism, a heresy which denies or denigrates the Fall of humanity. But he has done so while celebrating the dearness and freshness of the natural world, in a poignant contrast with human depravity.

Another way of looking at the poem is to see it as an allegory of poetry itself. Hopkins is renowned for the muscular inventiveness of his language, but we have seen already that this may well reflect a certain modernist suspicion of language, as well as a celebration of it. Language in its everyday state is, so to speak, fallen: it is bleared and smudged with trade, degraded to a mere instrument of commercial and bureaucratic communication; and to be stirred into life again, the poet must wreak what the Formalists, as we have seen, called a certain organised violence upon it. Hence all that Hopkinsian cramming and dislocating and burnishing of language, which some find gorgeous and others find merely eccentric. A hostile critic once remarked that Hopkins took the English language and left it a 'muscle-bound monstrosity'. Language in its common-or-garden state is no medium of grace and truth; but if you shake it and crush it, heightening, stretching and compressing its words, you may persuade it to release a precious insight. Poetry, like grace, does not come naturally. You have to work for them both. Yet poetry is not unnatural either. The creative imagination is a reflection of God's action within the individual; and like divine grace it 'redeems' the world by restoring it to us in all its pristine freshness.

There is a typically modernist 'extremism' behind this poetics. Truth is accessible only when you press things to their outer limit. Only in some Room 101 of the human spirit, faced with the vilest horror you can imagine, can you give voice to it. Everyday life, by contrast, is banal, illusory, inauthentic. You have to shake it very hard to get anything worthwhile out of it. The same goes for human beings, in a certain traditional conservative view of them. In their natural state men and women are indolent, selfish, violent creatures; only by disciplining and chastising them can you force anything half-decent out of them. Hopkins himself was a conservative, who found 'trade' distasteful from the standpoint of a spiritual aristocrat, not from that of a socialist. He was also something of an ascetic, concerned with subjugating the flesh. His poetics, like his politics, brood upon the way a stringent Jesuitical discipline (of rhythm, internal rhyme and so on) may bring the best out of its raw materials. If this is too gloomy a view of human nature, the opposing liberal vision tends to be too dewy-eyed. Human beings will do the right thing spontaneously if only you leave them to their own devices. It is pushing them around which causes all the trouble.

6.4   Edward Thomas, 'Fifty Faggots'

The final work to examine is Edward Thomas's 'Fifty Faggots', written early in the twentieth century:

> There they stand, on their ends, the fifty faggots
> That once were underwood of hazel and ash
> In Jenny Pinks's Copse. Now, by the hedge
> Close packed, they make a thicket fancy alone
> Can creep through with the mouse and wren. Next Spring
> A blackbird or a robin will nest there,
> Accustomed to them, thinking they will remain
> Whatever is for ever to a bird.
> This Spring it is too late; the swift has come,
> 'Twas a hot day for carrying them up:
> Better they will never warm me, though they must
> Light several Winters' fires. Before they are done

The war will have ended, many other things
Have ended, maybe, that I can no more
Foresee or more control than robin and wren.

It is a change to find a poet actually working in the midst of Nature. In Collins's 'Ode to Evening' we see no signs of labour at all, and the poet's stance to the landscape is purely contemplative. (Much the same is true of the novels of Jane Austen, which hardly ever portray anybody at work on the landed estates which form their backdrop.) Wordsworth is watching someone else working but not working himself, and the reaper's labour is not the focus of his attention. The Hopkins poem is sharply critical of work upon the natural world, which it can see only as a form of ravage and pollution. In this poem, however, Nature is not a landscape to be surveyed but a working environment to be engaged with. Work is the process by which human beings transform their natural environment in order to meet their needs, and Thomas makes no sentimental apology for hacking faggots (or bundles of firewood) from a copse. Country people need to keep warm in winter, and relate to Nature not primarily as an aesthetic object but in terms of its use-value.

It is generally town-dwellers who gaze upon Nature as a timeless aesthetic spectacle, in what one might call the day-tripper view of the countryside. They do not typically see Nature as fuel and food – as something to eat as well as something to stare at. Whereas 'Fifty Faggots' is clearly a poem by someone who lives in a rural environment, knows his way around and names the landscape in familiar local terms ('Jenny Pinks's Copse') rather than, like Collins, in the more exalted nomenclature of myth and allegory. Nature comes to us not 'in itself', but as socially mediated: Thomas is interested in the way it is woven through with human meanings and purposes, and not just human ones either: even the birds see Nature not as a reality in itself but as somewhere to nest.

Even so, this is not a natural landscape which is *centred* on the human. 'Man' is not lord of all he surveys, appropriating what he wants from Nature with the consumerist lack of effort of a Wordsworth plucking memories like pansies as he wanders on his way. Thomas's relationship to Nature is among other things one of sweat and struggle: carrying the faggots up to the hedge was an arduous business, which he tells us with a pleasant touch of wit has warmed him more than the fires that the wood is intended for ever will. Nature is not a blank text to be inscribed as the fancy takes you, but recalcitrant stuff with a life of its own.

The closing lines of the piece – '. . . many other things / Have ended, maybe, that I can no more / Foresee or more control than robin and wren'

– 'decentres' the supposedly privileged nature of human consciousness by stressing its ignorance and fallibility, thus putting humanity on the side of the equally agnostic birds rather than raising it above them. '. . . that I can no more / Foresee or more control than robin and wren' presumably means that the poet can no more foresee or control the future, or indeed events happening elsewhere in the present, than the birds can. But it is also possible to read 'robin and wren' as the objects of the verbs 'foresee' and 'control', so that the line comes to mean 'I can no more foresee or control these events than I can foresee or control robin and wren.' This involves some grammatical strain, since you can speak of foreseeing a disaster but not, normally, of foreseeing a bird. Yet this possible sense lingers within the more obvious meaning of the line, to suggest humanity's lack of control or dominance over its surroundings, the way it cannot second-guess either the natural or the human processes at work around it.

The human is also dislodged from any particularly exalted status within Nature by the poem's quiet insistence on how alien natural things are to us, as well as how intimate. Humans and animals interact within the same context, as mice and wrens may creep through the faggots which the speaker has stacked, and birds will later come to nest in them. Yet they also inhabit their own quite separate time-schemes, worlds of meaning and spheres of activity, and the very interaction of these with each other shows up, ironically, how different they are. A bird's idea of eternity is inscrutable to us, though we can assume it is not the same as ours. Its comings and goings intersect with our own history and practice, but also cut through them like an alternative universe. It is as though different worlds sit cheek by jowl, interrelated but non-interfering.

Whereas natural landscapes are often seen as static and changeless, Thomas's poem is alive with transformation. The faggots were once 'underwood of hazel and ash', and will soon be consumed to ashes of a different kind. What looks like a static object is just a kind of snapshot or cross-section of a complex temporal process. A world which is actually a set of processes appears to us like a set of fixed objects. Stacked by the hedge, the bundles of firewood 'make a thicket', which (since thickets are fairly fixed features of a landscape) lends a kind of deceptive air of permanency to what is actually a bunch of sticks in transit from copse to winter fires. This, presumably, is how the mouse and the wren will treat it, just as the nesting blackbird and the robin will behave as though this ephemeral pile of timber has always been there and always will be. Even so, it is too late for what will happen next year to happen this year; the two temporal frames are disjoint.

The speaker inhabits different time-schemes, too. The wood-carrying which took only a brief time to heat him up can be contrasted with the longer-term destiny of the faggots, one which will stretch the length of several winters. And this time-stream can be measured in turn against the great public time-frame known as political history, so that the First World War, in which Thomas fought and was killed, will be over before the faggots have been used up. It is odd to think of such a modest, local event as the consumption of firewood in an English village outlasting such a global narrative as the war. No grand totality of these various time-schemes appears possible: they do not seem to add up to some master-narrative which would make sense of them all. Instead, for Thomas as much as for Thomas Hardy, it is the ironic, contingent, purely random way they collide with each other which is most imaginatively compelling.

Things exist in the present, but also, in a ghostly, indeterminate kind of way, in the future. They have a similarly hazy existence, through memory, in the past. Memory and anticipation are faculties which only human animals possess, furnished as they are with the power of imagination. Robins presumably do not cherish fond memories of their infantile years, or blackbirds expect the farmer to return next Wednesday at ten minutes past three. Only an animal with language is able to do that. So the speaker knows more than mouse and wren, but much of what he knows concerns how much he doesn't know. One might almost claim that human beings have consciousness in order to know what they don't know. They are aware of their own ignorance and powerlessness, as birds presumably are not; and it is this alone, perhaps, which raises them above their fellow animals. Human beings live in the subjunctive mood, as well as in the indicative one.

If the poet has an edge over the birds in knowing that there is such a thing as the future, he is nevertheless as ignorant as they are of what it might hold: '. . . many other things / Have ended, maybe'. 'Things' is significantly vague, and the fact that they have ended is by no means sure. So one cannot even be certain of events which have already taken place, let alone those still to come. Only the future will disclose whether something which might have ended in the present really has done so, so that once more we have a crossing and merging of time-streams, this time within human history itself. Projecting ourselves forward in imagination lends our lives an anxiety and instability to which blackbirds are immune. The present is hollowed out by the way it intimates a set of possible futures, just as it is overshadowed by the various pasts from which it evolved. Yet it is not quite that living in time robs us of solid self-identity in a way that can be contrasted with the repleteness of the faggots. For they, too, as we have seen, have a history, and thus only an illusory self-completeness. The difference is rather that we live out the chancy, provisional nature of our history in the form of lack, desire and imagination, whereas the natural life-forms around us do not.

The fleeting, open-ended nature of things, despite many a poetic cliché to the contrary, is not simply to be lamented. In fact, this poem is not necessarily lamenting it at all. Transience means among things that the war will not last for ever, even if the poet's confidence that it will be over before the faggots are finished is somewhat at odds with his general agnosticism. Envisaging the future may make you dissatisfied with the present, but it may also prevent you from absolutising it. The 'many other things' that may have ended are not necessarily all positive. Just as a fugitive feature of the landscape (the faggots) can be mistaken by a bird for a customary one, so aspects of a customary way may have vanished overnight with the military upheaval. But we should not conclude that this is all to be regretted. It is the sheer fact of ephemerality, rather than the specific losses and gains that it brings, that seems to preoccupy the poem. The piece is full of a sense of clashing perspectives, ironic juxtapositions and relative standpoints. In this sense, its very form is 'liberal', questioning the kind of dogmatic rhetoric which was associated with the war itself. It makes a virtue out of not being sure, at the same time as its closing lines betray the insecurity which such a lack of assurance can breed.

The mood of the poem, then, is not elegiac. In fact, Thomas is too busy thinking in these lines to indulge in any very intense emotion. It is hardly the kind of compliment one could pay to, say, Tennyson. The language of the work is low-key, businesslike and briskly anti-rhetorical. It accepts in its level-headed way the clashing, ironic, untotalisable nature of things, but it is not excessively stoical about it. The tone of the last few lines is matter-of-fact and a touch wry, rather than nostalgic. The poet himself intrudes on the scene he portrays only at a couple of points. Sensibility is subordinated to description. There is no deep subjectivity at stake here. Yet the sense of a poetic personality – ironic, unassuming, coolly realistic, really rather English – comes strongly through. It is a poem which, in an understated, self-effacing English way, refuses to flaunt its superbly accomplished technique.

6.5 Form and History

The French critic Roland Barthes once observed that a little form could be a dangerous thing, while a large amount of it could be salutary. What he meant was that a narrow kind of formalism treats poems superficially, neglecting what they say for the way that they say it; whereas a more subtle attention to form grasps it as a medium of history itself. To speak of the politics or ideology of form is to speak of the way in which formal strategies in literature are themselves socially signifying. And the social or ideological messages poems emit may well be in conflict with what one might call the ideology of their content.

Take as an example the heroic couplet, as we have seen it deployed in Alexander Pope's mock-heroic poem *The Dunciad*. We have noted already how the elegance and economy of this device, with its trim balances, inversions and antitheses, its sense of words locking with preordained precision into their allotted places, reflects a certain notion of order, reason, harmony and cosmic necessity. It would not be difficult to relate this notion in turn to the traditional world-view of the English landowning and patrician class of which Pope is so eloquent a spokesman – so that what we get in the regular stressings and stretchings of these clipped pairs of pentameters is nothing less than a whole social ideology.

In Pope's own time, it was an ideology under threat from the dunces who constitute the subject of his satire – the literary hacks and timeservers who value the present over the classical past, innovation against tradition and mobility over hierarchy. This swarm of social parasites Pope associates with the rapid commercialisation of writing in his day, and so with the rising fortunes of the middle classes. There is a sense, then, in which the tension between the form and the content of his poem reflects a conflict between two social classes or world-views, one on the wane and the other on the ascendancy.

In fact, the iambic pentameter – the most common kind of English metre – is itself saturated with social meaning. What makes it so supremely serviceable is the interplay it sets up between the spontaneous flexing and flowing of the speaking voice, and the unobtrusive, impersonal framework which undergirds it. The line is a triumph of reconciliation between order and freedom, necessity and spontaneity, the rule-governed and the open-ended. In blending the distinctive tone of an individual voice with a sense of stability, it allows for just the kind of balance between the individual and the social order which liberal societies tend to favour. In avoiding the individualist anarchy of free verse, it equally rebuffs the kind of cultural form in which the collective dominates over the individual. 'Three Blind Mice', whose baffling aporias and ambiguities we have investigated already, would be an example of such a collectivist form, one in which the ritual chant and regular thuds of the rhythm allow the reader or speaker a minimum of personal freedom. You can't read such a nursery rhyme in an individualised, uniquely 'meaningful' way', as a

Stratford actor might deliver a Shakespeare speech; instead, the rhythm of the lines more or less determines how we are going to recite them.

It would have been possible, in discussing Blake's 'Tyger' poem, to relate the speaker's ambivalent awe and admiration of the tiger to some familiar responses to the Industrial Revolution, an historical episode which hovers in the poem's background. In such a reading, the ambiguous feelings of the piece might be seen among other things as an allegory of that revolution's internal contradictions – how it is both enslaving and emancipating, a sublime liberation of energy and a brutally dehumanising process. It might be possible, too, to read the tremulous melancholy of Tennyson, in 'Mariana' and 'In Memoriam', as a social as well as personal phenomenon – a response to the gradual haemorrhaging of spiritual meaning from an increasingly materialist, mechanistic Victorian England, with its tortuous crises of faith and deep-seated terror of social revolt.

The fact that Tennyson so often seems not to know why he is sorrowful – that his grief lacks an 'objective correlative' or determinate object – might be relevant here. Here, it is *mood* or sensibility – what Raymond Williams has called a 'structure of feeling'[1] – which provides the vital hinge between text and history. In the work of W. B. Yeats, by contrast, it is very often *tone* which alerts us to the wider historical context of the poetry: that of the precipitate decline of the Anglo-Irish governing class of which Yeats was a self-appointed representative, the collapse of whose fortunes can be dimly heard in the poet's guilt, *hauteur*, mournful resignation or defiant exultation.

Even syntax can provide the mediation between poem and history, as is clear from Edward Thomas's 'Old Man' and 'Fifty Faggots'. The knotted, flailing syntax of these pieces, with their bristling thickets of qualifications, reflects a modernist sense of the extreme elusiveness of truth, as time-schemes diffuse, identity falters, and experience fragments to the point where simple exactitude becomes a kind of sweated labour. It is surely not hard to trace in this crisis of knowledge the deeper upheaval which was the war in which Thomas fought and died, a trauma which seemed to many who endured it to call into question the foundations of Western civilisation itself. There is no longer a grand narrative of progress in a piece like 'Fifty Faggots', just a random collision of distinctive time-streams, in which the present is shot through with a haunting sense of absence and irreparable loss. If these works of Thomas are not 'just' Nature poems, it is because there is no such thing.

---

[1] See Raymond Williams, *Marxism and Literature* (Oxford, 1977), Ch. 9.

A full examination of these matters is not the task of this book. Yet it is worth noting that of all literary genres, poetry would seem the one most stubbornly resistant to political criticism, most sequestered from the winds of history. It has its own thickness and density, which are not to be summarily reduced to symptoms of something else. Yet it is not only that a rigorous distinction between poetry and history is itself historically quite recent, and would have bemused many an eminent poet of the past. It is also, not least in the modernist epoch, that the poem's very recalcitrance to social analysis, the way it cuts itself loose from conventional perceptions, is itself an eloquent historical phenomenon. What kind of society is it on which poetry feels it has to turn its back? What has happened to the content of social experience when the poem feels compelled to take its own forms as its content, rather than draw from a common fund of meaning? To write the history of poetic forms is a way of writing the history of political cultures. But to do this, we have first to grant those forms their material reality; and this book has been one attempt to do so.

Glossary

addressee: the actual or intended recipient of an utterance or work of art.

alexandrine: a line of six iambic feet, e.g. 'Which like a wounded snake drags its slow length along'.

allegory: a text or narrative whose literal meanings can be read as coded signs of other meanings, such as moral or spiritual ones.

alliteration: the recurrence of the same sounds at the beginning of adjacent words (e.g. 'Round and round the rugged rocks the ragged rascal ran').

ambiguity: a word or piece of writing whose meaning is difficult to determine because it allows for alternative interpretations (e.g. 'Refuse to Be Put in This Basket').

ambivalence: the holding of two determinate but conflicting meanings in tension within an utterance.

anapaest: a metrical foot (or unit) consisting of two unstressed (or 'short') syllables followed by one stressed (or 'long') one: *di-di-dum*.

assonance: a set of mutually echoing, half-rhyming sounds, usually vowel sounds, in the separate words of a line or phrase (e.g. 'dapple-dawn-drawn').

bathos: a movement from the sublime to the commonplace or ridiculous.

blank verse: unrhymed iambic pentameters.

bombast: pompous or extravagant language.

cadence: the spontaneous rhythms of the voice in ordinary speech, as opposed to the set patterns of poetic metre.

chiasmus: the linking of two phrases, the second of which reverses the order of items in the first (e.g. 'the majesty of death, and death of majesty').

conceit: a witty or fanciful image.

content: the substance of a literary work, such as its meaning, narrative, argument, action or moral vision.

dactyl: a metrical foot or unit with one stressed syllable followed by two unstressed ones (*dum-di-di*).

diction: a selection of words considered on social or aesthetic grounds, or both, to be suitable for poetry. Or, the type of language peculiar to a particular poem or poet, such as archaic, Latinate, Anglo-Saxon and so on.

didactic: concerned to teach a moral or lesson.

discourse: language considered in the material context of communication between human subjects, or as an historical phenomenon rather than an abstract system.

elegiac: mournful or lamenting, as in an elegy.

enjambement: the running over of meaning and grammatical structure from one line of verse to the next without a punctuated pause.

epic: a lengthy poem which narrates the adventures of legendary or heroic characters; also an adjective to describe such large-scale actions.

estrangement: Russian Formalist term for the kind of inventive or self-conscious language which compels us to refresh our experience of the reality portrayed.

figurative: metaphorical or non-literal language, such as 'the voice of your eyes is deeper than all roses'.

force: the impact or intended effect of an utterance, as opposed to its meaning.

foreground (used as a verb): the act by which a phenomenon, e.g. language in a poem, draws attention to itself.

form: all those aspects of a literary work, including tone, mood, texture, structure, mode of characterisation and so on, which are relevant to *how* the work presents its materials.

heroic couplets: pairs of rhymed iambic pentameters.

hyberbole: poetic exaggeration.

iamb: a foot (metrical unit) of two syllables, with the stress on the second (*di-dum*).

iambic pentameter: a poetic metre consisting of five iambs or units of one unstressed and one stressed syllable (e.g. 'perchance'). 'To err is human, to forgive divine' is an iambic pentameter.

iambic tetrameter: a line of poetry made up of four iambs (*di-dum di-dum di-dum di-dum*).

image: figurative language in poetry, especially similes and metaphors.

incarnational fallacy: my own coinage for the false belief that words in poetry somehow 'contain', or form an organic part of, the things they refer to.

indeterminacy: lack of clear or exact meaning.

inscape: a term coined by Gerard Manley Hopkins to denote the essence or typical inner form of a phenomenon.

metaphor: the use of language which is imaginatively but not literally appropriate (e.g. 'nobody, not even the rain, has such small hands'), or the representation of a thing by another thing which resembles it.

metonymy: the representation of a thing by another thing which is part of or associated with it, e.g. 'crown' for 'monarchy' or 'turf' for horseracing.

metre: a regular kind of poetic sound pattern, one generally determined by the length of a line and stresses of the feet (or groups of syllables) which compose it.

metrical foot: a group of stressed and unstressed syllables which forms the basic unit of a line of poetry, e.g. an iamb (*di-dum*) or a trochee (*dum-di*).

mimetic: imitative.

mimetic fallacy: the belief that, say, a poem about boredom should itself be boring.

mock-heroic: a literary work which uses heroic forms and images in a debunking, satirical way.

mood: the emotional climate or ambience of a piece of writing.

paradigmatic: in semiotic theory, the relations between units of a literary text and the totality they constitute, rather than their relations with their immediate neighbours.

para-rhyme: a near-miss of a rhyme; two words (e.g. 'bliss' and 'bless') which sound alike but do not rhyme exactly. More exactly, a semi-rhyme in which the consonantal sounds agree but the vowels do not.

parataxis: the juxtaposition of clauses without indicating the connections between them.

pathetic fallacy: the assigning of human feelings to natural objects.

performative: concerning language as an action or event, rather than simply as a structure of meanings.

phatic: language relating to the act of communication itself, e.g. 'Good to talk to you!'

phonic: relating to sound.

poetics: the study or theory of poetry.

pragmatic: concerning practical uses and consequences.

rhythm: the variable pattern of accented and unaccented syllables in an utterance, as opposed to the invariant pattern of metre.

semantic: relating to meaning.

semiotics: the study of signs.

signified: a concept or meaning.

signifier: a sound or written mark which denotes a concept or meaning.

simile: figure of speech comparing one thing with another.

sonnet: a poem of fourteen lines, usually iambic pentameters, the classical form of which divides into two sections: an eight-line octave and a six-line sestet.

stanza: a verse of a poem, composed in a particular metrical and rhyming form which is then repeated in the other verses.

structure: a phenomenon (such as a poem) considered as a set of organised, interconnected parts.

synecdoche: the use of a part of a whole to indicate the whole, e.g. 'There were three new faces at the meeting.'

syntagmatic: in semiotic theory, the relations of a literary unit with what immediately precedes and follows it, as in a syntactical chain.

syntax: the organisation of phrases and clauses into sentences.

tetrameter: a line of four feet (or metrical units).

texture: the pattern of sounds of a poem.

timbre: the distinctive quality of a voice, used metaphorically of the unique character of a poet's linguistic style.

tone: the sound, pitch, pace and intensity of a poem considered as expressing a particular emotion.

trimeter: a line of three feet.

trochee: a metrical unit with one stressed and one unstressed syllable (*dum-di*).

trope: figurative use of language.

Index

Addison, Joseph 16
addressee 28, 32–3, 51, 165
addresser 51
Adorno, Theodor 2
aesthetics, negative 50
aleatory writing 54
alexandrine 56, 65, 120, 165
allegory 3, 99, 100–1, 121, 146–7, 165
alliteration 46, 51, 76, 121, 155, 165
ambiguity 32, 165
  Gray 73–4
  Hopkins 124–5
  Larkin 125–6
  Shakespeare 126–30
ambivalence 125, 165
'Among School Children' (Yeats)
  120–1
Amours de Voyage (Clough) 62
anapaest 55, 165
anti-climax 138
anti-heroism 6, 7
anti-poetry 133
Antony and Cleopatra (Shakespeare)
  79–81, 114
Arendt, Hannah 17n10, 20n11
Aristotle 13, 35
Arnold, Matthew 16

art/Nature 148
'As You Came from the Holy Land'
  (Raleigh) 136
association 42, 61, 62, 110
assonance 121, 155, 165
'Atalanta in Calydon' (Swinburne) 46
Auden, W. H.
  concrete/abstract images 139, 166
  'In Memory of W. B. Yeats' 7–8, 90
  'Musée des Beaux Arts' 3–8
Auerbach, Eric 9
Augustine, Saint 13
Austen, Jane 66–7, 158
authenticity 59–60
automatic writing 54
'To Autumn' (Keats) 59–60
avant-garde artists 21

'Badger' (Clare) 37–8
Bakhtin, Mikhail 2, 9
Baldick, Chris 141n10
Balzac, Honoré de 29
Barbauld, Anna Laetitia
  'The Rights of Woman' 117
Barthes, Roland 2, 16, 161–2
Bateson, F. W. 91n4
bathos 4–5, 27, 83, 136–7, 138, 165

'Battle-Hymn of the Republic' (Howe) 43

beauty 58, 64

'Because I could not stop for Death' (Dickinson) 100–1

belief system 89

Benjamin, Walter 2, 9, 17–18, 20

Bennett, Tony 48n1

Blake, William 12, 14, 24
'Tyger' 70–2, 163

blank verse 25, 165

bombast 11, 116, 165

Brecht, Bertolt 21, 80, 80n1, 106, 106n1

Brecht and Company (Eagleton) 70

Breton, André 21

Brontë, Charlotte 33

Brontë, Emily
Wuthering Heights 67

Brooke, Rupert
'The Soldier' 60–1

Browning, Elizabeth Barrett
'How do I love thee? Let me count the ways' 118

Browning, Robert
'How They Brought the Good News from Ghent to Aix' 119
'Porphyria's Lover' 103–4, 116

Brownjohn, Alan
'Common Sense' 34–5

'Burbank with a Baedeker: Bleistein with a Cigar' (Eliot) 94

Burke, Kenneth 9

Byron, George Gordon 12, 35–6

Cambridge school 9

Cantos (Pound) 42

capitalism 17, 18

Carroll, Lewis
'Twas brillig, and the slithy toves' 46

'Charge of the Light Brigade' (Tennyson) 118

Chaucer, Geoffrey 17

chiasmus 14, 141, 165

'Chicago' (Sandburg) 113

children's emotion 107

Cicero 15

'The Circus Animals' Desertion' (Yeats) 83

citizenship 11

civilisation/philology 9

Cixous, Hélène 2

Clare, John
'Badger' 37–8

close reading 1–2, 10, 102–8

Clough, Arthur Hugh
Amours de Voyage 62

code 33, 51, 52–3

Coleridge, Samuel Taylor 13, 16, 19
Lyrical Ballads 12, 37–8

'The Collar' (Herbert) 116–17

Collins, William 158
'Ode to Evening' 143–9

colloquial idiom 4

colon 7, 131

comic effect 27, 137, 138

comma 94, 122, 131

commercialisation of writing 162

commodification 17, 18

'Common Sense' (Brownjohn) 34–5

communication 15, 57

compression 42, 52, 121, 124–5

conative function 51

conceit 56, 93–4, 165

concrete 12, 139, 141

connotation 110, 111

Conrad, Joseph 23, 25

consciousness 22, 145, 159, 160

consonants 120–1

consumerism 18

contact, communication 51

content 65, 166
and form 28, 64, 65–9, 70–88, 144–5
performative 148
politics of 8
semantic 66

content analysis 2–3
context
  communication 51
  conjuncture of 53
  cultural 106–7, 109–10, 118
  meaning 109
  social 105
  suffering 8
  tone 95
  words 54
contradiction 88–9, 150–1
conversation style
  'Musée des Beaux Arts' (Auden) 7
'Coole Park and Ballylee' (Yeats) 81–2,
  85, 123
Coriolanus (Shakespeare) 127
Corso, Gregory 25
Crime and Punishment (Dostoevsky)
  33
cultural studies 16
cultural theory 16
Culture 19
cummings, e. e. 130–1
Curtius, Ernst Robert 9

Dadaism 54
Dante Alighieri 89, 92
'The Darkling Thrush' (Hardy)
  121
Davie, Donald 144
'Days' (Larkin) 125–6
de Man, Paul 2, 15, 15n7, 62,
  62n7
De Rerum Natura (Lucretius) 30
decentring 5, 159
decoding 33
defamiliarisation 49
democracy 10–11, 12
Demosthenes 15
denotation 52, 110
depersonalisation 80
Derrida, Jacques 2, 15, 18
description/sensibility 161

'A Dialogue of Self and Soul' (Yeats)
  114–15
Dickens, Charles
  Oliver Twist 33, 35, 36
Dickinson, Emily
  'Because I could not stop for Death'
    100–1
diction 144, 166
didactic 89, 166
difference/identity 54–5
'Digging' (Heaney) 60, 61
disbelief, suspension of 30
discourse 2–3, 49, 90, 166
'A Disused Shed in Co.Wexford'
  (Mahon) 86–7
doggerel 43
dogma 89
Donne, John 117
  'A Valediction Forbidding Mourning'
    93–4
Doolittle, Hilda 140
  'Sea Violet' 36–7
Dostoevsky, Fyodr
  Crime and Punishment 33
double-reference 51–2
drama 3–4, 6, 25
Dryden, John 25, 52
The Dunciad (Pope) 87–8, 162
Dunkin, WIlliam
  'The Parson's Revels' 137–8

Eagleton, Terry 1n1, 10n4, 15n6, 16n9,
  24n12, 58n5, 70n1, 106n1
  Brecht and Company 70
'Easter 1916' (Yeats) 54
Eichenbaum, Boris 50
'Elegy in a Country Churchyard' (Gray)
  73–4
Eliot, T. S. 84, 92
  'Burbank with a Baedeker: Bleistein
    with a Cigar' 94
  experience 33
  Four Quartets 19–20, 59

Eliot, T. S. (*cont'd*)
'Gerontion' 151
'The Love-Song of J. Alfred Prufrock'
92–3
'Mr Eliot's Sunday Morning Service'
90–2
punctuation 3, 14
The Waste Land 21, 76–7, 92, 95–6,
103
'Whispers of Immortality' 123–4,
130
Elizabethan poetry 141–2
emotion 77, 106–7, 112–14, 117, 128–9,
133–5
emotive function 51
empathy 24
empiricism 11–12, 142
Empson, William 9, 16, 124n3, 125,
129
Some Versions of Pastoral 73–4
enjambement 7, 96–7, 119, 166
Enlightenment 11, 44
ephemerality 159, 161
epic 14, 166
epithets 115
equivalence 54–5
Erlich, Victor 48n1
Essay Concerning Human Understanding
(Locke) 11
Essay on Criticism (Pope) 33, 65
estrangement 49–52, 166
'The Eve of St Agnes' (Keats) 77
evening star/morning star example
65–6
exchange-value 41
exclamation marks 117, 130
experience 17–19, 20, 33
expressive behaviour 107
extremism 157

fact/fiction 31–2
feelings 106–7
see also emotion

fiction 69
emotion 113
fact 31–2
imaginary 33–4
morality 35, 36
truth 35
'Fifty Faggots' (Thomas, E.) 157–61,
163
figurative 14, 141, 166
Finnegans Wake (Joyce) 125
'For Johnny' (Pudney) 134–5
force 90, 166
foregrounding 48–9, 166
form 65, 166
and content 28, 64, 65–9, 70–88,
144–5
history 8, 161–4
metre 2
'Ode to Evening' 147–8
formalism 16, 59–64, 69, 161–2
see also Russian Formalists
Forms, Platonic 13
Forster, E. M.
A Passage to India 4
Foucault, Michel 2, 18
Four Quartets (Eliot) 19–20, 59
Frazer, R. 140n8
free verse 26
Freud, Sigmund 64, 68
Frost, Robert
'Stopping by Woods on a Snowy
Evening' 64, 96–9
Frye, Northrop 16
full stops 94, 131
Furbank, P. N. 139n6
Futurists 21

Garvin, Paul 52n2
generalities 146, 148–9
Genette, Gérard 2
genre 31, 51
Georgian poetry 144
Georgics (Virgil) 30–1, 89

'Gerontion' (Eliot) 151
'God Save the Queen' 38–9
'God's Grandeur' (Hopkins) 153–7
Goethe, Johann Wolfgang von 19
Grace/Nature 155–6
grammar 123–4
grand narratives 7, 163
Gray, Thomas
   'Elegy in a Country Churchyard'
     73–4
grief 107, 114
Grundrisse (Marx) 142

Haeffner, Paul 141n9
Haffenden, John 33n2
Hamlet (Shakespeare) 95, 113
Hardy, Thomas 145, 148, 160
   'The Darkling Thrush' 121
Hartman, Geoffrey 2
Heaney, Seamus 142
   'Digging' 60, 61
Hegel, Georg Wilhelm Friedrich
   13
Heidegger, Martin 17, 20
Hemingway, Ernest 19
Herbert, George
   'The Collar' 116–17
   'Love' 94
heroic couplets 25, 53, 166
   Keats 78
   Pope 87–8, 162
history 36, 160–4
history-as-heritage 18, 19, 20
Homer
   Iliad 33, 62
Hopkins, Gerard Manley 85
   'God's Grandeur' 153–7
   imagery 155
   inscapes 13, 167
   inventiveness 45, 156–7
   labour 158
   Roman Catholicism 154
   sound-patterns 155

'Spring and Fall' 124–5
verbal self-consciousness 42–3
'The Windhover' 43
Housman, A. E.
   A Shropshire Lad 63–4
'How do I love thee? Let me count
   the ways.' (Browning, E. B.)
   118
'How They Brought the Good News
   from Ghent to Aix' (Browning, R.)
   119
Howe, Julia Ward
   'Battle-Hymn of the Republic' 43
hyperbole 128, 141, 166

iamb 55, 166
iambic pentameter 33, 162–3, 166
   Clare 38
   Eliot 76, 92–3
   Jonson 53
   Keats 78
   Lowell 56
   Mahon 87
   O'Donoghue 46
   reception of 33
   Shakespeare 135
iambic tetrameter 56, 63, 133–4, 138,
   166
identity/difference 54–5
Iliad (Homer) 33, 62
image 139–40, 166
imagery
   aural 139
   Hopkins 155
   industrial 72
   Nature 72, 121
   pseudo-scriptural 75
   Romantics 140–1
   tactile 139
   visual 138–42
   Wordsworth 151–2
imaginary 33–4
imagination 13–14, 22–4, 140–1

Imagist poetry 140, 142
'In Flanders Fields' (McCrae) 133–4
'In Memoriam' (Tennyson) 112–13,
    117–18, 163
'In Memory of Major Robert Gregory'
    (Yeats) 83
'In Memory of W. B. Yeats' (Auden)
    7–8, 90
incarnational fallacy 59–64, 166
indeterminacy 125, 167
individualism 23–4, 127
Industrial Revolution 72, 163
information 55, 56–7, 58
inscape 13, 167
'Insensibility' (Owen) 132–3
intensity 118–19
inventiveness 62, 156–7
    see also verbal invention
inversion 4
'Inviting a Friend to Supper' (Jonson)
    53
Irish music, traditional 107–8
irony 51, 141
    artifice/nature 97
    Auden 6
    Forster 4
    performative contradiction 88
    punctuation 130
    tone 67
    vice/virtue 127, 129–30
Iser, Wolfgang 2

Jakobson, Roman 50, 51
Jameson, Fredric 2, 9, 9n2, 48n1
Johnson, Samuel 16, 17, 29–30, 146
    Lives of the Poets 30
Jonson, Ben
    'Inviting a Friend to Supper'
    53
Joyce, James 23
    Finnegans Wake 125
juxtaposition 63

Keats, John 12, 152
    epithets 115
    'The Eve of St Agnes' 77
    'Lamia' 77–8
    'To Autumn' 26, 59–60
    truth/beauty 58, 64
Kennedy, George 10n4
King Lear (Shakespeare) 33, 79, 95,
    110–11
Kipling, Rudyard
    'Tommy' 43
Koch, Kenneth 39–40, 41
Kristeva, Julia 2

labour 158
Lacan, Jacques 58
'Lamia' (Keats) 77–8
language
    citizenship 11
    distrust of 44–5
    empiricism 11–12
    estrangement 49–52
    freedom 139
    incarnation 59–60
    materiality 48–9
    modernism 44–5, 46
    morality 28–9, 63
    phenomenalisation of 62
    poetry 2–3, 41–7, 67–8, 69
    prose 25
    texture/meaning 46
    thing-like 140
    tone 67
    truth 11
    unpredictability 20, 56
    see also communication; words
Larkin, Philip 25
    'Days' 125–6
Larrissy, Edward 72, 72n2
Lawrence, D. H. 8
    'To Women, As Far As I'm
    Concerned' 26–8, 31

Leavis, F. R. 9, 16, 26, 26n1, 59–60, 59n6, 140, 140n7
Leibniz, Gottfried Wilhelm 13
lesbian readings 104, 105
limerick example 56
line-endings 25–6, 27
  see also enjambement
literariness 2–3, 48–9
literary criticism 1, 3, 28–9
  belief 89
  Cambridge school 9
  cultural theory 16
  imagination 22–4
  politics 9, 15–16
  as psychosis 22–3
  rhetoric 16
  Romantic 8–9
  semantics 67
  social history 9
  subjectivism 102–3
  see also Russian Formalists
literary theory 1–2, 8
Literature 12–13
literature 15–16, 23, 29–31
litotes 141
Lives of the Poets (Johnson) 30
Locke, John
  Essay Concerning Human Understanding 11
Longfellow, Henry Wadsworth
  'The Song of Hiawatha' 43
Lotman, Yury 52–3, 52n3
  concrete 142
  difference/identity 54–5
  information 58
  metre 53–4
  minus device 56
  poetic 56–7
  systems in poetry 57–8, 59
'The Lotus Eaters' (Tennyson) 119–20
loudness 117–18
'Love' (Herbert) 94

'The Love-Song of J. Alfred Prufrock' (Eliot) 92–3
Lowell, Robert 116
  'Mr. Edwards and the Spider' 55–6
  'My Last Afternoon with Uncle Devereux Winslow' 42
Lucretius 52
  De Rerum Natura 30
Lycidas (Milton) 30
Lyotard, J.-F. 18
Lyrical Ballads (Wordsworth and Coleridge) 12, 37–8

Macbeth (Shakespeare) 95, 127
McCrae, John
  'In Flanders Fields' 133–4
Mahon, Derek
  'A Disused Shed in Co.Wexford' 86–7
Mallarmé, Stéphane 52
Man, Death of 18, 19
'The Man and the Echo' (Yeats) 82–3
Mann, Thomas 19
'Mariana' (Tennyson) 111–13, 116, 163
Marvell, Andrew
  'To His Coy Mistress' 104–5
Marx, Karl 41
  Grundrisse 142
Matejka, L. 48n1
materiality of words 43–4, 48–9, 60, 61, 109
mathematics 34–5
Mayakovsky, V. V. 21
meaning 21–2
  context 109–10
  force 90
  incarnation 59
  medium 69
  readers 108–9
  semantic/non-semantic 67
  social 110, 162–3
  spiritual 163

meaning (*cont'd*)
    subjectivity 108–14
    words 21, 47
medium/meaning 69
melancholy 111–13
The Merchant of Venice (Shakespeare) 135
message, communication 51
meta-discourse 10
metalinguistic function 51
metaphor 54, 139, 167
    distrust of 44
    Elizabethan poetry 141–2
    metonymy 38
    Nietzsche 14
    Owen 133
    Romantics 141
metaphysical poetry 93–4
meteorological report example 33–4
metonymy 38, 139, 167
metre 102, 167
    emotion 133–4
    form 2
    formality 56
    information 55
    insistent 43
    line-endings 25
    Lotman 53–4
    'Mr Eliot's Sunday Morning Service' 91–2
    Owen 133
    rhyme 56
    rhythm 135–8
    unvaried 97
metrical foot 55, 56, 167
Mill, John Stuart 14
Miller, J. Hillis 2
Milton, John
    belief system 89
    diction 144
    form/content 65
    Lycidas 30
    Paradise Lost 44, 94–5

mimetic fallacy 112, 167
mimetic theory of form 65, 68, 167
'Mind the Gap' sign 29
minus device 56
mock heroic 87, 88, 167
modern poetry
    allegory 99
    Auden 7
    diction 144
    Eliot 91–3
    extremism 157
    'Mr Eliot's Sunday Morning Service' 91
modernism 8
    conservatism 20
    language 44–5, 46
    poetry 14
    subjectivity 17
monads (Leibniz) 13
Montagu, Lady Mary Wortley
    'The Small-Pox' 78–9
mood 66, 167
    emotional value 112
    'Fifty Faggots' 161
    sensibility 163
    'The Solitary Reaper' 152–3
    tone 105, 116
    value judgements 112
morality
    fiction 35, 36
    language 28–9, 63
    literature 29–30
    poetry 27, 28–31
    Wordsworth 153
Morris, Wiliam 14
Morrison, Van 107–8
'Mr. Edwards and the Spider' (Lowell) 55–6
'Mr Eliot's Sunday Morning Service' (Eliot) 90–2
'Musée des Beaux Arts' (Auden) 8
    anti-heroism 6, 7
    conversation style 3–4, 7

irony 6
rhyme scheme 7
syntax 7
word order 4
worldly-wise tone 4, 5, 6–7
'My Last Afternoon with Uncle
    Devereux Winslow' (Lowell) 42

national anthem 38–9
Nature
    allegory 146–7
    art 148
    Collins 143–9
    Grace 155–6
    imagery 72, 121
    labour 158
    polluted 155
    Roman Catholicism 154
    symbols 146–7
    Thomas, E. 158
    Yeats 85
neoclassical poetry 144, 145, 146,
    148–9
New Criticism 16, 19
Nietzsche, Friedrich 10, 14–15, 17, 68
non-pragmatic discourse 38–41
Norris, Christopher 15n6
'Not Waving But Drowning' (Smith)
    136–7
novel 14, 16, 35–6

'Ode to Evening' (Collins) 143
    diction 144
    form 147–8
    generalities 146, 148–9
    tone 144–5
'Ode to the West Wind' (Shelley) 119
O'Donoghue, Bernard
    'Pencil It In' 45–6
'Old Man' (Thomas, E.) 121–2, 163
Oliver Twist (Dickens) 33, 35, 36
Olivier, Laurence 135
Olson, Charles 52

onomatopoeia 62
Opus Posthumous (Stevens) 69
orators 10
    see also rhetoric
Orwell, George 16, 49
Othello (Shakespeare) 95, 113
overcoding 52–3
Owen, Wilfred 134
    'Insensibility' 132–3
oxymoron, semi 54

pace 67, 119–20
pantheism 154, 156
paradigmatic 57, 61, 63–4, 167
Paradise Lost (Milton) 44, 94–5
parallelism 27
para-rhyme 116, 132–3, 167
parody 39–40
parsnip example 51–2
'The Parson's Revels' (Dunkin) 137–8
particularities 37, 141–2, 146
A Passage to India (Forster) 4
pathetic fallacy 8, 167
pauses in lines 27
Pearson, Keith Ansell 10n3
Pelagian heresy 154, 156
'Pencil It In' (O'Donoghue) 45–6
perception 146
performance
    conceits 93–4
    contradiction 88
    Eliot 90–3, 94, 95–6
    Milton 94–5
    Morrison 107–8
    rhetorical 89–90
performative 11, 88, 148, 167
permanency 159
personification 141, 145
Petrarchian sonnet 118
phatic function 51, 167
philology 9
phonetic system 53
phonic 54, 55, 57, 167

pitch 67, 116–17
Pitman's phrases 34–5
Plath, Sylvia 116
Plato 11, 13
play 58
Poe, Edgar Allan
  'The Raven' 43
poetic function 49, 51
poetics 11, 56–7, 157, 164, 167
poetry 12–14
  Eliot 19–20
  fiction 31–8
  history 164
  language 2–3, 41–7, 67–8, 69
  as meta-discourse 10
  morality 27, 28–31
  non-pragmatic discourse 38–41
  as performance 88–96
  as phenomenology of language 21
  pragmatic 38–41, 99, 153
  prose 25–8
  rationalism 21–2
  readers 108–9
  signification process 21, 32, 48–9
  systems/sub-systems 52, 57–8
  truth 15
  see also content; form
Pol Pot 24
politics
  literary criticism 9, 15–16
  literary theory 8
  poetics 157, 164
  poetry 14
  rhetoric 10–11
  textuality 10
Pomorska, K. 48n1
Poor Law Commissioners 36
Pope, Alexander 125
  The Dunciad 87–8, 162
  An Essay on Criticism 33, 65
  heroic couplets 78, 87–8, 162
'Porphyria's Lover' (Browning, R.)
  103–4, 116

postmodernism 17
post-Romantics 141, 146
post-structuralism 15, 18–19
Pound, Ezra 14, 140
  Cantos 42
pragmatic 167
  didactic 89
  non-pragmatic 99
  poetry 38–41, 99, 153
  Pudney 134–5
  speech act 38–9
Prague school of structuralism 52
private sphere 6–8, 111
propaganda 90
prose 25–8, 38
Proust, Marcel 19, 25
public sphere 6–8, 12, 79, 111
Pudney, John
  'For Johnny' 134–5
pun 75, 125
punctuation 102
  colon 131
  comma 94, 131
  cummings, e. e. 130–1
  Eliot 3, 123–4
  exclamation marks 117, 130
  full stops 94, 131
  Lawrence 8
  rhetoric 14
  semicolon 14, 131
  Thomas, E. 122
  Yeats 84

Radcliffe, Alexander 137n5
Raleigh, Walter
  'As You Came from the Holy Land'
  136
rationalism 11–12, 15, 21–2, 140
'The Raven' (Poe) 43
readers 108–9
reality 30, 36, 61–2, 141
Redgrave, Michael 135
referent 49, 51, 52

referential function 51, 52
'A Refusal to Mourn the Death, by
   Fire, of a Child in London'
   (Thomas, D.) 74–6
'Remember me when I am gone away'
   (Rossetti) 118–19
repetition 27, 97, 98, 131–2
representation 139–40
reproduction, mechanical 20
resonance 37, 92
rhetoric 10–12
   Antony and Cleopatra 80–1
   force 90
   Herbert 94
   history of 14–15
   literary criticism 16
   Nietzsche 14–15
   rationalism 15, 140
   reality 141
   Thomas, D. 75
rhyme 54, 56, 102, 131–2
rhyme scheme
   Auden 7
   Dunkin 138
   Frost 97
   Keats 78
   Lotman 53
   McCrae 133–4
   Pudney 134–5
   Rossetti 118–19
   Tennyson 112, 120
rhythm 167
   bathos 137, 138
   emotion 117
   equivalence / difference 54
   iambic tetrameters 138
   insensitivity to 68
   irregular 92–3
   metre 135–8
   psychic level 135
   repetition 27
   resonance 92
Richards, I. A. 9, 16, 19, 125

'The Rights of Woman' (Barbauld) 117
Roman Catholicism 154
Romantic literary criticism 8–9
Romantic poetry 12, 13, 140–1
Rossetti, Christina
   'Remember me when I am gone
   away' 118–19
Ruskin, John 14
Russell, Bertrand 28
Russian Formalists 2, 16, 47
   estrangement 49–52
   literariness 48–9
   poetic function 49
   universal theory of poetry 50–2
   see also Lotman, Yury

Said, Edward 9
'Sailing to Byzantium' (Yeats) 84–5
Sandburg, Carl
   'Chicago' 113
satire 78, 162
Schumpeter, Joseph 16, 16n8
Scottish Enlightenment 11
'Sea Violet' (Doolittle) 36–7
self-consciousness 42, 45, 87, 112
self-interest 129–30
self-referentiality 49
semantic 53, 54, 57, 67, 167
semi-assonance 121
semicolon 7, 14, 124, 131
semiotics 52–8, 167
semi-rhymes 121, 167
sense-impressions 23–4
sensibility 161, 163
sensuousness 77–8
Shakespeare, William
   Antony and Cleopatra 79–81, 114
   Coriolanus 127
   diction 144
   Hamlet 95, 113
   King Lear 33, 79, 95, 110–11
   Macbeth 95, 127
   The Merchant of Venice 135

Shakespeare, William (*cont'd*)
  Othello 95, 113
  sonnets 110, 126–7, 128–9
  Troilus and Cressida 127
Shaw, George Bernard 21
Shelley, Percy Bysshe 12, 14
  'Ode to the West Wind' 119
Shlovsky, Viktor 50
A Shropshire Lad (Housman) 63–4
signification process 21, 32, 48–9
signified/signifier 21, 41–2, 46, 47, 49, 64, 68, 167
signifier 168
  floating 52, 110
  materiality 43–4
  'Mr Eliot's Sunday Morning Service' 91
  overcoding 53
  see also **signified**/signifier
simile 93, 138–9, 141–2, 168
singer/song example 108
'The Small-Pox' (Montagu) 78–9
Smith, Stevie
  'Not Waving But Drowning' 136–7
social class 15–16
social history 9
social meaning 110, 162–3
'The Soldier' (Brooke) 60–1
'The Solitary Reaper' (Wordsworth) 149–53
Some Versions of Pastoral (Empson) 73–4
'The Song of Hiawatha' (Longfellow) 43
sonnets 118, 126–7, 128–9, 168
sound-patterns 155
speech utterance 27, 51, 89
'Spring and Fall' (Hopkins) 124–5
statements
  factual 29
  moral/empirical 29, 30–1
Steele, Richard 16
Steiner, George 20

Stevens, Wallace 14, 25, 52, 108
  Opus Posthumous 69
'Stopping by Woods on a Snowy Evening' (Frost) 64, 96–9
Strauss, Leo 20
structuralism 52
structure 66, 67, 168
subjectivity 17, 18, 21, 108–14
suffering 5–7, 8, 80
Surrealists 21
suspension of disbelief 30
Swift, Jonathan 23
  'Verses on the Death of Dr. Swift' 45
Swinburne, Algernon Charles 116
  'Atalanta in Calydon' 46
syllables 4, 54–5, 60, 138
symbolism 13, 29, 146–7, 151
symbolist poetry 46, 52, 69, 152
synaesthesia 130, 131
synecdoche 14, 139, 168
syntagmatic 57, 168
syntax 5, 7, 121–3, 168
systems/sub-systems 52, 57–8

tabloid newspapers 49
Tacitus 10, 10n5
Tennyson, Alfred, Lord 14
  'Charge of the Light Brigade' 118
  'In Memoriam' 112–13, 117–18, 163
  'The Lotus Eaters' 119–20
  'Mariana' 111–13, 116, 163
tetrameter 56, 166
texture 68, 120–1, 168
'There was a young poet of Japan' 56
'This is Just to Say' (Williams, W. C.) 39, 40, 41
Thomas, Dylan 30
  'A Refusal to Mourn the Death, by Fire, of a Child in London' 74–6
Thomas, Edward
  'Fifty Faggots' 157–61, 163
  Nature 158
  'Old Man' 121–2, 163

Thompson, E. P. 16
'Three Blind Mice' 73, 162–3
timbre 116, 168
time-schemes 159–60
'To His Coy Mistress' (Marvell) 104–5
'To Women, As Far As I'm Concerned'
    (Lawrence) 26–8, 31
Tolstoy, Leo
    War and Peace 33
'Tommy' (Kipling) 43
tone 66, 102, 168
    Collins 144–5
    context 95
    language 67
    Marvell 104
    misinterpreted 114–15
    mood 105, 116
    social context 105
    Yeats 163
'The Tower' (Yeats) 115–16
Trilling, Lionel 9
trimeter 54, 56, 116
trochee 51, 168
Troilus and Cressida (Shakespeare) 127
trope 14, 168
truth
    beauty 58, 64
    Enlightenment 11
    fiction 35
    genre 31
    history 36
    language 11
    novel 35–6
    poetry 15
'Tyger' (Blake) 70–2, 163

universal theory of poetry 50–2
universalities 141–2
    see also generalities
use-value 41

'A Valediction Forbidding Mourning'
    (Donne) 93–4

value judgements 111, 112
vatic effect 116
verbal invention 41–2, 46, 62
'Verses on the Death of Dr. Swift'
    (Swift) 45
vice/virtue 127, 129–30
Vickers, Brian 10n4
Victorian poetry 118–19
Virgil
    Georgics 30–1, 89
virtue/vice 127, 129–30
voulu (willed) 112

War and Peace (Tolstoy) 33
war poetry 132–4
The Waste Land (Eliot) 76–7, 92, 95–6,
    103
'Whispers of Immortality' (Eliot)
    123–4, 130
Williams, Raymond 16, 163, 163n1
Williams, William Carlos 140
    'This is Just to Say' 39, 40, 41
Wilson, Edmund 9
'The Windhover' (Hopkins) 43
window pane image 69
Wittgenstein, Ludwig 62, 110, 110n2
Woolf, Virginia 25
word order 4
wordplay 27, 64
words
    authenticity 59–60
    context 54
    inverted 4
    materiality 43–4, 48–9, 60–1, 109
    meaning 21, 47
    sense-making 32
    syllables 4, 60, 138
Wordsworth, William
    consciousness 145
    imagery 151–2
    inspiration 151
    labour 158
    Lyrical Ballads 12, 37–8

Wordsworth, William (*cont'd*)
  moral lessons 153
  'The Solitary Reaper' 149–53
World Spirit (Hegel) 13
Wuthering Heights (Brontë) 67

Yeats, William Butler 14
  'Among School Children' 120–1
  'The Circus Animals' Desertion' 83
  'Coole Park and Ballylee' 81–2, 85,
    123
  dancer/dance idea 66, 120

'A Dialogue of Self and Soul' 114–15
'Easter 1916' 54
epithets 115
'In Memory of Major Robert Gregory'
  83
'The Man and the Echo' 82–3
Nature 85
'Sailing to Byzantium' 84–5
self-belief 82–3
syntax 123
tone 163
'The Tower' 115–16